THE POKER
-TOURNAMENT-
FORMULA

THE POKER
TOURNAMENT
FORMULA

— ARNOLD SNYDER —

CARDOZA
PUBLISHING

Cardoza Publishing is the foremost gaming publisher in the world, with a library of over 175 up-to-date and easy-to-read books and strategies. These authoritative works are written by the top experts in their fields and with more than 8,500,000 books in print, represent the best-selling and most popular gaming books anywhere.

FIRST EDITION

Copyright © 2006 by Arnold Snyder
- All Rights Reserved -

Library of Congress Catalog Card No: 2005930779
ISBN: 1-58042-203-9

Visit our web site—www.cardozapub.com—or write for a full list of books and computer strategies.

CARDOZA PUBLISHING
P.O. Box 1500, Cooper Station, New York, NY 10276
Phone (800) 577-WINS
email: cardozapub@aol.com
www.cardozapub.com

TABLE OF CONTENTS

PART 1:
A NEW APPROACH

PART 2:
THE STRATEGIES

4. MEET THE WEAPONS: ROCK, PAPER, SCISSORS

5. BASIC POSITION STRATEGY

6. CARD STRATEGY I: HANDS AND MOVES

PART 3:
THE FINE POINTS

PART 4:
THE MOST IMPORTANT CHAPTERS IN THIS BOOK IF YOU WANT TO MAKE MONEY

INTRODUCTION

or...

**Why a New Approach to Winning Poker
Tournaments is Long Overdue**

I am going to show you how to make money in the "fast" no-limit hold'em tournaments that are now so popular on the Internet and in poker rooms all over the country. I'm also going to show you how to stop being at the mercy of the cards you are dealt, and how to adjust your strategy for each tournament you play. You will also learn exactly why you must learn to do these things if you have any intention of making money in these tournaments.

What is a "fast" tournament? It's any multi-table tournament that has blind levels that last less than an hour. These events generally have buy-ins from $20 to $1,000, and last anywhere from two hours to six or seven hours at the maximum. If you think that the strategies for beating these tournaments are the same strategies that you would use to beat the major events featuring the world class players you see on television, you are mistaken. And if you think you can use a single one-size-fits-all strategy, you are mistaken again, and your mistake is costing you money.

Many players seem to believe that a no-limit hold'em tournament is a no-limit hold'em tournament, and they approach every event the same way. This is wrong. The blind structure of any specific tournament more than any other factor alters not only hand values, but optimal playing and betting strategies, as well as bankroll requirements. Even small changes in the blind structure require significant changes in your strategy. Structure is the key problem players in fast tournaments must deal with in order to win. My focus on structure means that I will quickly gloss over many of the topics that other books focus on. They are simply not all that important in fast tournaments. Topics other authors have not even considered will be expounded upon at length.

This book will be different from every other book on poker you've read, even if you've read them all. This is not a rehash of the same old stuff that all of the major poker authors have already said. This is something entirely new, from a different type of professional gambler's perspective, and it works.

If you picked this book up because you are a beginner, and you apply yourself, you should soon be making a lot of money in small buy-in tournaments from many more experienced poker players. If you are an advanced player and you've read all of the major books on this subject, this book will contain analyses and strategies that will surprise you.

In addition to the structure, the small buy-in tournaments also differ significantly from the major big money events in the quality of your opponents, which will run the gamut from knowledgeable, dangerous, and obviously experienced tournament players to downright oafs who do not even know the standard rules and procedures of poker. The fact is that you can use strategies against more knowledgeable players that will never succeed against an oaf. This book will deal with these types of problems too.

If you currently play regularly in small buy-in tournaments, you have probably noticed players who seem to make the final tables consistently. You may think that these players are just lucky, and get dealt more good hands than you do. You may think they suck out so much they must have some kind of a pact with the devil. In fact, if you read this book, you'll learn what they are doing. And soon you will be feeling a whole lot luckier yourself.

THE REAL MONEY-MAKING APPROACH: LIVE AND ONLINE

For every player who enters a major $10,000 buy-in tournament, there are at least a thousand players who enter a fast tournament. In Las Vegas alone, there are more than 400 fast tournaments every week. The number of these tournaments is also exploding in California's poker rooms and other poker rooms all over the country—to say nothing of the Internet poker rooms, where you will find thousands of online tournaments daily. The boom in tournament play represents an influx of unskilled players to the game that makes these fast tournaments one of the richest gambling opportunities I've seen in decades. And you don't have to be a poker star, or have a big bankroll, to take advantage of this opportunity.

This is a book for the 99.99% of no-limit tournament players who are more interested in making money in the tournaments they actually play than in reading about strategies that might work in the major $10,000 events they can't really afford. After all, if you make more money in the tournaments you're actually playing, you'll be able to afford the big events much sooner.

FILLING IN THE INFORMATION GAP

I've been writing about professional gambling for more than twenty-five years. If you're familiar with my blackjack books and the ways I've analyzed other casino games, you'll understand right off why I'm analyzing poker tournaments from a different perspective. In the mid-1970s, when I started counting cards at blackjack, all of the major authors seemed to provide the same advice. Here's your basic strategy. Here's your counting system. Spread your bets from 1 to 4 or 1 to 8 units at the high counts. You'll win.

What I found at the tables, however—moving back and forth between the single-deck games in Reno and the 4-deck shoes in Las Vegas—was that the major authors were so focused on how to play hands correctly that they had ignored the most important stuff. None of the blackjack authors had spent any ink at all dissecting the *structures* of the various games and how these structural differences affected optimal playing and betting strategies. In my first book, *The Blackjack Formula* (1980), I made my name in blackjack as the guy who analyzed the game's structure, so that strategies could be devised based on the specific game rather than some one-size-fits-all card counting system. With this book, I do the same for poker tournaments.

In my library, I have eighty-four books on poker. I just counted them. This is not a large poker library by any means, as it is primarily focused on the game of no-limit Texas hold'em, and especially poker tournaments. Reading these books, however, gave me much the same feeling I got when I first started reading blackjack books back in the 1970s. Most of the poker authors seemed to be rehashing a lot of the same ideas, focusing on how to play specific hands. My experience in the tournaments I was playing, however, told me that there was a huge gap in the information I was being given. In my first four weeks of play, I played twenty-five tournaments at various Las Vegas casinos, including Luxor, Sam's Town, Orleans, Mirage, Sahara, Sunset Station and Bellagio, with buy-ins ranging from $28 to $540. The number of players in each tournament ranged from 31 to 190, and they all had different amounts of starting chips and different time lengths for the blind levels.

As a professional gambler attempting to apply the strategies I'd learned from poker books, I realized that the major poker authors had ignored the structural differences between tournaments. I knew intuitively that these structural differences made for very different games that required very different approaches. I also knew that the structural differences between tournaments could be analyzed, and if these analyses could isolate the important differences between the tournaments, they would lead to improved strategies and greater profits.

STRATEGIES TO WIN FOR TODAY'S SMALL BUY-IN TOURNAMENTS

In the course of playing in these tournaments, analyzing them, and making final tables regularly, I met many poker players of comparatively vast experience who told me they'd *never* made a final table, and I knew exactly why they weren't getting anywhere. As players who came to these tournaments from a love of poker, and often after having studied all the best poker books, they were so focused on poker strategy, and so ignorant of tournament strategies and how to make money from gambling, that their poker skill and knowledge literally killed their chances of winning.

Part of the problem is that the renowned poker authors have probably not played many of the $40 or $100 or even $500 buy-in tournaments populated primarily by amateurs, where all players start out with very few chips and the blinds go up every fifteen to twenty minutes. And most of their opponents in the major tournaments have probably been very different from the opponents I found in the small buy-in tournaments—the same type that you will be facing in these fast tournaments. None of the authors describe the frantic state of never-ending all-in bets that usually starts about ninety minutes into a fast multi-table tournament, when hordes of desperately short-stacked players start facing blinds they can't afford. It's not that the great poker authors were writing about an entirely different game; they weren't. But they were writing about the game played with an entirely different *structure.*

This book has been written to fill in all these gaps. It covers the questions fast tournament players need to be asking before they buy-in, including:

- ♠ How much of a bankroll do I need?
- ♠ How should the number of players affect my game plan?
- ♠ How do I optimize a strategy for a specific tournament based on its structure?
- ♠ How do I analyze the profit potential of a tournament?
- ♠ How do I know whether I'm playing a winning strategy?

Do my methods of tournament analysis have any applicability to major events with long, slow blind structures? Yes, they do. But these types of tournaments require more advanced poker skills in addition to knowledge of poker tournament strategies. (To learn more about advanced poker skills and theory, I recommend reading books by Doyle Brunson, Mike Caro, T.J. Cloutier, Dan Harrington, Tom McEvoy, and David Sklansky. See the bibliography in the back of this book for recommended titles.) A player who has these advanced poker skills, but who lacks tournament skills, should find a huge value in the methods and techniques I describe. Players with less poker skill and experience can actually start using these techniques immediately in fast tournaments where traditional poker skills are a smaller factor.

SUCCESS CAN BE YOURS

This book is a gift to the up-and-coming pro gamblers of tomorrow who are trying to build a bankroll today in the small tournaments. These small buy-in tournaments won't make you rich overnight in and of themselves, but they can get you the bankroll and experience you need to take on bigger gambling ventures. Playing in these baby tournaments, you'll learn a lot about gambling and people.

And even if you have no aspirations toward becoming a professional gambler, poker tournaments are fun. Once you start playing them, it's hard not to develop a passion for the game, and making any money at all at a game you enjoy playing is reward enough for many players. This book is for you too.

I have great admiration for the top players I've met in the fast small buy-in tournaments, the players I've seen over and over again at the final tables. I learned a lot of what I know by watching the winning players who were already doing much of this stuff when I got there.

A friend asked about whether this book will open the eyes of the tournament hordes. I doubt any book could ever change the one basic fact of poker that has kept the pros going for decades:

There are a lot of fish in the sea.

PART ONE:
A NEW APPROACH

1

THE WAITING GAME VS. THE HUNTING GAME

The major no-limit hold'em tournaments whose final tables you watch on TV start out as "waiting games." Players begin with substantial chip stacks compared to the blind costs, and most of these tournaments require three to five days of play before the players reach the final table. The $10,000 main event of the World Series of Poker has been described as "hours of boredom interspersed with moments of terror."

The small buy-in no-limit hold'em tournaments, by contrast, are not so much waiting games as *hunting games*. Players in these tournaments start out with substantially fewer chips, the blinds go up much faster, and the final table is reached in a matter of hours as opposed to days. These fast tournaments do not allow you the luxury of boredom. And when your total dollar investment is in the neighborhood of $60, it's hard to characterize any situation that might occur as ever approaching "terror."

Many of the major authors describe the early stages of a big tournament as a "survival" period. During this time, they suggest taking few risks, avoiding dangerous confrontations with less than premium hands, and basically waiting for very strong cards and opportunities to make money. In these early stages, a major tournament is indeed a waiting game.

By contrast, there is no "survival" stage in a fast tournament. The reason the small buy-in tournaments are not so much waiting games as hunting games, is because if you know what you're doing, you don't wait very long. You're not just hoping for premium cards; you're also hunting for *shots*. And shots come a lot more frequently than cards. What is a shot? A shot is any bet you can make that is likely to earn you a pot whether or not you have the cards to back up your bet. In fact, in a fast tournament, your cards are immaterial more often than not.

Is the strategy required to win in these types of tournaments a high-risk strategy? Yes, in the short term, but there is no avoiding the short term risk factors if you intend to win in the long run. In the small buy-in tournaments, you need to make more money faster than you can expect to earn with quality cards, because you won't get the hands you need as frequently as you need them, and when you get them they won't pay off as much as they must for their frequency of occurrence. One of the first things you must learn to do in these fast tournaments is make money from all of the players who have read the major authors and who are trying to avoid early confrontations as they wait for strong hands during what they believe is the survival period.

Shot-taking is not easy. Some players seem to have a natural talent for it, and you should study these players. I am going to provide you with specific methods for taking shots based on easily discernable situations in the game. Once you get the logic of it, you can get creative and improvise all kinds of shots that will earn you the chips you need to get into the money more often. Even more important, I'm going to show you how to adjust your shot-taking based on the tournament structure. It's as costly (and common) an error to take more shots than the structure dictates as to take fewer than you should.

The chapter that immediately follows this one is a primer on how the game is played. After that, we do *not* go straight to strategies, as most how-to books on beating poker tournaments would do. I cannot begin with the strategies because the optimal strategies differ *based on the tournaments' structures*. So, after a basic introduction to the rules and procedures, this book will proceed to defining the tools you need to analyze tournament structures in order to determine the optimal approaches to the different speeds of tournaments available. The chapter on tournament structures involves some arithmetic. If you hate math, please accept my apologies in advance, but read this chapter anyway. I know nobody wants to open a book on how to beat poker tournaments and find a bunch of formulas, charts, tables, and new lingo, but you simply must understand a few new concepts in order to follow the strategies in the rest of the book. If I tell you to push all-in on your pocket tens from middle position if your chip stack is less than *competitive* and the tournament's *patience factor* is less than 5.0, you need to understand what I mean by these terms.

In this book, there is a specific definition of what constitutes a "competitive" chip stack, and "patience factors" are also defined in detail. If I advise you to adjust your *fast play* based on your opponents in *Skill Level 5* tournaments, you must know what "fast play" is in addition to knowing when a tournament is rated "Skill Level 5." None of these concepts are difficult; but they're necessary. So, read Chapter 3.

After Part One covers these basics, you'll learn simple strategies for how to beat fast tournaments that no other author has even hinted at. If you've got the heart for it, you're going to start making a lot of final tables, and a lot of money. And isn't that what these tournaments are about?

Do the math.

2

HOW TO PLAY TEXAS HOLD'EM

If you are already an experienced no-limit hold'em tournament player, you may skip this chapter. The typical no-limit hold'em tournament game is played with nine or ten players per table. If the tournament is played with seven or fewer players per table, this would be considered a "short-handed" tournament. In this book, I will primarily be concentrating on tournaments with nine or ten players per table, as these are the most common type of small buy-in tournaments available.

THE BLINDS

All forms of poker require some kind of forced betting before any cards are dealt so that there is a minimum pot to compete for on every hand. Most forms require every player who wants to receive cards to put in a small amount, called an **ante**, before the deal. In Texas hold'em, however, rather than using an ante system, only two players are required to put money in the pot prior to the deal. These bets are called **blind** bets, and they are posted by players in adjacent seats, with the requirement to post the blinds rotating clockwise. The **small blind** is typically half the size of the **big blind**, and is posted by the player on the right. (Sometimes the small blind is some other fraction of the big blind, but it is usually not a complete bet.) The big blind represents the minimum bet any player must make to enter the pot on the first betting round.

In non-tournament hold'em games, the blinds are static— throughout the course of the game, the amount of the blinds never changes. In tournaments, however, the blinds continually increase according to a predetermined time schedule. In a long, slow tournament, these blind increases may occur every sixty minutes or more. In a fast tournament, blind increases may occur every thirty minutes or less. In this book, we'll be concentrating on the tournaments that use the faster blind structures.

THE DEAL

After the blinds are posted, the dealer deals one card to each player clockwise, starting with the small blind, and continues dealing around the table until each player has two cards. These cards are dealt face down and are known as **hole cards** or **pocket cards.** The player hand to the right of the small blind is the **button**, and is the last position to receive cards. There is, in fact, a disk that is rotated around the table, moving clockwise one seat after each round, to denote the button position.

THE COMMON POKER BETTING ACTIONS

Call: To "call" a bet is to place the minimum amount of money into the pot that will keep your hand alive. Essentially, this means matching the amount of the previous bet. To call the minimum bet on the first betting round, which is the amount of the big blind, is called **limping** into the pot.

Check: To "check" is to place no money into the pot when no bet is necessary to keep your hand alive. On the first betting round after the initial two cards are dealt, only the player in the big blind would have the option to check, and then only if no player had entered the pot with a bet larger than the amount in the big blind. If any player entered the pot with a bet larger than the big blind, that would be a…

Raise: To "raise" is to place chips into the pot larger than the minimum necessary bet, a bet that other players must call if they want to keep their hands alive. In no-limit tournaments, the minimum amount of a raise allowed is generally a bet of twice the size of any prior bet, or—on the first betting round—twice the size of the big blind. But there is no maximum limit to a raise in a no-limit game or tournament, other than the total number of chips the player has.

Reraise: To "reraise" is to place a bet into the pot larger than the bet of a player who has already raised. Reraising is also called **going over the top** of a prior raiser.

Fold: To "fold" is to throw your hand away, also called **mucking**, rather than placing any required money into the pot to keep your hand alive.

HAND RANKINGS

Throughout this book, when I describe player hands, I will abbreviate ace, king, queen, and jack as A, K, Q, and J, respectively. All cards with numerical values will simply be described by that value from 2 through 10. A small "s" indicates "suited" cards. A-Ks means an ace and king of the same suit. A lowercase "o" means "offsuit." A-Ko means an ace and king of different suits. If neither "s" nor "o" is specified, it means that the suit is not critical to the discussion of that hand.

Texas hold'em uses the same hand rankings as any traditional poker game. From best possible hand to worst, these are the rankings:

> **Royal Flush:** Any A-K-Q-J-10 of the same suit.
>
> **Straight Flush:** Any five consecutive cards (such as Q-J-10-9-8) of the same suit.
>
> **Four of a Kind or Quads:** Any four cards of identical value, such as four 9s.

Full House: Three cards of one value, with two of another. Example: K-K-K-8-8.

Flush: Any five cards of the same suit.

Straight: Any five consecutive cards (such as Q-J-10-9-8) but not all of the same suit.

Three of a Kind or Trips: Any three cards of identical value, such as three 9s.

Two Pair: Two cards of one denomination, and two of another. Example: J-J-6-6.

One Pair: Two cards of one denomination, such as 10-10.

High Card: If no player has a hand in any of the above nine rankings, then the player with the highest card wins. Ace is highest and deuce is lowest. If both players have an identical high card, then the second highest card determines the winner, then the third, and so on.

Note: Any time two or more players have identical best hands, the pot is split equally between them. Note that every player's hand is a five-card hand. Two players that each have a pair of aces would use the rank of the next highest card in their hands, then the next, and so on, to determine the winner. The pot is split only if both hands are of identical rank on all five cards.

THE PLAY OF THE GAME

After receiving their initial two hole cards, each player must decide if he wants to enter the pot with a bet that either matches the big blind, matches the bet of any player who has already entered the pot with a raise, or raise or reraise himself. The player to the left of the big blind—a position called **under the gun**—is the first to act, and all players either bet, call, raise, or fold, clockwise in turn. The big blind is the last player to act on this first betting round. If no player has raised the big blind, then he is automatically in the hand. Since his money is already in the pot, he has the option to either "check" or raise the bet himself. If there has been a raise, he must decide if he wants to call the raise, reraise, or fold.

Ultimately, each player in the pot will use his hole cards to make the best five-card poker hand possible utilizing the **community cards** that will be dealt face-up on the table. So, each player's decision to enter the pot on this first betting round is often determined by his assessment of the strength of his hole cards, either as they stand, or according to their potential to make a strong poker hand when the community cards come down.

The Flop

After the initial betting round is completed, and all players have decided whether or not to enter the pot with their two hole cards, three cards are dealt face up in the center of the table. This is called the **flop**. Each player must now decide on his betting action. If no bets have been made, a player may check or bet. However, once a bet is made, checking is no longer permitted. The bet must either be matched for a player to stay in the pot, raised if he wants to make it more expensive for this opponents, or the player must fold. If all players in the pot check after the flop, which is to say no player places a bet, then all hands remain alive and all players get to see the next card for free.

This betting round starts with the small blind, or if he has folded, the first active player to his left, and rotates to the button, who is last to act. If the button has folded, then the first active player who sits to his right will be last to act.

Basically, each player must look at the three cards on the table to determine how well they combine with his two hole cards to make a good poker hand. There are still two more cards to come, so each player's current five-card hand may improve to a better hand, and a big part of skillful hold'em play is evaluating this potential. For example, a player may have four cards to a straight or flush, but otherwise no ranked hand. He must decide if he wants to continue playing in an attempt to draw to one of these high ranking hands.

The Turn

When the betting on the flop has been completed, the fourth community card is dealt face up onto the table. This card is called the **turn**. Each player must now decide on his betting action—checking or betting if no bets are due, or calling, raising or folding if a bet has already been placed. This betting round again starts with the small blind or the first active player to his left, and rotates to the button or the last active player clockwise, who is last to act.

The River

After the betting on the turn has been completed, the fifth community card is dealt face up onto the table. This card is called the **river**. After the river card is dealt, there is another betting round. When this betting round is completed, any players still in the pot show down their hands, and the highest ranking hand wins. This is called the **showdown**.

If any player places a bet that is not called by any other players in the pot, that player will win the pot uncontested, and he need not show down his hand. This is true at all points in time in poker; if all players fold, then the lone remaining player wins the pot by default.

THE BETTING STRUCTURE

Limit games follow strict betting structures for each round, and often limit the number of raises that can be made on any round. In no-limit games, the betting structure is much looser. The bet for calling the blind, and a minimum raise of double the big blind, are commonly specified for the first betting round. Larger raises of any size, however, are allowed, up to the total number of chips a player has in front of him. After that, raises must usually be at least twice the prior bet (if any) but can be any amount greater than this as the bettor elects. There are also typically no restrictions on the number of raises on any betting round in no-limit games.

3

THE PATIENCE FACTOR

One of the most important factors in your tournament success will be your ability to choose the best tournaments for both your skill level and your bankroll. Some tournaments are overwhelmingly luck-fests, and if you enter these tournaments you might as well regard your buy-in as a lottery ticket. Other tournaments provide more of a chance for skilled players to consistently earn money commensurate with their skill. In this chapter, we'll discuss how you should choose a tournament, based on your level of skill, when you have such a vast array to choose from. (In a later chapter, we'll discuss how you should choose tournaments based on bankroll requirements.)

If you flip through this chapter you'll see various charts and tables and formulas. You don't have to get out your pocket calculator or try to memorize anything here. If you just follow the logic, you'll learn how to choose the best tournaments to enter for value. None of this is rocket science. If you read this chapter carefully, you will know more about tournaments than 99% of your opponents. In this chapter, we're going to put numbers on things that nobody has ever put numbers on before, and I promise you will use what you learn.

We'll start by defining every tournament as fast, medium, or slow. A single-table satellite, designed to come up with a winner in an hour or so of play, is the quintessential fast tournament. That's because the players start out with small chip stacks and the blinds escalate quickly. The WSOP main event, which takes the better part of a week to determine a winner, is the ultimate slow tournament. That's because the blinds start small relative to the players' starting chips and go up slowly, so that players can be very selective in the hands they play and how they deploy their chips to their advantage.

Fact: *The faster a tournament is, the more likely it is that the winner will be determined by luck, as opposed to skill.*

Q: What makes a tournament fast or slow?

A: The blind structure in relation to the number of chips each player starts with are the primary considerations, but a few other factors can also affect a tournament's speed. The number of players in a tournament will have an impact on a tournament's speed, and can even cause a slow tournament to become fast as the tournament progresses, as we will discuss in a later chapter. **Rebuy** formats that allow players to purchase more chips in the early stages of a tournament, also affect the speed. But the small buy-in tournaments are generally fast from the very start.

TOURNAMENT SPEED AT A GLANCE

Although amateurs' chances of winning any tournament are greater with fast tournaments, and go down more or less proportionately as the speed of play slows down, a fast tournament that lasts even four or five hours will leave many of the rankest amateurs in the dust. The more time there is to play poker, and the more chips there are to play with, the more skill becomes a factor in determining the winner.

So let's further define fast and slow. Here are some general guidelines.

FAST TOURNAMENTS

Any multi-table tournament where you start out with a chip stack that is equal to the cost of 25 or fewer big blinds is **fast**. If blind levels increase every fifteen minutes or less, it's **lightning fast**. If you get $1,000 in chips, and the blinds start at $25 and $50, you've got a chip stack equal to exactly 20 big blinds to start with. If the blinds go up every fifteen minutes, you—as well as every other player in the tournament—are starting out short on chips. There's no time to fool around. If you've read other tournament books that tell you not to feel threatened until your chip stack amounts to only ten big blinds, forget it! Those books were written by players who assumed blind levels would last sixty minutes or more.

With the blinds going up every fifteen minutes, you'll be entering the fourth blind level, with blinds of $150/$300 (assuming typical blind levels with these starting blinds), just forty-five minutes from the start. So, you must get to work fast. You have a lot of chips to earn in the first hour. With a lot of players in the field, this tournament could last a couple of hours, but a format this fast in a multi-table tournament is as luck-based as a tournament gets.

A tournament with equally few starting chips but a slower blind structure, on the other hand, will be comparatively much more skill-based. Consider what happens if you have the same starting blinds of $25/$50, and the same $1,000 in chips to start, but the blind levels increase only once per hour, instead of every fifteen minutes. This tournament is still fast because all of the players are starting out under-chipped. But with this 60-minute structure, at the end of two hours, you'd just be entering the third blind level, which is $100/$200. Even if you hadn't played a single hand in those first two hours, you'd still have a couple hundred in chips in front of you. This is a real tournament. With 15-minute blind levels, by contrast, after two hours you'd be entering the ninth blind level. This would typically put the blinds at $600/$1,200 with a $200 ante! That puts a lot of pressure on your starting chip stack of $1,000, because you must either grow it fast or die. And because all of the players in this fast tournament are under the same pressure, with many entering pots out of desperation to survive, the winners tend to be the players who were dealt the luckiest cards.

So, it's the combination of starting chips and the rapidity with which the blind levels advance that define the speed of a tournament, and fast blind levels are generally the more important factor. (If you are in a tournament where the blinds start at $5/$10, and you have $200 in starting chips, this would be equivalent to the examples above. Your starting chips in this case again equal the cost of exactly 20 big blinds. It's not the dollar amounts of the starting chips and blinds that define the speed, but the *relationship* of the starting chips and blinds to each other.)

MEDIUM-FAST TOURNAMENTS

With starting chips totaling 30 or more big blinds, and 20-minute blind levels, a tournament is still fast, but it's a noticeably slower event than with 15-minute blind levels, and you'll feel the difference. With this format, you might start with $1,500 in chips and blinds of $25/$50. At the end of forty minutes, you'll be entering the third blind level, which is $100/$200. It's still true that if you don't make some money in the first hour of play, you will already be in big trouble. Even assuming that all you do is pay the blinds once at each level—$25/$50, $50/$100, $75/$150—you'll have paid $450 in blind costs in the first hour alone, reducing your starting chips to $1,050, just as the blinds reach the $100/$200 level. That's tight. But a $1,050 bet with the big blind at $200 would still be an intimidating raise to any player who didn't have a pretty strong hand, especially with the general chip shortage on the table. That's what makes this a better tournament format than the lightning fast one described above.

MEDIUM TOURNAMENTS

With a starting chip stack equal to the cost of 50 big blinds, and 30-minute blind levels, you've got some time to play poker before the blinds become a threat. What do I mean by "play poker?" I mean you can be even more selective in choosing the hands you want to play and how you want to play them. You can afford to lose some chips without being desperate. You can take some chances without jeopardizing your survival. This is a **medium-speed** format. If the field of players is bigger than 100 (and we'll discuss field sizes in detail later), and if 10% or so of those players are fairly proficient tournament players, expect these skilled players to consistently occupy three to five seats at the final table. Luck will still be a factor for many players in the money, but its effect is greatly diminished.

SLOW TOURNAMENTS

With 50 or more big blinds to start with, and 60-minute blind levels, a tournament has a slow structure that will weed out most of the less-skilled players in the first five to six hours. This tournament, in fact, may not end on day #1 unless the field of players is small. A rank amateur will make it to the final table in a format like this only when there is a huge pool of amateurs to start with (and these days, that amateur pool is often there), and then only by having some phenomenal luck with cards. But any unskilled players in a tournament this slow are exactly the types of players every pro wants to see—*dead money*.

Slow tournaments are where the big money pros play. These tournaments often have high buy-in costs, which deter most amateurs. This is where the big money is. Many tournament pros benefit from the large number of amateurs now entering these expensive tournaments on satellites.

Amateurs enter these events because they want to compete with the best players, or because they fantasize about getting on TV. They also want to make the big bucks, but in most cases, they are badly deluding themselves and just giving their money away. In many cases, they don't actually know how bad they are, and how poor their chances of making it into the money are.

Poker is a very unusual "sport," in that anyone with the money can compete with the world's recognized champions. If you want to compete with professional tennis players, you cannot just buy-in to the next U.S. Open. Same with golf, boxing, baseball, hockey—name a sport, any sport.

Poker tournaments, on the other hand, are open to anyone and everyone who's got the cash to buy-in. So, the tournament pool has minnows and goldfish swimming with the sharks. In my opinion, the amateurs who dive into this pool are making a huge mistake. They would be much wiser to earn their way up to the major poker tournaments the same way athletes enter professional-level sports—by coming up through the ranks.

THE VALUE OF FAST TOURNAMENTS

In evaluating tournaments in order to maximize your earnings, keep the speed factor in mind. If you are not an experienced tournament player, you stand your best chance of getting into the money in a faster tournament. Don't be lured by dreams of big money and the possible fame you might acquire by excelling in the slow tournaments. The truth is that too many of your competitors in those tournaments will have the skill to outplay you. If you are already a skilled tournament player, on the other hand, the slower the tournament the more you will be rewarded for your skill.

Fast tournaments are excellent tournaments to start out in anyway, and also provide excellent practice for skilled players, because fast play is an art form in itself, and you will use it and encounter it at some point in every tournament, even the slow ones. In a fast tournament, the desperation level starts high and never stops accelerating. These tournaments will force you to recognize hands of value based on the combination of your position, your chip stack, and the players you are confronting. When you're taking a shot with a marginal hand, these are hugely important factors, and the only way to learn how to evaluate these factors—to play as fast as required at any point in a tournament, but not too fast—is by putting yourself under pressure to do or die. Fast tournaments also force you to identify the weak players and the dangerous players around you quickly.

If you can get to the point where you can win money in fast tournaments, you'll find the skills you develop in these tournaments invaluable in all tournaments. Every tournament becomes a fast tournament for every player who ever gets short-stacked. There is an art to playing a short stack successfully, and nothing teaches this art like playing in tournaments that start out fast and never slow down.

If you never develop the art of speed play, you will also be at a disadvantage when you encounter other players who are short-stack experts. Any player who can "change gears"—that is, move from fast play to slow play and vice-versa, at will—is a dangerous player. It's a general rule in no-limit hold'em that you don't go up against the player with the big stack of chips, as that player can really hurt you. But if that big stack is sitting in front of a wimp who simply acquired those chips with a few lucky hands, you might well prefer to take a shot at that player rather than the short-stacked pro who's capable of putting you to a test with a reraise. Any player who gives no indication of whether he's playing his cards or his guts is a dangerous player. You not only want to be able to recognize that player, you want to *be* that player. These are the players who win the fast tournaments. And, you know what? They're the players who win the slow tournaments, too.

Many players who enter slower tournaments do well until around the halfway point, then they die. They can never seem to figure it out. Why did the good cards stop coming? In fact, their experience has nothing to do with the cards they were getting. Every tournament gets faster as the tournament progresses. That's what a tournament does. It speeds up continually. These players who do fine early on are often among the best poker players, but they simply can't change gears for the faster portion of the tournament. They ought to forget about the slower tournaments for a while and get into some of these hair-raising fast tournaments. These players may know poker, but they need a crash course in tournament speed play.

Fast play. That's a term I'll be using a lot. I will explain **fast play** in great detail in an upcoming chapter, but for now, let's just say that fast play is how you play when you are starting to feel the pinch of the blinds (and antes). In fast tournaments, this is a constant occurrence and you must adjust to it quickly.

Finally, fast tournaments teach you satellite skills, and these skills have a huge value to players who want to play in the bigger tournaments, but don't have a sufficient bankroll to risk the big buy-ins. Satellites can get you in cheaply. There are real differences between satellite structures and regular tournament structures that we will discuss later, but just about all satellites require speed play for success.

ESTIMATING THE "PATIENCE FACTOR"

In order to compare tournaments with each other, both to get a handle on the importance of luck versus skill in any particular tournament format, and to figure out the best strategy based on the tournament's speed, you need to quantify the speed of play required more precisely than just defining a given tournament as fast, medium, or slow.

We all know that the main event of the World Series of Poker is a slow tournament and that your local Tuesday night $40 buy-in tournament that starts at 7 p.m. and ends around midnight is quite a bit faster. But is there a way to put some numbers on these tournaments that would indicate exactly how slow or how fast they are? What if you want to compare the speed and value of the $40 buy-in tournament available at one poker room with a $60 buy-in tournament offered at another poker room on the same night? They're both fast tournaments, but one has fewer starting chips, the other has faster blind levels, etc. As a matter of fact, it's fairly easy to hone in on precise tournament speed and value if you return to the parameters that contribute to a tournament's speed:

1. The number of starting chips
2. The blind structure

What you are looking for specifically is what I call the tournament's **patience factor**. The more patience and flexibility a tournament allows players in selecting the pots they enter and the way they play a hand, the greater a factor skill will be in determining the winners and the more money skilled players will make over time. The more players are forced to take shots with marginal hands just to try to keep up with the blinds, the more luck will play into any player's chance at winning.

But how do you quantify "patience" in a poker game?

To solve this problem, I used a trick I learned from the great gambling mathematician, Peter Griffin. If you are attempting to solve a very complex gambling puzzle, start by simplifying it. Isolate the factors that make the biggest difference, and consider them in a simpler game to see how they work.

The World's Most Patient Player

To simplify the complex problem of quantifying a tournament's speed, I started by creating the World's Most Patient Player, a player who will not enter any pot unless he is dealt two suited aces. Since no deck of cards contains two suited aces, the World's Most Patient Player is fully content to wait forever, never playing a single hand. Obviously, this player is a fiction, but he allows us an easy way to solve this problem of quantifying tournament speed—or the patience factor.

The first step in determining the patience factor is to estimate how long the World's Most Patient Player (WMPP) would sit without playing a single hand before he was **blinded off**, that is, all his chips were lost to the forced blinds without playing a hand. You have to make some assumptions based on experience in order to come up with an answer to this problem. Let's first assume that this player is playing at ten-handed tables and that he will go through the blinds once every twenty minutes, which is a pretty good assumption for a live ten-handed game in my experience. (Online play moves much faster, but we will address that later.) Obviously, 20-minute rounds will not be true for every table in every tournament, but this is a pretty good assumption for ten-handed live tournaments.

Then, how do you estimate the cost of the blinds (and antes, if any) per hour, so that you can calculate how long it will be until the WMPP is blinded off? For a tournament with 60-minute blind levels, figuring out the cost of the blinds per hour is an easy calculation once you have the tournament's blind schedule. You simply assume that the WMPP will go through the blinds three times (once every 20 minutes) at each blind level, and you reduce his starting chip stack by the cost of the blinds until his stack is depleted.

First Example of Tournament Speed

As an example, let's figure this out for the $1,000 buy-in Seniors' no-limit hold'em event at the WSOP, which had 60-minute blind levels. The first blind level is $25-$25, and the WMPP will go through this blind level three times (at a total cost of $50 once every

20 minutes) in the first hour. Here's a chart that shows the costs of the first four blind levels:

Level	Blinds	Total	x3/hr	Cumulative
1	$25-$25	$50	$150	$150
2	$25-$50	$75	$225	$375
3	$50-$100	$150	$450	$825
4	$100-$200	$300	$900	$1,725

Notice that in the Cumulative column, we're totaling the blind costs from the start of the tournament through each succeeding level. The first thing to note from this chart is that the WMPP's $1,000 in starting chips will cover the cost of the blinds through the first three levels ($825), but not the blind costs of the fourth blind level. In fact, since the WMPP will have already paid $825 in blind costs by the end of the first three blind levels, he will have only $175 remaining—not even enough to cover the $300 cost of going through the blinds one time at the fourth level. Of course, where the WMPP sits in relation to the blind will determine how long his remaining $175 will last on the fourth level.

We're ignoring the possibility that the WMPP will accidentally win on one of his blind hands since he is so tight that he will immediately muck his cards as soon as he sees that they are not suited aces. Thus, he cannot possibly win a hand, even by accident. We're just trying to get a blind-off time here, not debate technicalities.

We'll figure out exactly what percentage of those final twenty minutes the WMPP can cover, on average, with his remaining $175 in chips, by simply dividing the total cost of the blinds on the final round ($300) by the number of remaining chips the WMPP has at this point ($175). It looks like this:

$$\$175 \ / \ \$300 \ = \ .58 \ or \ 58\%$$

Since 58% of 20 minutes = 11.6 minutes, we'll estimate that the WMPP will stay alive in this tournament, on average, approximately three hours and twelve minutes before he gets blinded off. To express this in decimals, he would be blinded off after 3.19 hours.

Second Example of Tournament Speed

Now, let's compare this tournament to another tournament with the same $1,000 in starting chips. As of this writing, the Flamingo Hotel and Casino in Las Vegas has a popular no-limit hold'em tournament held twice daily that has a buy-in of just $60. (For up to date information on both live and online poker tournaments, see my website www.pokertournamentformula.com.) Players get $1,000 in starting chips, and blinds go up every twenty minutes. The 20-minute blind levels mean that the WMPP will go through each blind level just once. Also, the amounts of the blinds are slightly different from the WSOP event. Here's a chart that shows the costs of the Flamingo tournament's first four blind levels:

Level	Blinds	Total	Cumulative
1	$25-$50	$75	$75
2	$50-$100	$150	$225
3	$100-$200	$300	$525
4	$200-$400	$600	$1,125

You can see that with his $1,000 in starting chips, the WMPP has sufficient chips to last through three blind levels (cumulative cost of $525), but again, he will not make it through the fourth level. Paying $525 in blind costs through the first three levels means that he'll have $475 remaining of his initial $1,000 in chips. But the fourth level blinds cost $600 total, so, again, he won't last twenty minutes at this level. So, let's figure out the percentage of those twenty minutes he'll last, on average, based on the $475 in chips he has remaining:

$$\$475 / \$600 = .79 \text{ or } 79\%, \text{ and}$$
$$79\% \text{ of } 20 \text{ minutes} = 15.8 \text{ minutes}$$

Since each of the first three blind levels last twenty minutes, for a total of one hour, the WMPP can expect to be blinded off in this tournament after about one hour and sixteen minutes, or, expressed decimally, in 1.26 hours.

The Patience Difference

You now have a measure for comparing the WSOP tournament that starts with $1,000 in chips with this Flamingo tournament that also starts with $1,000 in chips. This "blind-off" time tells you that we'd last 3.19 hours in the WSOP tournament, but only 1.26 hours in the Flamingo tournament. This difference is due entirely to the different blind structures of these tournaments. The Flamingo blind levels last only twenty minutes, while the WSOP has 60-minute levels. Also, the Flamingo blind levels are higher right from the start. If you hadn't noticed this before, go and look at the blinds at each level in both of these tournaments.

But what does this mean in terms of the difference in playing these two tournaments? Nobody is really going to sit for hours without playing a hand. A player in the WSOP tournament would last longer than a player in the Flamingo tournament if indeed neither of these players played a single hand from start to blind-off. But the time difference between 3.19 and 1.26 is almost two hours. Does that time difference matter all that much if you're actually playing?

The answer is yes. In these fast tournaments that time difference is far from insignificant. Think of the positions two players will be in if they play these two tournaments, and in both cases, never have a playable hand in the first hour. In the Flamingo tournament, as we've seen, the player will have paid $525 in blind costs in the first hour, and could not cover the cost of the blinds ($600) for the next round with his remaining $475. In the $1,000 buy-in WSOP tournament, on the other hand, the player will have paid only $150 in blind costs in the first hour, and will have $850 remaining when the cost of the big blind goes up from $25 to $50 for the second hour.

In other words, a player can afford to be more patient in a tournament with a slower blind structure. But that doesn't even begin to describe how huge the patience difference really is between these two tournaments.

Consider where these players would stand at the end of two hours, assuming both actually played, and actually made enough chips on a couple of plays to increase their chip stacks by $1,000 in the first hour. In the WSOP tournament, at the end of two hours, the blinds would be going up to their third level, $50-$100, so that even though the player will have paid $375 in two hours of blind costs to this point, that $1,000 in wins will have him at $1,625 two hours into the tournament.

Meanwhile, the Flamingo player's $1,000 in wins won't even help him get through the second hour. He'll be blinded off long before the second hour is up unless he makes a lot more chips than that. Just to survive to the two-hour point, he will have to cover more than $5,600 in blind costs! And after two hours with those 20-minute blind levels and the Flamingo's lightning fast structure, he will find himself entering the seventh blind level, which happens to be $2,000-$4,000.

Adjusting the Blind-Off Times

Even small differences in blind-off times are significant differences. You might think from looking at the blind-off times of these two tournaments (3.19 v. 1.26 hours) that the Flamingo tournament would only be two to three times as fast as the WSOP event. Not so. This would be true only if the blinds were not going up. Because the blinds are continually escalating, however, differences in blind-off times should not be read as linear differences, but as *exponential* differences.

In order to help you appreciate this difference, we're going to make a simple mathematical adjustment to the blind-off times to produce a tournament's patience factor. We're simply going to square the blind-off time for comparison purposes. Squaring a number means multiplying the number by itself. That's all. Here's how these tournaments compare after you square the blind-off times to produce the patience factors:

WSOP blind-off = 3.19.
Flamingo blind-off = 1.26.
WSOP patience factor = 3.19 x 3.19 = 10.20
Flamingo patience factor = 1.26 x 1.26 = 1.59

Now you can see that these two tournaments are really extremely far apart when it comes to how fast they will play out.

The patience factor is simply a tournament's blind-off time squared. That's the entire definition. And that number will tell you a lot of what you need to know to devise a strategy for any tournament.

COMPARING REAL WORLD TOURNAMENTS

Let's look at the patience factors of a variety of real tournaments. We'll start with the WSOP tournaments, using the blind structures from 2005, and we'll stick with the no-limit hold'em tournaments that were played nine- or ten-handed. (Note that with the large fields of players in 2005, most of these tournaments began with ten-handed play, then became nine-handed when tables started clearing.) For convenience, I'm going to analyze all as ten-handed.

WSOP Tournament Patience Factors						
Event	**Cost**	**Starting Chips**	**Starting Blinds**	**Blind Time**	**Blind Off**	**Patience Factor**
$10K	$10,000	$10,000	$25-$50	100 min	8.67	75.24
$5K	$5,000	$5,000	$25-$50	60 min	4.85	23.48
$3K	$3,000	$3,000	$25-$25	60 min	4.77	22.78
$2.5K	$2,500	$2,500	$25-$25	60 min	4.47	19.98
$2K	$2,000	$2,000	$25-$25	60 min	4.17	17.36
$1.5K	$1,500	$1,500	$25-$25	60 min	3.75	14.06
$1K*	$1,000	$1,000	$25-$25	60 min	3.19	10.20
*Seniors						

None of these tournaments would qualify as a "fast" tournament by my definition. Even the $1,000 buy-in "Seniors" tournament is a long slow tournament compared to the small buy-in tournaments you'll find in your local poker room. You'll rarely find a small buy-in tournament with a patience factor of 10 or more.

With long slow tournaments like these, and patience factors this high, skill will always be the dominant factor in determining the winner. In fact, the winners will usually be determined by which truly skillful players get lucky, because skill alone will rarely get you through days of play without a crippling blow to your chip stack. Expect any tournament with a patience factor higher than 10.00 to be dominated by pros and skilled semi-pros.

PATIENCE FACTOR ADJUSTMENTS

I recommend some simple patience factor adjustments for a few situations that significantly alter tournament speed. The first of these adjustments is for events with a *rebuy structure*. When rebuys are allowed, play tends to be looser, and betting wilder, during the rebuy period. Therefore, when players are allowed to rebuy, you are forced to play faster to keep up with the chip stacks of those who are getting lucky. Patience simply does not pay off when other players are buying more chips and playing much more loosely. Therefore, rebuy periods have the effect of reducing patience factors.

To calculate the patience factor for a rebuy tournament, you first need a method for estimating your starting chips when rebuys are allowed. This is not difficult. If a single rebuy is allowed, with no further rebuys or add-ons, then estimate your starting chips as the total of your initial buy-in chips, plus the rebuy chips. I am assuming here that you intend to make the allowed rebuy—which is a good idea and will be discussed in the upcoming chapter on rebuy strategies.

If one rebuy and an add-on are allowed, then assume that your total starting chips are the total of your buy-in chips, rebuy and add-on. Again, I am assuming you intend to make these purchases.

If multiple rebuys and an add-on are allowed, but you can only rebuy if you are at or below your starting chip level, then estimate your starting chips as the total number of chips you can get with your initial buy-in plus one rebuy and the add-on. If you are allowed two rebuys at the start, and two if you go below your starting chip level, then consider your starting chips to be your buy-in plus two rebuys and the add-on.

The point is to estimate your starting chips as the amount of chips you would be allowed to buy at once, plus any allowed add-on. Do not estimate your starting chips as greater than this amount even if you intend to make as many rebuys as needed throughout the rebuy period to keep your chip stack healthy.

After calculating the patience factor of a rebuy event based on these amounts of starting chips, make one more adjustment and reduce the patience factor by 20%. For example, if a patience factor is 4.00, but one or more rebuys are allowed, reduce the patience factor by 20% to 3.20.

To give you a better idea of how rebuys affect the patience factor of fast tournaments, and how these tournaments compare to the WSOP events analyzed above, let's look at a few of the regular weekly no-limit hold'em tournaments recently available in Las Vegas poker rooms. The purpose of this chart is not to provide a comprehensive list of available tournaments, but to give you an idea of the range of patience factors in typical small buy-in tournaments.

For the "cost," I added the cost of one rebuy where only one rebuy is allowed, while for tournaments that offered one or more rebuys and an add-on, I added the cost of one rebuy and the add-on—the maximum chips you can buy at one time.

Likewise, for starting chips, I added the chips you may acquire via one rebuy and an add-on, where allowed. If no rebuys are allowed, there is an "N" in the Rebuy column. If one or more rebuys are allowed, there is a "Y" in the Rebuy column. Also, after calculating the patience factor, I reduced it by 20% in any tournament with a rebuy format.

The chart includes just a small sample of the regular weekly or daily tournaments available in Las Vegas. Personally, with all the choices available, I wouldn't play in a multi-table tournament that had a patience factor below 4.00. Anything below

			REGULAR LAS VEGAS TOURNAMENT PATIENCE FACTORS (PF)				
Casino	Cost	Start. Chips	Start. Blinds	Blind Time*	Rebuy	Blind Off	PF
Wynn	$540	$3,000	$25-$50	45	N	3.23	10.42
Bellagio (FSa)	$1,060	$3,000	$25-$50	40	N	3.00	9.00
Mirage (S)	$430	$4,000	$25-$50	30	N	2.76	7.64
Orleans (Sa)	$230	$3,250	$25-$25	20/25	Y	2.93	6.89
Bellagio (STh)	$540	$2,000	$25-$50	40	N	2.58	6.63
Orleans (F)	$105	$1,625	$10-$15	15/20	Y	2.80	6.29
Caesars	$220	$4,500	$25-$50	40	Y	2.78	6.18
Mirage (Th)	$430	$3,000	$25-$50	30	Y	2.76	6.12
Binion's (S)	$200	$3,500	$25-$50	25	Y	2.75	6.03
Orleans (MT)	$85	$1,275	$10-$15	15/20	Y	2.62	5.50
Mirage (TW)	$330	$3,000	$25-$50	30	Y	2.53	5.11
Rio	$130	$3,000	$25-$50	20	Y	2.09	3.50
Harrah's	$90	$3,000	$25-$50	20	Y	2.04	3.33
Plaza	$100	$3,500	$25-$50	20	Y	1.89	2.87
MGM	$65	$1,200	$25-$25	20	N	1.67	2.80
Aladdin	$110	$2,000	$25-$50	20	N	1.56	2.42
IP	$80	$2,300	$25-$50	15	Y	1.64	2.14
Bally's	$60	$2,000	$25-$25	15	N	1.39	1.93
Flamingo	$60	$1,000	$25-$50	20	N	1.26	1.60

*number of minutes

3.0 is just lightning fast, and the luck factor is so high that there will only be a very small return on investment for skillful play. It's okay to play single-table satellites that are this fast, but in multi-table tournaments you might just as well draw straws to see who gets the lucky hands. All of the players get so short-stacked so fast, that there is no time for any finesse. There is not much you can do in a multi-table tournament this fast to increase your chances of winning, other than play with maximum speed and aggression and pray for luck.

One obvious general trend here is that, as with the WSOP events, the more you spend to buy into a tournament, the higher the patience factor tends to be, and the more of a skill event it is. With the small buy-in tournaments, however, this is not always the case. You might note that the $540 Wynn tournament beats out a couple of more expensive events. (The Wynn has a $330 tournament with the same format and patience factor on weekdays.) Note that the Orleans in Las Vegas has $105 and $230 Friday and Saturday night tournaments have patience factors that beat a number of more expensive events. The Orleans weekend tournaments are among the best values for inexpensive tournaments that award skillful play.

You see that the number of starting chips is not in itself a good criterion for evaluating a tournament's speed, though I've found that many small buy-in tournament players assume that it is. The Orleans $85 M/T tournament, with only $1,275 in starting chips, has a patience factor of 5.50, beating out many tournaments with greater numbers of starting chips and higher buy-in costs. The Orleans' first two blind levels in these tournaments are $10/$15 and $10/$20, significantly lower than the more typical $25/$50 and $50/$100. Those small starting blinds make *all* the difference.

More Patience Factor Adjustments

Now let's discuss a few other patience factor adjustments.

If the blind levels change at 20-minute intervals, it's easy to calculate how much the blinds are going to cost you per hour. You simply assume that you will pay the blinds at each level once. Likewise, if the blind levels last sixty minutes, the calculation is straightforward. You simply total the cost of going through the first blind level three times, then the second blind level three times, etc.

Length of Blind Levels

But how do you estimate the blind costs if a tournament has 30-minute blind levels, when you are going to be paying the blinds every twenty minutes? Simply divide the actual blind level length by twenty minutes to estimate how many times you will pay at each vel. For 30-minute blind level, divide 30 by 20 (which comes to 1.5), and assume that you'll be going through the blinds at each level 1.5 times. Likewise, if a tournament has 15-minute blind levels, assume you'll go through each blind level 15 / 20 = .75 times. We're just trying to get an average here, and other methods of averaging I've tried don't change the patience factor significantly.

Nine Players Instead of Ten

What if the tournament uses nine-spot tables instead of ten? How can you adjust the patience factor for this? Well, I'd assume that I'd be going through the blinds every eighteen minutes instead of every twenty minutes, so I'll go through 6.67 blinds in two hours, not six. But if you hit the ante level, remember that you'll only pay nine antes as you go through a full round, not ten. Or, you can do it the easy way. If you use these numbers to figure out patience factors, you'll usually find that a nine-spot tournament is about 5% faster than a ten-spot tournament. So, just subtract 5% from your patience factor.

I have an Excel spreadsheet I have set up to automatically figure out not only the patience factor of any tournament structure, but the length of time until I can expect to hit the final table. It also calculates the bankroll requirements for any tournament based on the buy-in costs, number of players entered, and other factors you will find in this book. If you're good with spreadsheets and you play a lot of tournaments, this is pretty easy to set up, and it saves a lot of time when you're just trying to make a quick decision on a tournament's desirability. In later chapters, we'll provide simple formulas for estimating all of these things. (Another way to save time is to just check the complete data at: www.pokertournamentformula.com.)

Adjusting for Automatic Shufflers

One other variable that slightly affects a tournament's patience factor is the use of automatic shufflers on the tables. These devices speed up the play of the hands, allowing slightly more hands to be played at each blind level. The effect is equivalent to having slightly longer blind levels. I have not included this effect in any of the specific tournaments analyzed in this chapter, though some do use automatic shufflers. If you are calculating a specific tournament's patience factor, and you know that this poker room uses automatic shufflers, add 5% to the patience factor. That is, if the patience factor is 2.00, simply make it 2.10 (2 x 5% = .1, so 2 + .1 = 2.1).

PLAYING THE RIGHT SPEED

Now, let me ask you something. Do you think you would be correct in applying the same no-limit tournament strategy at the Wynn tournament (patience factor = 10.42), as at the Bellagio Sunday tournament (patience factor = 6.63), and the Mirage Tuesday night tourney (patience factor = 5.11)?

No! They may all be no-limit hold'em tournaments with essentially the same rules and procedures, but if you approach these tournaments as if they all require the same strategies, you will be making a huge tactical error and reducing your expectation of winning. These tournaments are as different from each other as night and day.

The faster a tournament is, the *faster* you must play. This means playing more hands, and playing those hands more aggressively. That is, putting more chips at risk earlier, and also challenging your opponents to put more of their chips at risk. In a long slow tournament, players can afford to play more cautiously in the early stages, being very selective about the hands and situations they get involved with. Playing too fast—investing too many chips in too many pots—is a mistake in a slow tournament. You will inevitably run into premium hands that your more selective competitors will be playing, and you will not survive.

But playing too slowly in a fast tournament is as big a mistake as playing too fast in a slow tournament. Right from the start, you've got to turn on your aggression, take shots at those players who are waiting for stronger hands, and steal, steal, steal. Later chapters of this book will give specific suggestions for fine-tuning your speed of play for the best results in any particular tournament, but all adjustments begin with getting a handle on that tournament's patience factor. Again, there is no single correct strategy for no-limit hold'em tournaments. There are many constantly changing strategies that all revolve around the specific tournaments' patience factors.

THE PATIENCE FACTOR DETERMINES THE "SKILL LEVEL"

Later, this book will provide specific strategies for tournaments according to "skill levels" based on their patience factors. Here's my ranking system:

PATIENCE FACTOR & SKILL LEVEL		
Patience Factor	Skill Level	Comments
1.49 or less	0	a crapshoot
1.50 to 2.99	1	still too fast, pray for good cards
3.00 to 4.49	2	very fast, good for learning speed play
4.50 to 5.99	3	fast, excellent for good speed players
6.00 to 7.49	4	medium fast, requires more skill
7.50 to 9.99	5	slower, requires much more skill
10.00 and up	6	slow, highly skilled players only

There is a mathematical basis for these distinctions in skill level, based primarily on the likelihood of premium hands being dealt preflop at a ten-handed table, and the statistical likelihood of your being the lucky player dealt any of those premium hands. In other words, you can easily calculate that you will be dealt a pair of aces on approximately one hand out of every 221 hands you play. It is the same for a pair of kings, or any other specific pair. If you take a range of hands that are considered "premium," and assume that these will be the only hands you'll enter a pot with, you can figure out approximately what percentage of pots you'll play.

For example, let's say I consider a premium starting hand to be any A-A, K-K, Q-Q, J-J, A-K, or A-Qs, and these are the only hands I'll play. The odds against my getting dealt one of these starting hands are about 29 to 1, which is to say, I will be playing only about one hand out of every thirty that I'm dealt. This means I will be playing only one hand per hour, which is unlikely to earn me enough chips to survive in any tournament, fast or slow. In a fast tournament, however, a starting hand strategy this tight would be suicidal. Since the blind-off time in most fast tournaments is under 2.5 hours—or only seventy-five hands—I'd be resting my entire tournament outcome on only two to three hands of play. No two starting cards can be counted on to deliver enough chips to keep you alive with a strategy like that.

Also, even a medium-fast tournament rarely lasts more than five hours—or about 150 hands for each player who survives that long—before reaching the final table. In a tournament this fast, I'd be dealt one of these premium starting hands, on average, only about five times. There is no guarantee that I'll get any action on these hands, or even that any of my premium starting hands will hold up. Aces get cracked all the time. I may be dealt pocket jacks then have to abandon my hand in the face of aggressive betting when overcards come down on the flop.

So, the slower a tournament is, the more selective and flexible I can be in my starting hand strategy. The faster a tournament is, the more hands I must add to my list of pot-entering hands, and the more I must make plays to steal chips when I have no legitimate hand to speak of.

Skill Levels 0-1

If you look at the patience factor range of the Skill Level 0 tournaments, you can see that in these tournaments you could pay the blind costs only three times or fewer before falling below the stack required to cover the cost of the blinds for the next round. That's why I call these tournaments crapshoots. Everyone's got to throw his money into the pot with mediocre hands and take shots at the pot with nothing, and most of these bets must be all-in bets that can eliminate a player if he is called. Very little skill can be employed in tournaments with Skill Levels of 0 or 1. They're just too damn fast and make all players too desperate.

Skill Levels 2-3

As the patience factors go up, the skill levels rise because players have more time to be selective and flexible in the pots they enter. With Skill Levels of 2 and 3, there still isn't much time to wait for premium starting hands, but you can use aggressive tournament strategies to take advantage of players who *are* waiting for premium hands. These tournaments give players enough chips to make them feel "alive" and protective of their stacks. Advanced poker skills are not required to beat these tournaments, because they are still too fast for any playing finesse. But *tournament* strategies are very strong in these weak fields and will pay off handsomely.

Skill Levels 4-5

As you move up to Skill Levels 4 and 5, more advanced poker skills are needed to survive. At these levels, you'll start running into players who will be reading you like a book, taking shots at you with nothing more than position on you, slowplaying, check-raising, and doing all sorts of other tricky plays. You will have to learn to do plays like these yourself, and to guard against them, in order to make money in these slower tournaments. A lot of these moves will be discussed in this book, but no book can cover every situation, and some of the best stuff comes only with experience. So I'll tell you the best ways to go about getting the right experience.

Skill Level 6

As for Skill Level 6 tournaments, you'd better be a damn good poker player if you plan to make money in these events, because you will be up against some very fine players who want to make money from you.

More Comprehensive Overview of the Skill Levels:

Skill Level 0

If the patience factor is 1.49 or less, then unless this is a single-table satellite, skill will have very little to do with the determination of the winners. (Many single-table satellites have Skill Levels this low, but can be played profitably. We'll discuss satellite play in a separate chapter.) In a Skill Level 0 tournament with five or more tables, the players who are dealt the best cards win. Simple as that.

Skill Level 1

With a patience factor from 1.50 to 2.99, tournament skill will start to be a factor in determining the winners. Skill Level 1 tournaments are best with small fields—under sixty players. With large fields (200+ players), these tournaments are not much better than Skill Level 0 tournaments. The more skillful players simply won't have the chips or the time to outplay the desperate all-in hordes. Even with huge fields, these tournaments finish quickly. (Field size effects will be covered in detail in a later chapter.)

Skill Level 2

With a patience factor of 3.00 to 4.49, this is a very fast tournament, but it's excellent for learning speed play. With any size field, luck will still be the dominant factor in determining who finishes in the money. This is the lowest skill level, however, where knowledgeable speed play will pay off. To make money in Skill Level 2 tournaments, you must take early advantage of weak opponents who are clueless about how fast this tournament will get, and how quickly they will become short-stacked, as the minutes tick by.

Skill Level 3

This is the lowest tournament skill level that I advise you to play once you have mastered the skills in this book. With a patience factor from 4.50 to 5.99, this is an excellent fast format for speed play. The weaker the field, the better you'll do. Don't expect to find many pros attracted to tournaments this fast, but you will start bumping into other players who understand and employ speed play techniques and you must watch out for them. They will probably recognize what you are doing as well, and will usually steer clear of you. You should do well in these tournaments if you follow the strategies in this book.

Skill Level 4

With a patience factor of 6.00 to 7.49, these are medium speed tournaments. Speed play is definitely a factor in these tournaments, but you also need more poker skills to thrive, as you will start to bump into better players who will play back at you and test you more than in the faster format events. In weak fields, speed play in the first two hours will be very strong, and should set you up for a decent shot at the money.

Skill Level 5

Tournaments with patience factors between 7.50 and 9.99 are medium-slow tournaments. To survive the early blind levels, you must adjust your speed play much more to your opponents than is necessary in faster tournaments, which is to say you must have some fairly well-developed poker skills. And some of the players in these tournaments will be reading your bluffs, taking shots at you, and otherwise testing both your skill and your courage. In other words, players in these tournaments have sufficient chips to play poker, and in order to survive, you will need poker skills that go beyond the primary focus of this book.

Skill Level 6

Any tournament with a patience factor of 10.00 or higher should be viewed primarily as an event for the most highly-skilled players. Also, although large fields make fast tournaments overwhelmingly luck-based events, this is less the case in a long slow tournament. In slow tournaments, the greater the number of players, the more impossible it becomes for an unskilled player to survive to the end. With a huge field of unskilled players, some will likely make it into the money while many of the top pros may not, but it will usually be a combination of luck and skill that will get any player into the *big* money, with skill a crucial factor.

ONLINE TOURNAMENTS' PATIENCE FACTOR

Many online poker rooms have excellent small buy-in tournaments, often with patience factors higher than those available in live poker room tournaments. Online poker rooms can offer these better tournaments at a relatively cheap price for a number of reasons. One is that they have substantially lower overhead costs than live poker rooms. There are no dealers to pay, nor is there any real furniture, cards or chips. Once an online poker room has its operating software, setting up a tournament for a few hundred (or a few thousand) players requires little more than the bandwidth to handle the connections.

Also, online games play at a much faster rate than live games. Whereas you assume that in live tournaments you will go through the blinds at a ten-handed table approximately once every twenty minutes, playing on average about thirty hands per hour, in online games you will go through the blinds about once every twelve minutes, playing approximately fifty hands per hour. This will vary from one online poker room to another, and sometimes from table to table, but if you play online, you cannot help but notice this difference. What this means is that a long slow tournament that would take ten hours to play in a live casino would finish in about six hours online.

There are a number of reasons for this increased speed of play online. Not only is the shuffle time eliminated online, but the dealing is also speeded up considerably. Most players use automatic features, such as automatic blind posting, checking, and folding, and these really speed things up. Also, there are never any arguments or mistakes. No player can bet out of turn, or raise an incorrect amount. When a player pushes all in, everyone at the table knows the exact amount of the bet. In fact, every player's chip stack is displayed both graphically and numerically. Nobody ever asks for a chip count. Players don't stop to study the faces of their opponents, looking for "tells" before deciding on how (or whether) to play a hand. There are no misdeals. The cocktail waitress doesn't interrupt the action.

Online tournaments are the most difficult for which to make general estimates of speed factors because the rate of hands played per hour can differ widely from one online poker room to another—much more so than in live tournaments. I have played in online tournaments where the speed of play was not that different from a live tournament, and in others where the speed of play seemed unbelievably fast compared to live games. I have clocked some online tournaments at seventy-five to eighty hands per hour. The number of hands played per hour in online poker rooms also seems to speed up as time passes, and I suspect this is due to more and more players having high-speed DSL or cable Internet connections as opposed to dial-up.

Adjusting for More Hands per Hour

I'm going to assume fifty hands per hour as the "standard" rate for online tournament play in this discussion, just as I assumed thirty hands per hour for live tournaments. What this increased speed of play means is that online tournaments are essentially following a different clock. You can use patience factors to analyze the speed of online tournaments, but you must make an adjustment for this increased speed of play online.

At fifty hands per hour, twelve minutes of online play is equivalent to twenty minutes of live play. Therefore, if an online casino has 12-minute blind levels, this is the same as a live casino having 20-minute blind levels and you can assume you'll be going through each of the blind levels once in that span. Then you can calculate the patience factor exactly as for any live tournament, by squaring the blind-off time. If you made the false assumption that you would be going through the blinds only once every twenty minutes in an online tournament, that tournament would appear to have a patience factor much lower than what it really is.

Getting an Accurate Patience Factor Online

The actual length of time to blind-off that this method would give you for online tournaments would be incorrect, but that is not important. What you are concerned with is getting an accurate patience factor, not an accurate blind-off time. Here's a chart for converting real online blind level lengths to their live tournament equivalent (based on fifty online hands per hour):

Online Blind Level Length	Live Tournament Equivalent
5	8
6	10
10	17
12	20
15	25
20	33
25	42
30	50
40	67
45	75
60	100

In other words, if an online tournament has fifteen minute blind levels, simply use twenty-five minutes when you calculate the blind-off time, and square this result to get the patience factor. Let's take a quick look at a few of the best regular daily or weekly tournaments available online.

REGULAR ONLINE TOURNAMENT PATIENCE FACTORS							
Casino	**Cost**	**Start. Chips**	**Start. Blinds**	**Blind Time**	**Live Equiv**	**Adjusted Blind-Off**	**PF**
UltimateBet	$109	$2,500	$5-$10	15	25	4.13	17.04
UltimateBet	$55	$1,500	$5-$10	12	20	3.06	9.39
Full Tilt	$109	$2,000	$15-$30	10	17	3.02	9.12
Party Poker	$109	$3,000	$20-$40	15	25	2.85	8.11
Poker Stars	$109	$1,500	$10-$20	15	25	2.78	7.75
Full Tilt	$55	$1,500	$15-$30	10	17	2.75	7.54

Note that these patience factors are comparable to the best regular tournaments in Las Vegas. In fact, the Utlimate Bet $109 online tournament has a patience factor higher than any Las Vegas regular tournament. And this chart includes only a very small sample of what you'll find available online, with many equally good tournaments available at other buy-in levels. (None of these tournaments, incidentally, allows rebuys, which is why there is no column to indicate whether or not rebuys are allowed. For more comprehensive online tournament data, see www.pokertournamentformula.com.)

ARE ONLINE TOURNAMENT STRATEGIES IDENTICAL TO LIVE TOURNAMENT STRATEGIES?

The methods I describe in this book for beating tournaments are applicable to both live and online tournaments, with some limitations. The math doesn't change just because you can't see your opponents. But the inability to look at online opponents definitely gives a different *feel* to the game. In live tournaments, I often base decisions on "player types," and I find it more difficult to categorize online players than players in live tournaments. Online pros compensate for the lack of visual information with things like watching the timing of their opponents' bets, taking copious notes on opponents that can be pulled up when needed, and even using player tracking software to collect data on players' hand histories in advance of tournaments.

But it can't be denied that eliminating the ability to read opponents visually removes a psychological skill factor from the game. And any time a skill factor is eliminated, luck will play a bigger part in deciding the winners. But I suspect there are many players who are poor at reading opponents, and who are likewise poor at disguising their own feelings about their hands, who will do much better online than in live tournaments. And I'm also certain that there are players who are extremely talented at reading opponents, and at disguising their own hands, who will do better in live games than they can achieve online.

Playing Live or Online

Those high online tournament patience factors, however, indicate to me that these tournaments are high skill events. The players in these tournaments have enough chips to be very selective in the hands they play and how they play them. It's easy to see why so many of the best young players today have been able to make the transition to live tournaments from online play. Despite the lack of visual information on opponents, these online tournaments are much closer to long slow live tournaments in terms of strategy than many of the lightning fast small buy-in events that are popular with tourists and amateurs in live poker rooms.

One other important difference between live and online tournaments with similar patience factors is the overall superior quality of play in some of the live tournaments. The Bellagio and Wynn tournaments, for example, are dominated by local pros and semi-pros, while the less costly online tournaments always include a huge segment of poor players equivalent to the tourists who show up for the cheaper fast tournaments in Vegas. There are a good many pros who play online precisely because of the weak fields. These tournaments are an excellent profit opportunity for skillful tournament players who can live without the visual clues.

Getting Ready for the Next Lesson

In any case, it's time to move on to the playing and betting strategies for fast tournaments. I know that by this point in most other books on tournament strategies, you would already have been presented with charts covering the starting hands to play and the ones to throw away. So, you're probably chomping at the bit to finally learn what to do with your pocket 8s on the button.

Well, sorry, but that's not the strategy lesson coming up. Look, cards are just not all that important in these fast tournaments. We'll get to them eventually, but first you've got to get a grasp on the underlying strategic principles of the game.

And that's the next chapter...

PART TWO:
THE STRATEGIES

4

MEET THE WEAPONS: ROCK, PAPER, SCISSORS

The first step to victory in no-limit hold'em tournaments is knowing the three distinct weapons you will have at your disposal. Many of your opponents in fast tournaments will know nothing about these weapons or how to use them at anything but a novice level. If you follow my step-by-step instructions, this chapter will raise your consciousness above that of your opponents.

The three weapons in no-limit hold'em tournaments are cards, chips, and position. Cards and chips are self-explanatory; position is simply where you are sitting in relation to the dealer button. **Early position** means that you are in one of the seats that must play your hand before most of the other players at the table. **Late position** means that you will play your hand after most of your opponents.

The easiest way to understand the power relationship between these three weapons is by looking at a simpler game that has very similar power relationships. Essentially, a no-limit hold'em tournament is an elaborate version of the game *Rochambeau*, or rock-paper-scissors.

Most of us played rock-paper-scissors as kids, but if you didn't, it's essentially a game of fixed power relationships, where two opponents each simultaneously display a hand symbol for one of the three weapons, and the more powerful of the two weapons wins. In rock-paper-scissors, rock beats scissors, scissors beat paper, and paper beats rock.

In no limit hold'em tournaments, the three weapons of cards, chips and position have this same kind of fixed power relationship. Specifically:

- ♠ Cards beat Chips
- ♠ Chips beat Position
- ♠ Position beats Cards

I can already hear objections being raised. Obviously, position isn't going to beat a royal flush. Nothing is, which leads most players to believe that cards beat everything, when the fact is that your cards are the least important of your three weapons. Players hold the **nuts**—the best possible hand given the cards on board—so seldom that such hands play only a small part in tournament success.

I owe the initial inspiration for this tournament strategy to David Sklansky's *Tournament Poker for Advanced Players*. This is not to say that Sklansky suggests a strategy anything like that which I provide in this book, or that he would endorse my strategy. But he presented an idea that I had not seen in any other book on tournament strategy, and his idea was my starting point.

In his book, Sklansky provides an optimal no-limit hold'em tournament strategy for beginners. Unfortunately, Sklansky's all-in strategy doesn't work very well in *fast* multi-table tournaments. That's because he devised his strategy specifically for a non-poker player who was entering the main event of the WSOP—a long, slow tournament where players waiting for premium hands could actually expect to catch one here and there in the hours while the blind costs are inconsequential. In fast tournaments, by contrast, you will rarely see one of these all-in opportunities based on a premium starting hand, and by the time you must make a move with a lesser hand, other desperate players will be forced to call you.

There are some differences between fast no limit hold'em tournaments and rock-paper-scissors. In no-limit hold'em tournaments, for example, you do not get to decide when you will get strong cards. Suddenly, they appear—or, more often, they do not. You also do not get to choose your position. The weak and strong positions rotate. As for chips, everybody starts out with the same strength, but the relative strength of that weapon for each player changes as the tournament progresses.

To further complicate the game, each player actually has some amount of each weapon at his disposal, and two of those weapons—

position and chips—are constantly visible to all. You can see who has the big chip stack, and who is desperate. And you can see who's on the button, and how far out of position every other player at the table is. Players' hole cards are not visible to opponents, but cards can only exert their full power if there is a showdown. Position and chips, by contrast, can often scare winning cards out of the pot.

CARDS, CHIPS, AND POSITION

At first, you may be confused by which weapon beats which weapon, but if you are familiar with the game of rock-paper-scissors, there is an easy way to remember the power relationship. Cards are made of paper. Chips are something you could throw, like a rock. If you can remember those two, there's nothing left for position except the scissors. Paper beats the rock. The rock beats the scissors. And the scissors beat the paper.

I can't overstate the importance of this power relationship. As you will see in the chapters that go into detail on strategies, this power relationship is the key to making final tables regularly. If you are an experienced poker player, but have limited tournament experience, this power relationship may strike you as incomprehensible. That's because this power relationship does not exist to the same degree in non-tournament poker. Chips, for example, get their power directly from the tournament structure with its ever-escalating blinds and the inability of players to either cash out or buy more ammunition.

The overall strategy of "Texas Rochambeau" is to make money by playing whatever strength you have at hand. If you are low on chips, you'll have to make money by capitalizing on your cards or your position. If your position is poor, you can't get involved in a hand unless you have a lot of chips or strong cards. If your cards are bad, then stay out of the fray unless you have a dominant chip stack or a strong position.

Position is an important weapon in hold'em tournaments partly because it comes around frequently. Strong cards are a rarity. It's a joy to find big slick or aces in the hole, and more of a joy to flop a monster hand. But while these occurrences are few and far between, position keeps coming around like clockwork.

And unlike good cards that suddenly surprise you with an appearance, you never just look down and suddenly find a huge chip stack. Nor does the big stack rotate around the table with the button. There is a separate strategy for playing each weapon, and in the coming chapters we will define each of these basic strategies in detail. For now, let's take a closer look at the properties of each of these three weapons.

Cards (Paper)

With good cards, you have power, and with great cards, you are a dominating force—if you play them well. Good cards before the flop, however, do not always hold up, which brings us to the first rule of good fast tournament strategy: *In fast tournaments, good cards must be played fast.* The worse your position, and the smaller your chip stack, the faster you must play your cards. What do I mean when I say you must play your cards *fast?* To play fast means to be aggressive—to raise and reraise rather than to call, and to raise bigger amounts, perhaps even all-in, rather than more standard raises of about half the pot size.

Even when you are in a strong position and you have a dominating chip stack, you are never wrong to play a strong preflop hand fast in a fast tournament. You should just about always raise with aces, kings, queens, jacks, A-K or A-Q. The only time it's correct to limp in with these hands preflop is when you feel certain that one of the aggressive players still to act behind you will raise. Then you can reraise him.

In fast tournaments, it's often correct to push all-in with any medium pair, no matter what your position. The reason is that you just don't have time to play much poker in a fast tournament. When you've got the premium paper, you must put any opponent who wants to take you on to a tough decision. Slowplaying must be reserved for those occasions when you have a truly scary chip lead on your opponents and can afford more risk, or when you have such a powerful hand, postflop, that there is no reason for you to fear a **suck-out**, an underdog hand that wins with a lucky draw.

Again, because strong cards are such a rarity, they are the least important weapon in your arsenal. You do not need "lucky cards" to get into the money, and you cannot rely on good cards coming. If a player with a big chip stack raises, and you have a strong hand, push all-in. You've got to play the cards you have *now*. Remember, *cards beat chips* (paper covers rock).

Fast tournaments just don't leave room for a lot of second guessing. What do you do if you call his raise with pocket 10s, the flop comes down Q-9-3, and he bets an amount that would either put you all-in, or leave you with too few chips to continue to be competitive in the tournament if you lose? A player with a lot of chips often plays loose. He may have raised with nothing more than a **suited ace**, an ace with another card of the same suit. Or he may be betting on nothing more than a straight draw.

If you have a strong hand you want to play against a player who has a big chip lead, you have two choices: either you push all-in on him, putting him to a test, or you fold. Once you call that raise, you've set yourself up for a very tough postflop decision, which more often than not will result in your forfeiting the chips you already put in the pot. In any case, you can't play your cards against those chips anymore, since you can't test him without the risk of busting yourself. You gave up the power of your strong preflop hand when you just called his raise instead of reraising.

When you have a hand like pocket 10s in a fast tournament—and I know what you learned in cash games, but forget it—you don't fool around with a call. If an opponent makes what may be a loose raise, you don't let him see the next three cards for nothing. You won't get a hand as strong as pocket 10s but maybe three or four times in the whole tournament. When you get them, you've got to make money on them. You have to make chips with your money hands. So you either fold if you believe this is a tight player who would only raise from that early position with a high pocket pair, or you put the raiser to the test. Here and now.

You take the attitude that there ain't going to be any poker playing at this table, buddy. It's all or nothing. How much do you like your hand? I like mine *this much!*

Position (Scissors)

As Doyle Brunson first pointed out in *Super System*, position is the most important weapon you have in no-limit hold'em, and it's the most important weapon you have in a fast no-limit hold'em tournament as well. To **have position** on an opponent simply means that you get to act after him. The closer you are to the button, the more players have to act before you, and the stronger your position overall. Strong position continually rotates around the table, so it's something you can count on. In fact, it's the only thing you can count on. As a general rule, position beats cards (scissors cut paper). In the right circumstances, you can call bets and raises when you have position on an opponent, and reraise if you sense any weakness in your opponent, regardless of your cards. Betting based on your position, rather than your cards, is called **position play**.

When facing a well-chipped opponent in a tournament, however, don't forget that *chips beat position* (rock breaks scissors). You can make a position play on this opponent if he is an overly tight or fearful player who will often fold good cards in the face of aggression. But the rock-paper-scissors power relationship means it's usually best not to tangle with a big chip stack when you're really just making a position play. It's much easier to steal a pot from a player with a strong hand who fears elimination than it is to steal from a player who has any competitive hand backed up by a mountain of chips.

Note that position changes after the flop. Preflop, the blinds are in the latest positions, with the big blind being the last to act. If you are in one of the blinds and you have a hand you want to play, it is rarely correct to call a big raise in a fast tournament. If you have a big pocket pair, jacks through aces, or a hand like A-K, A-Q or A-J suited, you should usually either reraise all-in, or get out of the way.

> I will be using terms like "usually" throughout this book when prescribing strategies. Every play is situational—dependent on the opponents you face, your relative chip stacks, and other relevant factors.

Reraising from the blinds is even more important with medium or small pocket pairs. You can call small raises from the blinds with these hands if you have a lot of chips and you simply want to try and flop a set, but these are awful hands to play after the flop from early position. Unless you flop a set, you usually have to abandon your hand postflop simply because of overcards on the board. You can call raises with all kinds of "playable" and even mediocre hands if you're on the button, since you'll get to see how other players play their hands on the flop before you decide what to do. But if you're in one of the blinds, you have to try to take that pot down preflop, while you still have position to wield.

Here's an example of a position-beats-cards play: A player made a standard raise from a middle position, three seats in front of the button. The player was a fairly smart and conservative player and did not play a lot of hands. I was on the button with 10-6 offsuit, a trash hand with little earning potential. I called the raise.

The flop came down K-8-2, rainbow (three different suits). The preflop raiser checked. I bet about half the size of the pot. He folded.

In folding, he turned up his cards—pocket queens—and said something like, "Every time I have the queens, a damn king or ace comes down on the flop!"

I mucked my 10-6 with a smile, happy to have beaten him with my imaginary kings.

This player made a huge mistake in not betting on the flop. There is a standard dictum in hold'em that you "do not give up the lead." This means that if you are the preflop raiser, you continue to bet after the flop, even if the flop doesn't improve your hand, and even if it scares you! In fast small buy-in tournaments, however, players are always and forever giving up the lead in the face of scare cards on the board. Players in these tournaments tend to hold their chips precious, knowing that they cannot acquire any more and knowing that the blinds are about to go up. They just don't want to take risks.

In any case, this a good example of *position beats cards*. Had I not been in late position, I would never have played a 10-6 offsuit. I wouldn't have been in the hand. And this hand is not a rare

THE POKER TOURNAMENT FORMULA

example. In the small buy-in tournaments, you will make a lot of money by calling raises on the button, then betting on the flop when your opponents check. It's just a basic strategy position play in these tournaments.

Chips (Rock)

In hold'em ring games, where the blinds remain constant, chips do not have the power that they have in no limit hold'em tournaments. It's the tournament format that makes your chip stack a power in the rock-paper-scissors relationship. Because players cannot purchase more chips, because they cannot pick up their chips and cash out whenever they want to, and because the blind costs keep getting higher, chips are very precious in tournaments. Every player knows that chips will be the ultimate deciding factor in who makes it into the money and how much money they will make. Any substantial bet by a player with a massive amount of chips relative to most other players at the table is a threat to any player in the pot because he can take away any player's shot at making money in the tournament.

Chips are what it's all about. If you are the chip leader at your table with the capability of eliminating any opponent who goes up against you, you have a lot of options on how to play your hands. Note that you must have substantially more chips than your opponents to really be able to wield the rock as a weapon. Having $5,500 in chips when an opponent has $5,300 is no big rock in your favor. Although the opponent can't put you out, he can cripple you and he knows it. When you have a big chip lead, however, position and cards become much less important in your decisions. If you prefer to wait for premium hands to get involved in a pot, you can do so without fear of being blinded off. If you want to play your position aggressively, which is the smarter way to use your chips, you'll find it even easier to steal pots than it was when you had position but fewer chips.

The only thing you have to watch out for is superior cards. *Cards beat chips.* You don't want to give away your chips trying to bully players whose hands are so strong—or whose chip positions are simply so desperate—that they will not relinquish the pot without a fight. When you have a lot of chips, you can use them to bully players out of pots, but you must also be concerned with protecting your chips.

When you have a big chip stack, all of your decisions will be more complex because you have many more options on how to play. It's actually much easier to play when you are short-stacked. When you're desperate for chips, you have only one move—all in. You make this move on any competitive hand, or on a position play when the opponent(s) in front of you have shown weakness. When you have a big chip stack, however, you really want to get reads on your more desperate opponents. If you've got a decent hand, and a player makes a move on the pot, you want to know if he's so desperate he'll try pretty much anything, or if he might just be taking a position shot. You have to know when you'd best get out of the way.

When you've got a big chip stack, use it as a weapon, but you must also protect it. You don't want to take unnecessary chances. Most of your aggressive plays will pay off when you have a big stack of chips in front of you. But you've got to let the more dangerous ones go. For players who are not yet masters of reading opponents, I'll provide a more detailed strategy for using your chips as a weapon in a later chapter.

ROCK, PAPER, OR SCISSORS?

Again, unlike rock-paper-scissors, you don't get to pick your weapon in no limit hold'em tournaments. Your weapon chooses you. Before every round of play, and before every decision—bet, check, call, raise, or fold—take stock of your weapons. Is your chip stack dominant, average, or on life-support? Is your position strong, weak, or somewhere in the middle? If you are short-stacked and out of position, then you are looking for a strong hand to play with maximum aggression. When the rock is small and the scissors are dull, you need some premium paper. If you're in late position with a better than average chip stack, then without even looking at your cards you can call any normal raise. If no players or only limpers have entered the pot in front of you, you can raise and often take down the pot, regardless of your cards.

Your weaponry will change throughout a hand. You may have an average chip stack in a middle position and call a standard raise with A-J offsuit, not exactly the best starting hand or position. But if all the players behind you fold, you're no longer in middle position. Calling that raise bought you the scissors (position). If your chip stack is substantially bigger than any other player in the pot, then even if you're not the chip leader at your table, you've got the rock for this hand. If you enter a pot with pocket 5s—not exactly superior paper—but the flop comes down A-9-5, you've now got the paper to challenge any and all comers. As you go through every hand you play, continually reassess your weapons.

You will make very few mistakes if you ask yourself where you stand in terms of the rock-paper-scissors power relationships. If you find yourself involved in a hand, and you are not sure about whether you should continue, stop and ask yourself which weapon you've got, and just as important: What does your opponent have? Not what cards does he have, but what weapon does he appear to be using?

In fast tournaments, you can't be afraid of busting out. If it happens, it happens. You will never make it to the money if you do not take advantage of every weapon, and use every weapon aggressively. Don't just wait for the paper. You will get the scissors far more often. In a fast tournament, if you get to the final table, you will have made more money on position play than with any other weapon. That is a fact. And 95% of the time, when you bust out, it will be with good cards. Cards are the weakest weapon you have. Don't overvalue them. Don't overplay them. Don't wait for them. Good cards are so rare, and you must increase your chip stack so much and so fast, that you must look at cards as icing on the cake. While you're waiting for cards, you've got to survive a lot of rounds with ever-increasing blinds.

In the next chapter, we'll look at how you do this.

5

BASIC POSITION STRATEGY

If you get nothing else from this book, I hope you'll get a real understanding of the concept of position—its importance in hold'em, how strong a factor it is in no-limit hold'em tournaments, and how to capitalize on its value.

Most of the hold'em books I've read discuss the relationship between position and starting hands. I struggled through a number of tournaments trying to match my decision to enter a pot with my position, my cards, the players and action in front of me, if any, trying to decide if I should check, fold, call, or raise—and if raise, how much?

In *Super System*, Doyle Brunson was the first author to put the proper emphasis on position in no-limit hold'em. Brunson discusses getting involved in pots with trash hands just because he has position, even raising with trash hands, and playing some hands without looking at his cards!

But there are real differences between the games we're discussing in this book and those Brunson was writing about. First, his chapter on no-limit hold'em isn't focused on tournament play, but no-limit hold'em ring games. The desperation factor that tournaments introduce as the blinds continue to rise is not a factor in ring games. Second, Doyle was playing in much bigger games. Players who sit down to play poker with tens of thousands of real dollars have a different perspective on the game than players in tournaments whose total money investment might be $40 to $60, or even a couple hundred, or even a couple thousand, because a tournament buy-in is always money the player can't get back anyway. And third, Doyle was often playing with some of the best poker players in the world. Most of the competition you will face in the small buy-in tournaments is composed of local low-limit ring game players, online players whose tournament experience is primarily cheap Internet tournaments, and rank amateurs who have no poker experience other than watching WPT final tables on television.

This chapter will provide a basic strategy of position for fast multi-table no-limit hold'em tournaments. You must have this strategy down cold if you intend to make money in these tournaments. The majority of your opponents do not know this basic strategy, and simply knowing and following these plays will put you way ahead of them in your survival chances.

This **basic strategy** is the mathematically optimal way to play your position, assuming you have no information other than your seating position in relation to the button and any opponents already in the pot. Any violations from basic strategy must be mathematically justified by other information you may have.

The basic position strategy, like any basic strategy, is not in itself a winning strategy. It's a survival strategy. Most of the money you make in a tournament will come from those hands where you violate the basic position strategy, based on either the strength of your cards or other factors. But the basic strategy will keep you alive and competitive during card droughts.

I must emphasize that the basic strategy of position play for a fast multi-table no-limit hold'em tournament is based *exclusively* on position. Starting hands are not a factor, nor are legitimate hands postflop. The chapter on card strategy that follows this one will show you how to incorporate cards into position strategy. Until you get there, simply ignore your cards.

THE IMPORTANCE OF POSITION

It may surprise many poker players that the basic position strategy for fast no-limit hold'em tournaments is not based on your cards, but exclusively on your position in relation to the button and the betting action in front of you. If you play other types of gambling tournaments, however, such as blackjack tournaments, this will make more sense, because competitors in these tournaments are often correct to violate the basic strategy for the normal casino game. Plays that would be "wrong" in a normal game can be correct in a gambling tournament based on a player's chip position—and seating position—relative to his opponents.

The reason basic position strategy works irregardless of your cards is that you don't win a fast tournament by betting on your strong hands so much as by betting against your opponents' weak hands. You will win many more pots by representing strong hands than you will by actually being dealt strong hands. And there is one truth about this game that has plagued every hold'em player since the first blind he ever posted in the first game he ever played:

Any two cards can lose

Most of the poker math I've seen in the excellent analyses by Sklansky, Caro, and others analyzes the probability of one hand either holding up or improving versus some other hand, or versus some number of opponents. There is nothing incorrect about this math, but it is incorrect to base an overall tournament strategy on these concerns. Instead of looking for the odds of your cards holding up versus your opponents' cards, you should be looking for the odds of improving your chip position versus your opponents' chip stacks. These are two entirely different considerations.

There will be a few key hands in every no-limit hold'em tournament where you must consider the mathematics of a hand holding up, or whether a bet is mathematically justified by the odds. When you are at a ten-player table, however, the bigger overall concern is not these few rare hands that you are dealt, but the likelihood of some other player having a hand so strong that he will not lay it down.

The later your position at the table, the smaller the likelihood that you will be surprised by an opponent's holding such a hand. And, just because a player has a premium starting hand before the flop, that doesn't mean he will like his hand as much after the flop, when "scary" boards are common.

You accomplish your first objective in every tournament—which is keeping ahead of the blind costs—by betting that your opponents do not have hands that they cannot lay down in the face of aggression when you are in late position.

PREFLOP BASIC POSITION STRATEGY

One misconception I've found many players have about position play is the idea that these types of strategies are based more on psychology than math. They believe that to raise a player on a stone cold bluff, you have to have a "read" on that player—that is, feel fairly certain based on his behavior that he has a weak hand, or is on a draw, or is just taking a shot at the pot with a probe bet. Players who are aware that they are not particularly talented at reading opponents believe their opportunities for bluffing players out of pots must be few and far between. And it's true that bluffing can be terrifying. It's easy to envision your opponent sitting there with the nuts, just aching for you to take a shot at him.

The truth, however, is that position play is based on math, though not the mathematical likelihood of my hand beating your hand. Instead, it's based on the likelihood of my bet being too much for your hand to get involved with. You've got to stop envisioning how powerful your opponent's hand might be, and just consider the odds. Position play is based on the mathematical truths of hold'em: One, premium starting hands are few and far between. Two, flops more often miss a starting hand than hit it. And three, strong hands on the flop, turn, or river, are rarely the nuts.

The preflop position basic strategy provided below does have some limitations. Again, this is a basic strategy for fast, multi-table, no-limit hold'em tournaments, played with nine or ten players per table, preferably with three to thirty starting tables (thirty to 300 entries). I would use this preflop basic strategy in all tournaments with patience factors up to 5.99, which is to say, primarily in Skill Level 2 and Skill Level 3 tournaments.

I would also use this strategy, but more selectively, in medium-speed tournaments with patience factors up to 7.49 (Skill Level 4), because these are definitely slower tournaments where you must play with more poker skill. But when I say "selectively," I do not mean infrequently. What I mean is that slower tournaments allow all players to be more selective in the hands they play, as well as in the way they play them. As a general guide, in Skill Level 4 tournaments, I would follow the preflop position basic strategy about 80% of the time. Which 80% you might ask? How do you make a decision on when to follow it and when not to follow it?

Unfortunately, the answer to this question gets into the subtleties of poker and your observations on the players you might be taking a shot at. You will find more deceptive slowplay and check-raising in slower tournaments and you will find opponents who are much more knowledgeable about moves that appear to be position-based, and who will shoot back at you if they suspect you are making a move. Again, the slower a tournament is the more real poker skill and experience is required, but if you really have no clue about whether you should or should not make your position play, then make it. It's better to be right 80% of the time than wrong 80% of the time, and only by taking action will you learn to recognize when danger lurks.

In Skill Level 5 tournaments, I would cut back on position basic strategy plays to about 60% of the time. And, again, there is no simple formula for when you should or should not make these plays, but you should make them more often than not. You can only learn when to make your moves and when to refrain from experience. If you start advancing to these slower tournaments, and you feel clueless about when to make a position play, then make your moves and watch what happens. Every time you make a position move, you are also testing your opponents. As a general guide, you might start by eliminating position moves on some of the worst starting hands. Make your moves with hands that have potential such as high cards, connected cards, and suited cards. This way if you are called you have a better chance of flopping a decent hand or a good draw. However, real position moves are not based on cards and keep in mind that flopping "good" draws, or top pair with a bad kicker, can get you into a lot of trouble.

As for Skill Level 6 tournaments, remember the definition earlier: *Any tournament with a patience factor of 10.00 or higher must be viewed primarily as an event for the most highly skilled players.* If you try to use the strategies in this book, or any book, in pro-level tournaments, you're on your own.

These strategies do work well in slow tournaments if you test them with commercially available poker bot software, like *Poker Academy* or Wilson Software's *Tournament Hold'em*. But real players in real games, especially in major big money tournaments, will be much more dangerous than poker bot opponents. I am not opposed to practicing tournament strategies on this type of software. In fact, when you are first learning the basic strategies of position, cards and chips, this type of software can be an excellent learning tool because you can play super fast to build good tournament habits. Just be aware that live skilled players are not poker bots.

Even in the fast tournaments for which this basic position strategy was developed, you must use judgment in making these plays. If you have an aggressive position player to act behind you—one who is capable of reraising with no hand to speak of but just because he plays position with aggression—then you will have to use these basic strategy plays more cautiously and less frequently. You must also pay close attention to the size of your chip stack in relation to those who will act after you. If you are desperately short-stacked, then the only position bet you can make is all-in—if you make any position move at all. Likewise, if a player to act after you is desperately short-stacked, and he is smart enough to know that he must play any moderately strong hand to survive, this is not a player to make a move on if you have nothing yourself. You don't want to risk doubling him up.

Pure position play—and by that I mean raising with no regard whatsoever to what your cards are—works best when you have enough chips to abandon your hand if necessary without serious damage to your survival chances, and the opponents you face are neither desperate nor out-chip you by any massive amount. These moves work best early in a fast tournament, when most players feel they have enough chips to be competitive (and I'll define "competitive" more precisely later). This is generally in the first two hours or so of a fast tournament, after which you must be much more selective in making any moves based purely on position. This doesn't mean you stop making position plays in the later stages of a tournament. You never stop making these types of plays if you have any intention of winning. You simply must use more judgment in picking your spots, primarily because more of your opponents will be desperate and forced to fight back.

Given these limitations, here is the preflop position basic strategy that I recommend for fast multi-table tournaments. Again, the cards you hold are immaterial. The strategy is presented according to the order in which players enter the pot:

PREFLOP BASIC POSITION STRATEGY

Seat	Action
Position 1 (under the gun):	Fold
Position 2 (early):	Fold
Position 3 (early):	Fold
Position 4 (early):	Fold
Position 5 (early/middle):	Fold
Position 6 (the raising seat):	Raise if first in, otherwise fold
Position 7 (the cut-off seat):	Raise if first in, otherwise fold
Position 8 (the button):	Raise if first in, call any number of limpers, call one raiser (up to 3-4 x big blind), otherwise fold
Position 9 (small blind):	Call in an unraised pot, otherwise fold
Position 10 (big blind):	Raise if small blind limps in with no other players in the pot; call if small blind raises 3-4 x big blind with no other players in the pot; otherwise fold

---

Note that according to preflop basic strategy, there are only five positions (#6, #7, #8, #9, and #10) from which you would *ever* play a hand. This is not to say that you will actually never play a hand from any of the other positions, but that to violate this basic strategy there must be considerations that override it—generally, either exceptional cards or your desperation for survival when your chip stack is getting too small.

Let's look more closely at how this strategy is actually applied at the table. Think of this as the strategy that you would be correct to apply if you couldn't look at your cards. It's true that as soon as you look at your cards, you have information that goes beyond this basic strategy—obviously, if you find pocket kings in one of the first five "folding" positions, you're not going to fold. But we will discuss departures from the basic position strategy later. The reason I'm not providing these departures here is because I want you to get a handle on the power of late position in and of itself.

Playing Positions 1 through 5 Preflop
Fold.

The first five positions are bad positions because you must enter the pot with no information on too many opponents. Information is power, and lack of information is weakness. So, the basic strategy in these positions is to fold.

Playing Position 6 Preflop and Postflop
Raise if first in, otherwise fold.

Think of Position 6 as "the raising seat." This is the easiest position from which to steal the blinds in fast tournaments. From this seat, with five players folding in front of you, there are only four to act after you, and only two of those players would have position on you after the flop. Entering the pot with a raise from this seat gets a lot more respect than a raise from either of the next two seats that have position on you. Blind defenders don't defend as readily as they do when raised from the button. In fact, if you get a call from either one of the blinds, you should assume that your opponent has a pretty good hand, and if he bets after the flop, just fold.

If you are called from one of the hands that will act after you postflop—the button or the cut-off seat—this is more problematic. Calls by one of these players are rare, and usually indicate that the calling player has a legitimate hand, as these players will not be assuming that you were just taking a shot with nothing. For the rest of the hand, however, this player will have position on you, and you will never be certain of what he's going to do, or whether he's playing his cards or his position. And never think that you're the only position player in the tournament.

If your poker skills—and by this I mean your skills at reading and exploiting other players and situations—are superior, then you might reraise a position player who raises behind you. But the basic strategy if you are ever reraised by a player who has position on you is to *fold*. (And, again, I'll discuss departures from this basic strategy based on your actual cards or other factors later.)

When I say that your Position 6 basic strategy, given the above preflop conditions, is to raise, I mean that regardless of what your cards are, you should make a **standard raise**, a bet of three to four times the size of the big blind. It doesn't matter if you have a 7-2 offsuit, you raise. Don't even think about not raising. You will make money with this play. It's that simple. Usually, you will simply steal the blinds. But you will also make money when you are called by one or both blinds and you bet when they check after the flop. And you will make a lot of money when your bets are called on the flop and turn, and you fold your opponents with a bet on the river. Obviously, none of these results are guaranteed, but you're going for the long run wins with this play, and they will be substantial.

You will lose money on this play when you are reraised and must fold your junk hands, or when an opponent is slowplaying you and calls you down to the end. Slowplaying is rare in fast tournaments, however. Most players will reraise when they have strong hands, and you can get out of the way with minimal damage. If you can start to recognize the player types who are capable of tricky plays, as well as the calling stations who will not lay down a pair to save their lives, you will know when to crank up your betting to get rid of an opponent and when to shut it down. Your overall success with basic position strategy will improve as you come to recognize a few important player types, so you can play against them accordingly.

Playing Position 7 Preflop and Postflop

Raise if first in, otherwise fold.

Position 7 is known among poker players as the **cut-off seat**. In limit games, or in long slow tournaments, this is probably the best seat from which to steal the blinds. Enough hold'em players know this, however, that in fast tournaments, it is more difficult to steal the blinds from the cut-off seat than it is from the raising seat specifically because every raise from the cut-off seat, as well as from the button, tends to be viewed as an attempt to steal. Players are just as suspicious of this move in slow tournaments and limit games, but the desperation factor in fast tournaments makes all players less risk-averse and more likely to fight back against anything that looks like a "move."

Your betting strategy from this seat, however, is identical to your Position 6 strategy. You run a greater danger of the button reraising you, because a position player on the button will rarely respect a raise from the cut-off seat, viewing it instead as an attempt to steal the button from him—which it is. He'll often try to put a quick end to it by reraising you, especially if you make this move more than once. If the button simply calls your raise, your post flop play is risky. He may really have a hand, or he may simply represent one, and unless you have some kind of a read on this player, you won't know which is true. The basic strategy play when you are involved in a pot postflop with multiple players is to check and fold to any bet if any one player has position on you. This is just too dangerous a situation if you do not have a strong hand yourself.

In a fast tournament, Position 7 is a trickier position to play from than Position 6. However, in addition to a raise usually winning the blinds, aggressive play will also give you more opportunities postflop to make some of the strongest position plays you can make in fast tournaments.

If the button player calls your preflop raise, and you get heads up against him, you should automatically bet half the size of the pot on the flop. Most of the time, your opponent will fold. If you are called, then you should do the same thing on the turn and river. This strategy assumes that both you and your opponent have sufficient chips to play some poker here. You cannot allow either your or your opponent's chip stack to be placed in serious jeopardy by these bets. If making these bets, or your opponent's call, would mean that either of you had more than half of his chips in the pot, then you must either raise all-in, or simply check and fold against a bet and wait for a better opportunity.

Never risk short-stacking yourself on a position play with a "standard" bet or raise. If you are not well-stocked with chips, you either go all-in, or get out of the way. And you cannot allow an attempt to steal force your opponent into a showdown just because he has so many chips already in the pot.

Despite the risk, in a fast tournament when both you and your opponent have sufficient chips to play poker, the basic strategy play is to keep the lead in the betting. If you were the preflop raiser, then you should bet after the flop, and keep betting at each street unless you are reraised. You will almost never go out on a play like this. Instead, you will almost always bust out when you actually have a strong hand. It is always *less risky* to play bluffs than it is to play your actual cards. This is because it's easy to abandon your hand on a bluff, but much more difficult to get away from a truly strong hand. Some players never realize this.

If you bet on the flop, simply keeping the lead, and your opponent raises, the basic strategy play is to fold. You are probably facing an opponent who has a hand he likes. Even a minimal raise here could be dangerous to call, as he may like his hand a lot more than the size of his raise indicates. Unless you have some kind of a read on this player, don't test him to see how much he likes his hand. You'll have many less dangerous opportunities to make money.

If you know this player to be an aggressive position player, however, you do have a chance here to make some real money by playing back at him. You will first have to make the tough decision. Does he really like his hand, or is he just doing what you do—betting that his opponent doesn't have a hand, or at least not a hand strong enough to continue out of position? If you decide the latter case is most likely, then you are making a big mistake if you fold. Your only decision here is whether you should call or reraise.

If you feel fairly certain that the button player who has position on you is simply making position moves when he raises you after the flop, then your strongest play is to call his raise on the flop, check and call again on the turn, then push all-in on the river before he has a chance to bet at you.

When you check and call, it means one of three things to your opponent. Either you are on a draw, you flopped a monster, or you don't believe *he* has a hand. If the raiser was simply playing position, he must decide which of these three possibilities is more likely. The least likely possibility is that you were simply planning on stealing all of his position bets on the river with a trash hand of your own.

You will only get a few opportunities to make this type of play in any tournament. If both you and your opponent have big stacks, then you can play this out to the river, which is the most dangerous but also the most potentially profitable way to make this move. The danger comes from the fact that your opponent may have a strong hand that he won't abandon, or worse—he may make a real hand as more cards hit the board. For example, he may backdoor a runner-runner flush or straight while you are bluffing at slowplaying him.

So, if you believe his reraise to your bet on the flop is just a position bet, and you want to play with less risk, you should immediately go over the top of his raise (and, in a fast tournament, it will probably have to be an all-in bet) and put an end to this hand before the turn or river cards are dealt. But whatever you do, do not try to check-raise him on the river. When the river card is dealt, you must push all-in yourself. Don't give him a chance to push all-in on you!

Sometimes, you will backdoor a powerful hand yourself while you are making this play. In this case, you may go ahead and try the check-raise move on the river if you're fairly certain your opponent will bet.

All postflop position play is very high-risk, but if you do not make occasional high-risk plays, you'll never make it into the big money. You'll need to make these plays once or twice in a fast tournament, and only when you can pick up a substantial pot. The preflop basic position strategy will keep you alive for a long time on stolen blinds, but it's the position moves postflop that put you into contention with the chip leaders.

Playing Position 8 (the Button) Preflop and Postflop

Raise if first in, call any number of limpers, call one raise (up to 3 to 4 times the big blind), otherwise fold.

Position 8 is the button, the strongest position at the table. If you get into the pot, you will have position on the flop, turn, and river on every other player. This is a huge advantage, so your cards are of minor importance in your decision to enter a pot. In fact, the only time you will fold your hand preflop is when there is a raise greater than a standard raise of three to four times the size of the big blind. (And again, as you will see in the chapter on chip strategy, if you are really short-stacked, this will not apply. All basic position strategy plays assume that you have sufficient chips to keep from jeopardizing your tournament survival as a result of the play.)

The position basic strategy also indicates that you should raise from the button if you are the first player in the pot. This will often be viewed as an attempt to steal the blinds—which it is. If one or both blinds are rabid defenders who will automatically call your raises, then you may find it more valuable to call from the button, rather than raise. You can then bet on the flop when the blinds check. In fact, although the basic position strategy play is to raise, it's generally best to mix up your play on the button with raises and calls, simply for camouflage. Occasionally, you might even fold a hand from the button in an unraised pot, but this is always a mistake in a fast tournament unless you are doing it purely for show, to convince the blinds as well as other players at the table that you primarily play your cards, rather than your position.

Against an opponent who consistently defends his blind, you should experiment with bigger raises, assuming you have the chips. If he calls your raise a couple of times when you bet three times the blind, make your next bet four times. If he calls this bet, try five times. Most players, even staunch blind defenders, have a threshold above which they won't get involved in a pot out of position unless they truly have a strong hand.

You may also find that, if you simply call from the button, one of the blinds will take a shot at the pot by raising *you*. This is a pain in the ass because you don't really know whether he has a hand or is just assuming that you don't and that you won't pay to see the flop. The basic strategy play here is to call the raise, then take it away from him when he checks on the flop.

But this decision must always be colored by your take on the player. If it's a tight player who raises you from the blind, I'd throw my hand away in a heartbeat. If it's some aggressive shot-taker, I'd give that bet no respect. He's going to have to maintain his aggression out of position after the flop if he wants to take this pot. And even if he bets after the flop, I may raise him if I feel he's just taking another shot to avoid giving up the lead.

Playing Position 9 (the Small Blind) Preflop and Postflop

Call in an unraised pot, otherwise fold.

From the perspective of pure position play, the basic strategy from the small blind would simply be to fold. You have no position after the flop on any player. The only reason you should call from the small blind in any unraised pot is because you're getting at least 3 to 1 odds on your money, and more if there are other limpers in the pot. If you flop a monster you might be able to take down a huge pot with a disguised hand and a very small initial investment. The exception to this rule is if the big blind is a position player who is likely to raise you if you limp in as the only other player in the pot. In this case, don't waste your money calling.

Without cards, the small blind is as weak as a position gets. You can't play position if you don't have it.

Playing Position 10 (the Big Blind) Preflop and Postflop

Raise if small blind limps in with no other players in the pot; call if small blind raises 3 to 4 times the big blind with no other players in the pot; otherwise, fold.

The basic position strategy from the big blind is to fold if there is any player in the pot who will have position on you postflop. So, the only time you will ever play this hand as a pure basic position strategy play is if the only other player in the pot is the small blind, because you will have postflop position on him. If the small blind is an aggressive player who will always take a shot at your blind when he's the first one into the pot, then always call his raise, or even reraise him. You will have position on him after the flop, so he will be the one who has to make the tough decisions.

MULTIWAY POTS

Multiway pots, which are pots with three or more players involved, are always more dangerous for position play. When you raise from position 6 or 7, you are always hoping that positions 7 and 8 won't call behind you, because you really want position on your opponents postflop. Although the position basic strategy is to keep the lead in your betting, you may have to alter the basic strategy in a multiway pot if any player enters the pot with position on you and is a player whom you've observed playing solid hands only. Although aggression must be your most consistent strategy, you must be ready to throw in the towel in the face of real danger. When you are facing more than one opponent, the danger is multiplied.

HOW TO LEARN THE BASIC POSITION STRATEGY

One thing I know from thirty years of learning all kinds of gambling strategies is that it's best to learn any complex strategy one step at a time. The temptation for many aspiring pro gamblers is to try and do everything at once. Inevitably, this learning method fails. It's frustrating and confusing to try to learn and apply multiple new skills at the same time.

I suggest that you learn to play position at hold'em the same way I did, by playing "in the dark," which means ignoring your cards completely. Don't even look at your cards as they'll only tempt you to violate the position play when they're strong, or scare you off of the play when they're weak. Ultimately, the problem is that you won't learn the position strategy. Start out by just getting the basic position strategy down cold. You simply bet or fold according to the guidelines defined above.

TOURNAMENT SIMULATION SOFTWARE

One of the best ways to learn position play is by practicing with a software program that provides "bots" as opponents in simulated tournaments. Don't expect any great deal of realism from these programs. The only reason you're playing these simulated tournaments, and playing without looking at your cards, is to learn the basic position strategy. Pay no attention to the results.

If the poker tournament simulation software you use does not provide an option for you to have your cards dealt face down, then simply tape a small square of cardboard over the area of your computer screen where your cards are displayed. As you play your hands, don't give in to the temptation to peek at your cards. If you take down a pot, don't look to see what hand you won with. You have to get used to your cards not mattering at all, and that's the most difficult aspect of position play.

Because of this, you should violate the position basic strategy rule to call in any unraised pot when you are in the small blind. Since you will not be looking at your cards at all, you cannot play this hand. Just fold it. Otherwise, just open this book and follow the preflop strategy chart on page 78 as you play.

If you use the 2002 *Tournament Texas Hold'em* software, don't be surprised if you finish in the money more often than not with position play, even when you're not looking at your cards. If you play the simulated WSOP main event on this software, you will finish in the money about 60% of the time without ever looking at your cards! That, of course, is ridiculous. Do not expect to get close to making money in real tournaments strictly with position play. All you're trying to do with this practice software is build one key skill. (I should note that this software has been updated since I tested it, reportedly with more realistic players.)

If you use the *Poker Academy* software, you will never finish in the money with nothing but preflop position play. The bots on that software, however, are much more susceptible to postflop position play, and you can occasionally finish in the money without looking at your cards if you take more risky position shots after the flop when more money is at stake. But don't take such results too seriously. Again, you are simply using the simulation software to practice the basic strategy position plays. One nice feature the *Poker Academy* software offers is the option of receiving your cards face down.

If you have the tournament software "tutor" or "advisor" feature turned on, you will frequently be told that you are playing incorrectly. Ignore the advice. Most amusing is when you fold to a raise and the Advisor asks if you are sure you want to fold since you have a very strong hand. Just fold. Don't play your cards. You're just trying to get the position plays down.

Let me mention here that you should not waste your time trying to learn how to beat the bots in these programs. The bots are way too easy to beat. Real players are much more complex in both their poor play and their expert play.

PRACTICING AGAINST REAL PLAYERS IN REAL MONEY TOURNAMENTS

Once you have the basic strategy position plays down cold— and it won't take long—I suggest you start playing in the dark in inexpensive live tournaments. Believe me, this is incredible fun. You'll be amazed at how far you'll get in tournaments just by using position plays. Every time you take down a pot you'll feel like the legendary blind Samurai, slaying opponents left and right with your eyes closed. And definitely take a few of the more risky postflop position shots. Test your reads on your opponents when you don't have a hand or, at least, you don't know if you have a hand!

Again, you shouldn't expect to make it into the money in real tournaments with all of your play in the dark. The value of playing without looking at your cards is to demonstrate to yourself how truly strong position play is. Many times, experienced hold'em players who have come to the tournaments from the ring games have told me that they get to a point in a tournament where they can see that their chip stack is getting dangerously short, and know they have to take a shot, but just can't bring themselves to push in their chips without a legitimate hand. In fact, you'll be amazed at the number of players in the small buy-in tournaments who never even take a shot at the blinds! If you make the basic strategy of position play part of your regular strategy, you will get short-stacked much less often, and you will be so comfortable with pushing in your chips without a legitimate hand that you'll be aching for opportunities to take position shots long before you're dangerously short-stacked. To me, one of the greatest thrills in poker is taking down a substantial pot without a hand. And this is what the fast tournaments are all about. If you don't really get a kick out of this kind of kamikaze play, and if you think the fun of poker is in being dealt pocket aces or flopping a set, you'll rarely make money in the fast tournaments.

Once you get good at combining your pure position plays with actually playing your cards, you'll find that you will almost never bust out of a tournament, or even lose any substantial portion of your chips, on position plays. You will lose your money when you're playing your legitimate hands and you get sucked out on, or your pocket kings just happen to bump into pocket aces. That is a fact. You will see this over and over again. It's good cards that get you in trouble.

If the thought of playing in real money tournaments without looking at your cards strikes you as a very expensive way to learn, ask yourself how often you're making it into the money when you *are* looking at your cards. If you want to beat these tournaments, you've got to pay a little for the education. The cost of a few small buy-in tournaments played in the dark is a pretty cheap price to pay for an education you can't get any other way.

One very important point to keep in mind when playing in the dark in a live tournament is that you must absolutely appear to be looking at your cards. You must cup your hands around your cards and appear to be peeking at the lifted corners, when in fact you're leaving your cards flat on the table and looking at nothing but the darkness inside your hands. Also, you shouldn't tell any of your opponents later that you played in the dark. If you are suspected by your opponents of playing in the dark, you'll be raised and reraised on every hand you play. This is your secret. You do it for a few tournaments until you have the basic position strategy down cold, then you'll never have to do it again.

Some players to whom I've described the basic position strategy have asked whether other players at the table get suspicious of these consistent raises from the same late positions. The fact is that there will be nothing all that consistent about your play. You only make these plays under specific conditions that depend on the prior actions of other players at your table—usually, they must all fold in front of you before you even enter the pot—so you do not keep raising from the same positions round after round. Many rounds, you will not play any hand at all. If anything, your opponents will think you are a very tight player looking for exceptional cards. After your initial practice plays in the dark, you will be adding plays from other positions based on your cards and/or your chip stack, and that will mix up your play quite well.

Postflop Basic Position Strategy 101

There are two major postflop basic strategy position plays that cover the majority of the postflop situations in which you have position on your opponents. Here are the two secret strategies for making money after the flop:

> **1.** He checks, you bet
> **2.** He bets, you fold

That's it. If you've played in a few tournaments already, then you know this is no big secret. You see it all the time. *But do you do it?* You have to do it! In fact, about the only time you shouldn't bet when your opponent checks is when you've flopped such a monster hand that you want to give your opponent every possible chance to make something so that he'll be willing to put some money in the pot.

Let's dissect the logic of these two postflop strategies.

He Checks, You Bet

He-checks-you-bet is just a standard basic strategy play when you have position. Standard. Requires no thought. Just do it. As your skill level increases and you begin to get meaningful reads on your opponents, you will occasionally make an exception to this play, but don't make a habit of violating this strategy.

If your opponent didn't bet, it is far more likely that he disliked the flop than that he is slowplaying you. About 90% of the time, the routine is: *He checks. You bet. He folds.* Forget about the 10% of the time when he is either slowplaying you, or likes his hand just enough to call, or has a strong draw and wants to see the next card even if he's not getting sufficient pot odds, or just thinks you're taking a position shot and is determined to be the sheriff. Unless you have some kind of an actual read on your opponent, ignore these possibilities. Follow the basic strategy.

If your opponent calls your bet, you continue with the he-checks-you-bet strategy on the turn, though in fast tournaments there's a good chance your bet on the turn may have to be all-in. It doesn't matter what your cards are. The simple math of this situation is that your opponent is unlikely to have a hand he can call an all-in bet with. If this play knocks you out of a tournament, so be it. You're going to get knocked out of most tournaments before you reach the money, and if you get knocked out on aggressive plays, that's a hell of a lot better in terms of your long-term prospects than getting knocked out by being slowly ground down by the rising costs of the blinds and antes. You want to go down fighting, not whimpering.

He Bets, You Fold

The postflop he-bets-you-fold move is also basic position strategy, but it will be one of the basic strategy plays that you will be correct to violate most frequently. Basic strategy decisions are never based on any specific player who is betting at you. Assuming you have no read on your opponent and no legitimate hand yourself, the correct play is to just get out of his way when he bets. Now let's look at the times when it's correct to violate this basic strategy.

The main reason you will often depart from this strategy and play back at your opponent is because experienced hold'em players all know that they should not "give up the lead" in their betting.

Any skilled opponent knows that to check here just because the flop didn't hit him would simply be giving you an opportunity to take a position shot at the pot, which he couldn't call. So, if you believe that the player who is betting has a pretty good grasp of traditional hold'em theory, there's a good chance that this postflop bet of his is meaningless. If you raise him here, he'll often fold.

One guideline to use on whether to play back at this player is the *size* of his bet. If his bet is a standard postflop bet, somewhere around half the size of the current pot, you should call. This is most likely a meaningless "don't give up the lead" bet in which he is simply not giving up his aggression. The reason you just call is to try and get him to make another of these don't-give-up-the-lead bets on the turn, so that you can get even more chips out of him.

If his postflop bet is much smaller than half the size of the pot, then make a substantial reraise to take the pot right here. Don't just call if he makes one of these half-hearted stabs at the pot. That weak bet usually means that he won't bet again on the turn unless the turn card gives him a strong hand, and you just don't want to give him a free chance to beat you. Take that pot now. You won't get any more chips out of him. Some players hope that a small bet like this will make you believe they've got a strong hand and are just trying to get more chips out of you. But in the fast tournaments, that's almost never the reality. Push all-in on that sucker and take the pot.

If his postflop bet is much greater than half the size of the current pot, however, get out of his way. He probably has a pretty good hand and he's unlikely to give it up.

SETTING UP POSTFLOP POSITION PLAYS

If you are well stacked in chips, you can set up postflop position plays by calling tight players who come in with a standard raise before the flop. These players only raise with legitimate hands, so you can assume they have a medium to high pocket pair, or something like A-K, A-Q, or A-J. These conservative players who enter very few pots are known as **rocks**. The nice thing about rocks is that you can be pretty sure that they've got high cards.

Never reraise a rock preflop unless you've got the goods. These players will call almost any bet before the flop, even an all-in, when they have truly strong hands. But after the flop, these players can get wimpy when the flop looks dangerous, and flops that don't hit them usually *do* look dangerous to them.

Tight players just don't bluff. If a rock raises preflop with pocket kings, and an ace comes down on the flop, he won't bet. He won't even take a shot. Since you called his raise preflop, he will be absolutely positive that you must have a solid starting hand. Weak players often believe that their opponents play as they do, and there are so few showdowns in a fast no-limit tournament that they can keep this illusion forever. Maniac bluffers are always assuming that opponents are trying to steal, and rocks live in mortal fear of the nuts. Since solid starting hands often include an ace, if you bet, the pot is yours. If he calls your bet, or check-raises you, then you do have to get out of the way, because he either flopped a set or two pair or something else that he won't lay down.

With a lot of chips you can also call limpers or standard raises from positions 6, 7, or 8. When you have a massive chip stack in addition to position on your opponents, you are truly a scary prospect at your table. But that gets into chip strategy, which is covered in detail later.

First, let's look at how you play when you know what your cards are. I mean, even though they're of minor importance, there are cards in this game...

6

CARD STRATEGY I: HANDS AND MOVES

If you are an experienced hold'em player, you already know that position affects the starting hands you should play. But in tournaments, the structure also alters optimal starting hand selection. The advice in this chapter applies specifically to the fast multi-table no-limit hold'em tournaments that are the focus of this book. These strategies are not meant for non-tournament ring games, single-table satellites, or major tournaments with long, slow blind structures. Don't take this playing advice into your local poker room's $2/$4 limit game. It won't work.

We've already discussed the rock-paper-scissors power relationship between chips, cards, and position and the basic strategy position plays you should make regardless of your cards. This chapter is about fast tournament card strategy. Cards are the most complex of the three weapons in poker tournaments not only because there are so many possible hands, but because the best way to play these hands varies according to your position, your chip stack, the tournament structure, and the time point in the tournament.

To keep this discussion simple, we'll start with the assumption that you are in a "competitive" chip position. You're not short-stacked, nor are you gloating over some mountain of chips that's terrifying your opponents at your table.

To be more precise about what I mean by a "competitive" chip stack in a fast tournament, I mean that your chip stack would cover the cost of at least 30 big blinds, but not more than 50 big blinds. For example, if you have $2,000 in chips, and the blinds are $25 and $50, your chips would cover 40 big blinds (2,000/50 = 40). You're not desperate, but neither are you particularly chip-rich. You're *competitive.* I will discuss how this changes when the antes kick in later. Now let's talk cards.

THE VALUE OF YOUR CARDS IN RELATION TO YOUR POSITION

In Texas hold'em, position is information, and in all forms of advantage gambling, information is power. When I have early position at a hold'em table, I have no information about what the other players may be holding preflop, yet I must make a decision about whether or not to bet, raise or fold. In late position, after other players have already acted, I know a lot.

Let's say I'm holding an A-10 under the gun, the first position to bet preflop. How do I play this hand? If I bet with it, then get raised, should I call? I'm in pretty bad shape if the raiser has an ace with a better kicker than my ten. And what exactly am I hoping for on the flop? If an ace comes down, and I bet, then get raised again, there's a good possibility my kicker is already beat by the raiser. If instead a 10 comes down, and I bet and get raised, does the raiser already have my 10s beat? Did his preflop raise mean he already had a bigger pocket pair? Or is he just raising with a hand like A-K or A-Q, assuming my bet was just because I didn't want to give up the lead? And what if the flop comes down K-10-5? Now if I bet and he calls, what does that mean? Does he have a king with a poor kicker? Is he slow playing a set, or calling on a straight or flush draw?

Under the gun, A-10 is a throw away. It's just too hard to play this hand without advance information on your opponents.

But, what if I'm in late position? First, if no one raises the pot, I can pretty well assume that there are no high pocket pairs at the table, and any aces in the hands of the limpers probably have poor kickers. If the flop comes down with an ace, and any player bets, I'll bet my kicker is better than his and I'll reraise him. If the flop comes down K-10-5 and no one in front of me bets, it's a pretty good assumption that my 10s are the best hand. I'll bet, and probably take the pot. If I'm called, it will likely be a player on a straight draw, not a player holding a king.

Late position to a hold'em player strengthens the value of every hand. Position provides information, and information spells money.

EARLY, MIDDLE, AND LATE

Let's define the positions at the hold'em table, from the perspective of playing your cards, rather than from the perspective of taking position shots to steal pots.

First, the button is the strongest position. Preflop, the only players who have more information before betting are the blinds, and they immediately go to the weakest position after the flop. After the flop, and through the turn and river, the button always bets last.

The two seats to the right of the button are late position seats. At a 10-player table, with all hands in action, these players would be betting 8th and 9th after the flop and through the river.

The three seats to the right of them—the players who would bet 5th, 6th, and 7th after the flop—are in middle position.

The two blind positions, as well as the two seats to the left of the big blind—meaning the players who will bet 1st and 2nd preflop, then 3rd and 4th postflop—are all early position seats.

In determining whether or not you should enter a pot, and then whether or not you should continue in a pot, and whether you should do so with bets, raises, or calls, it's important that you play your cards based on your position—early, middle, or late.

PREFLOP CARD STRATEGY

These are the hands to enter the pot with based on your position, and how to enter the pot:

Early Position

If first in, raise with all pocket pairs from 7-7 to A-A, and A-K, A-Q, A-J. If not first in, raise any limper or reraise any standard raise with J-J to A-A, as well as A-K. Call any standard raise with 7-7 to 10-10, as well as with A-Q, and A-J. Otherwise fold.

Middle Position

Follow early position card strategy, plus raise (if first in), or call any standard raise with K-Qs, Q-Js, and J-10s. Otherwise fold.

Late Position

Follow all of the early and middle position card strategy, plus call any standard raise with all pocket pairs from 2-2 to 6-6, as well as with A-10, A-9s, 10-9s, 9-8s, and 8-7s. And don't forget your position basic strategy plays in late position—if first in, raise with any two cards; if on button, call any standard raise with any two cards. Otherwise fold.

More Thoughts

Ideally, you will adjust these guidelines by the number of players already in the pot, and the number of players to act behind you. The more players in an unraised pot, and the later your position, the more marginal hands you may play.

This is an aggressive strategy because that's what fast tournaments require. In a long slow tournament or ring game, it would not be a basic strategy play to raise from early position with a hand like 7-7 or A-J. Nor would you usually call raises from late position with weak pairs like 2-2 or 3-3. In fact, the biggest mistake amateurs make in limit games is playing too many hands, and the above strategy would strike many experienced limit hold'em players as way too loose.

It's a general rule in hold'em that it's a much less costly mistake to play too few hands than it is to play too many. In the fast tournaments, however, playing too few hands is as big of a mistake. So you call standard raises with all pocket pairs from late position. If you flop your set, you'll make a bundle. And if you don't, you've got a good setup for a position shot.

In these fast tournaments, you will be surrounded by both players who play too few hands and players who play too many hands. The players who play too many hands generally enter pots and call raises with no consciousness of position, and little real understanding of card values. You'll see many players who will enter pots or call raises with any suited ace or king, or any two high cards, like K-J or Q-10. You might be correct to play cards like these when you are either short-stacked and desperate, or big-stacked and able to loosen up your play and take more shots with marginal hands. Use the guidelines above as a basic strategy for entering pots. In slower tournaments, Skill Levels 5 or 6, you must make adjustments based on your opponents. Adjustments based on your chip stack will be discussed in a later chapter.

Don't Ignore the Position Strategy

Once you start playing card strategy, don't stop playing position strategy. For example, the position basic strategy is to automatically fold from any of the earliest five positions. But the card strategy above dictates that with certain hands you will definitely enter the pot from these positions. Or, you may not have one of the "playable" late position hands listed in the card strategy above. But if you are the first player into the pot, then your position strategy is to raise with any two cards.

One easy rule to remember is that you should look at your cards first, and if your card strategy is to fold, then revert to position strategy. Any time you don't have the cards to play, you play the position strategy.

POSTFLOP CARD STRATEGY

Playing your hand after the flop is the most complex part of card strategy. There is no easy basic strategy for postflop play because so many interrelated factors are involved. How strong is your hand? How many players are in the pot? Do you have position on any or all of the other players involved, or do one or more have position on you? Who are these other players? Are they loose, tight, calling stations, timid, shot-takers, tricky players? Does the flop itself strengthen your hand, or does it present dangers such as overcards or potential straight or flush possibilities for your opponents? So many possible scenarios exist after the flop that any attempt at creating a "simple" basic strategy for postflop play would require a chart with hundreds of asterisks and footnotes.

Once the flop has come down, you must weigh all of the factors and play the situation in addition to your cards. But there is a logical process you can go through in assessing your postflop situation and best strategy. That process starts with looking at your cards in relation to both the flop and any other players in the pot to get an initial evaluation of where you stand. This is called **reading the board**.

READING THE BOARD

You must be fast and accurate in reading the board. The first thing to look for is how the flop may have helped or hurt your own hand. If your cards are a pocket pair, for example, you need to know if you've flopped a **set**, a third card of your denomination to give you trips, which is a very powerful hand.

If your cards are suited, you must ascertain whether two or all three of the flop cards match your suit. With two cards matching your suit, you have a decent shot at making a flush on the turn or river.

If your cards are connected—meaning consecutive values like 8-7 or J-10—you want to know if the board has given you a straight, an open-end straight draw, or even a gutshot straight draw. If one or two of the board cards match one or both of your cards, then you want to know if you have top pair, second pair, bottom pair, or two pair. You also may have a combination of possibilities. You may have top pair in addition to a straight or flush draw, etc.

Just as important as looking at the flop from the perspective of how it may have helped your cards is looking for possible dangers. If your cards are a pocket pair, and you do not flop a set—which will be most of the time—you must be concerned about any overcards to your pair that came down on the flop. For instance, if your cards are Q-Q, and an ace or king comes down on the flop, you may have to throw your hand away at a loose table with many callers, as there are likely to be some aces and kings in your opponents' hands. If you are heads up against a single opponent, then you will have to make a tough judgment call on this hand. He may have an ace or king or he may not. This is where more advanced poker skills come into play, because you must decide based on who your opponent is and how he plays his hand, if he has you beat.

If all three cards on the flop are suited, or if all three are connected with no more than two gaps total, then some player may already have a flush or straight. If only two cards are suited, or if only two cards are connected or separated by two gaps or fewer, then some player may be on a flush or straight draw.

Here's an example of how you must read the board, and think about your hand.

Let's say you are in early position with Q-Q, and the flop comes down K-Q-6, with two of the cards suited. You have a truly strong hand right now. In fact the only hand that could beat yours at this point is a set of kings if another player called your preflop raise was holding K-K. But both the flush and the straight possibilities are dangerous. Any player with two cards in the same suit as the two suited cards on the board would make a flush if another of that suit came down.

The straight possibilities are scary because the K-Q are right within the range of cards that so many players play. Any player holding A-10 A-J, J-10, J-9, or 10-9, could make a straight if a single card came down to complete it. When you're holding trips, you should fear straights and flushes more than anything else.

So, how do you play your Q-Q after reading this board?

You make a bet or raise that is at least the size of the pot, and if a bet that size would put more than half of the chips you started this hand with into the pot, then just push all-in. And if this is a multiway pot, meaning you have more than one other player involved in it, then always push all-in. You leave your fear of some player holding K-K behind you, since that is the most remote possibility, and you make anyone who is drawing to a straight or flush pay dearly to see the next card. When you make this bet, you're really hoping that there is a player in the pot with A-K or K-Q, because this player may very well call your bet, even if you go all-in.

You can't afford to check your set of queens with this flop, hoping to check-raise any bettor who might have a king in hand, because you may end up giving a free card to your opponents if no player bets. And if the turn card brings a third card to a straight or flush, you can no longer play with the same confident level of aggression.

In fast tournaments, you must bet with aggression when you make a strong hand, and with maximum aggression (all-in) whenever there is serious potential danger on the board.

One other important factor you must bear in mind when reading the board is that any time there is a pair on the board, some player could be holding a full house (or even quads). Also, if a player pushes all-in on you when there is a pair on board and you're sitting there with a flush or straight, you've got a real tough judgment call because he may be holding a full house. This is a situation where you've got to look at your opponent, think over the betting on the round, and make your best guess.

It's very difficult to lay down a set, a straight or a flush, and in fast tournaments especially, it's usually a mistake. In any case, you must first learn to read the board both for what it means to your own hand *and* what it might mean to other possible hands at the table.

UNDERSTANDING THE NUTS

To have the nuts in hold'em means to have hole cards that when combined with the community cards make the best possible poker hand at the moment, a hand that cannot be beaten no matter what hole cards any opponent may have. The concept is most easily explained by example.

Let's say the flop comes down: Q-8-6. The queen is a spade and the 8 and 6 are both diamonds. At this point, what are the nuts? Which two cards in your hand would make the best possible hand with the cards on that board? Let's use the process of elimination, starting with the best poker hands and working down.

Obviously, both royal and straight flushes are impossible with this flop. And since no pair is on the board, it's also impossible for any player to have quads or a full house. Also, since only two of the cards on board are suited, no flush is possible. And with three gaps between the queen and eight, no player could have a straight.

This brings us down to the next highest poker hand—three of a kind. Any player holding pocket queens, 8s, or 6s will have flopped a set. The nuts at this point would be the top set—queens.

When a five of spades comes down on the turn, the board looks like this: Q-8-6-5, now with two spades (Q-5) and two diamonds (8-6). What are the nuts at this point?

With this board, you can immediately eliminate all of the premium hands down to straights. Obviously, with no paired cards on board, and no more than two cards to any one suit, quads, full houses, and all flush possibilities are nixed. But that five on the turn does combine with the eight and six to make a possible straight for any player who had either a 9-7 or 7-4 in the hole. And the "nut straight," the hand that is the best possible at this moment, would be the 9-high straight. Those pocket queens may have just gotten sucked out on.

But the river card pairs the board with a five of diamonds. The board now looks like this: Q-8-6-5-5, with two spades (Q-5) and three diamonds (8-6-5). That river card changes everything. First of all, any player with a straight is now beaten by a flush if any player has two diamonds in the hole, since there are three diamonds on the table. And any player who has a suited ace of diamonds might believe he has the nuts, but he would be wrong. Since the five paired, a player with pocket queens now has a full house, and it's the nut full house since no higher full house is possible. There are also other smaller full house possibilities. You could have a full house with this board if you had hole cards of: 8-8, 6-6, Q-5, 8-5, or 6-5. Woe be to any player with any of those hole cards if an opponent holds pocket queens, because it is nearly impossible to lay down a full house.

And although the queens full of fives may be the nut full house, it's still not the nuts. Any player holding pocket 5s just made quad fives when that river card came down, and four-of-a-kind beats a full house.

But, unfortunately for any player with pocket 5s who just made quads, he still doesn't have the stone cold nuts. The real nuts with this board would be either a 9-7 or 7-4 of diamonds, because either of those hole cards would combine with the board cards to make a straight flush. And by the way, if a player has the 7-4 of diamonds, he should know that he doesn't have to worry that some other player will have the 9-7 of diamonds for the higher straight flush, because there is only one 7 of diamonds in the deck and he's got it.

An excellent way to learn how to read the board is to drill yourself on "finding the nuts." Take out a deck of cards, shuffle it, deal three cards face up onto the table and look for the nuts. After you've figured out the highest possible hand, deal a turn card and see if the nuts have changed. Then deal a river card, and once more, find the nuts. Put these five cards back into the deck, and do the exercise again. Take your time to get it right, and repeat until your speed increases and you never miss a straight. Note that unexpected straights are the hands that give most players the most trouble.

If you remember these four rules, you'll get very quick and accurate at reading the board:

FOUR RULES FOR READING THE BOARD

1. Unless there is at least one pair on board, it is impossible for any player to have quads or a full house.

2. Unless there are at least three suited cards on board, it is impossible for any player to have a flush.

3. Unless there are at least three cards on board that have two or fewer gaps between them (and a gap is a space between consecutive cards: 9-7, for example, has one gap), it is impossible for any player to have a straight.

4. If none of the above premium hands are possible, then the nuts would *always* be a pocket pair that makes a set with the highest card on board.

When you do this exercise, be sure to figure out not only the nuts, but all of the possible strong hands. At a poker table, you need to know them all because it will help you to figure out if your opponent could actually have the hand that could beat yours. For instance, in the example above, you might deduce that no player in the pot at the river would have the straight flush, because they would not have called a preflop raise with either a 9-7 or 7-4 suited. You might also deduce that no player would have the quad 5s, since the two fives on board came down on the turn and river, and any player with pocket 5s would have folded to the raises on the flop.

Reading the board, and thinking about the way the hand has played out, is the primary basis for making your postflop decisions.

BETTING ON THE FLOP

The way to make money with your cards in no-limit hold'em tournaments is to bet your strong hands aggressively in order to increase the size of the pot for your wins, and throw your weaker hands away so that you give up less money to stronger hands when you lose. Weak players tend to stay in pots—continuing to throw in more money, sometimes all the way to the showdown—far too long. This is not a calling game.

There are times when there is so much money in the pot, and you feel your chance of taking the pot is good enough, that it is correct to slow down your betting, prepared to call to the end in the hope that your hand will hold up. You only have to win a big enough percentage of these big pots to pay for, and profit from, these appropriate calls. But if you find yourself continually calling with marginal hands because the pot is so big, or because you made *something*, you are playing too many hands and staying in too many pots too long.

Playing Top Pair on the Flop

Basically, you should bet any premium hand, including top pair with a good kicker, aggressively. That means you should place a bet that is at least half the size of the pot, and more if the board may be providing your opponents with strong drawing opportunities. With three to a flush or straight on board, however, and another player reraising, you must slow down. If all you have is top pair, don't be averse to throwing it away against aggressive betting.

Almost all hold'em players have flush consciousness. If there is aggressive betting with three to a flush on board, this betting is either coming from a player who has already made the flush, or who has flopped a very strong hand such as a set or two pair, and wants to kill the action before someone draws out on him by making the flush if a fourth card of that suit comes down.

Never fall in love with top pair. The inability to surrender after making a pair of aces costs many poor players—who play far too many aces to start with—a lot of money. With three to a flush on board, or three to a dangerous-looking straight—such as 9-10-J—discard your top pair in the face of two aggressive bettors. Against a single opponent, you must make judgment calls based on the player and the precise situation.

Playing Second Pair on the Flop

If you make second pair, you must be even more cautious. Say you entered the pot with J-10 suited on the button, and the flop comes down K-J-7 rainbow. If everyone checks to you, bet. It is unlikely that any player has a king. The only real danger would be a player slowplaying a set. It is possible that a player in front of you entered the pot with Q-J, and has your J-10 beat, but that player is now being penalized for playing such a hand from early position. He was afraid to bet his jacks because of the king on board, and now—with your bet—he must assume you have a king.

It is possible that he will call your bet on the flop, hoping for his hand to improve, but he cannot play with any aggression at this point. You have both position and first strike aggression over him. If this is a very poor player—and there are a lot of them in fast tournaments—he may call again on the turn, then fold when you bet on the river if his hand doesn't improve, thinking you had him beat from the start with your kings. Poor players are always afraid of an ace or king on board if they cannot beat aces or kings. A smarter player will often call you down, based on his read on you, as he will realize that you could very well just be playing your position.

There is also the distinct possibility that the caller has your jacks beat with a bad king, possibly a K-3 suited or something, that he's afraid to bet because of his terrible kicker. In this case, he will probably call you down and take the pot at the showdown if you do not make it too expensive for him. That's life with players who play crappy cards.

In the above examples, I would view the calls to my bets as weakness, even if I did feel my opponent had me beat with top pair with a poor kicker, or that he had a jack like me, maybe even an A-J, but was afraid of the king. I would not allow these players to continue in the pot after that first call on the flop. When the turn card hits, if they check, I'm all-in.

What if you called a raise from middle position with A-Q, and one or more players entered the pot after you? Then the flop comes down K-Q-7. How do you play this hand? This is a tricky situation and how you continue will depend not only on how your opponents play this flop, but who those opponents are. If the early raiser bets half the size of the pot or more, with multiple players to act behind him, fold. He probably has a king and multiway pots are dangerous and can become very expensive if you don't have a really strong hand. If he checks or significantly underbets the pot—say he bets $250 into a $1,000 pot—and you have only one player to act after you, then you should bet or raise the bet to at least half the size of the pot. I'm assuming here that a bet this size will not severely affect your chip position. This is the only way to find out if the player who has position on you has a king. If he reraises, fold. If he just calls, and the early position player either calls or folds, you get to see one more card. And if you judge your callers to be weak—possibly calling on a straight draw—you should push all-in on the turn if the turn card does not appear to have helped a straight possibility.

If there are multiple players to act after you, betting out with second pair in the face of that king should only be done if you can easily afford to give up the chips if you are reraised. Playing marginal hands aggressively when you are out of position is generally best avoided. With aggressive players acting behind me, I would often just check and fold with this hand. You'll have lots of less risky opportunities for making money.

Taking Aggressive Shots with Marginal Hands

These types of aggressive shots taken with marginal hands like second pair when you sense weakness in an opponent almost always pay off. Or at least, they should. If you continually bust out of tournaments on these types of plays, then you are making them too often, or in the wrong situations. These are the kinds of mistakes you'll want to go over mentally afterward to identify any signs that should have indicated to you that your opponent was stronger than you judged him to be.

Plays like this are way beyond any basic strategy, and you'll never learn when to make these plays and when not to if you don't start trying them. This is something you'll get better at as you develop your player-reading skills. Online players compensate for the lack of visual information by keeping copious notes on their opponents. In the beginning, these will be difficult moves to make, so pick your spots carefully and think of them as experiments. As your successes increase and your failure rate goes down, you will find yourself in possession of two of the most lethal weapons that any poker player can have—confidence in your own judgment, and the courage to act on your gut feelings.

Strong Hands You Can't Get Away From

When I say that it's your cards that get you in trouble in tournaments, and that you'll usually go out on your good hands, I'm not talking about these all-in shots you take with marginal hands when you believe an opponent is weak. I'm talking about really strong hands that you just can't get away from. If you flop a set in a fast tournament and an opponent pushes all-in, you really have to call unless you are among the top players in the world when it comes to reading opponents. In many cases he'll be on a flush or straight draw, or maybe he'll have flopped two pair, and in most cases you will have the best hand. But it's *calling* these all-in bets with really strong hands that will most often knock you out of a tournament, not *making* the all-in bets.

Some All-In Thoughts

Your all-in position shots simply won't get called very often, because you make these bets when you face a weak opponent, and he goes away. Pushing all-in on second pair is really a position shot more than a card shot, and it just about always takes the pot. Don't be afraid to make these moves. You'll much more often go out with a hand like pocket aces when the 8-7 suited takes a kamikaze preflop all-in shot from the button and you call from the big blind. He'll make his flush and you're gone. That's the way it goes.

Nothing on the Flop

What if the flop doesn't hit you at all? Say you have a small pair in the hole and all overcards come down. Or you have A-Q and the flop comes down with midrange cards like 10-8-5. Then you're not playing your cards, are you? Either you bet to keep the lead if you were the preflop raiser, or you have a position play, or you let it go. With two strong overcards like A-Q, I might call a bet of half the size of the pot or less if I had sufficient chips to be able to afford folding if the next card didn't hit me, but I wouldn't get seriously involved with these cards on a poor flop like this one. It's a nice preflop starting hand, but that's all. Let it go if you face any aggression.

Flopping a Monster

What if you flop a monster, say, the nut flush, nut straight, or a full house? Is it ever wise to slow play? In my opinion, there's not much value to slowplaying in a fast no-limit tournament unless you have an aggressive bettor you know to be a smart player who is betting at you. Raising, or check-raising, his bet on the flop may cause him to fold and you'll only have gotten one bet out of him. By calling, he may believe you are on a draw, and he will probably bet at you again with a bigger bet on the turn. Aggressive players also often bet when they are on draws, hoping to take down the pot without hitting the hand they want. Most of the time in a fast tournament, you should bet and raise with every strong hand.

BETTING ON THE TURN

The deeper you get into the board, the trickier it gets. As each card is dealt, the possibilities for premium hands become greater. Essentially, you do the same thing on the turn that you did on the flop. You consider what the turn card means to your hand, if anything, and what it may have done for opponents' possible hands.

One major difference at this point, however, is that the field may have thinned after the flop, and you will know which players, if any, played with aggression on the flop.

Slowplaying the Turn

Keep in mind when playing the turn that it is impossible to have four cards on the table, with no pair among them, without the possibility of a straight draw. If there is a possible straight or flush draw, you must play two pair or any set aggressively on the turn. Never give a free card here unless you have the stone cold nuts and truly believe that you will get substantially more action on the river by letting other players make what they may believe to be competitive hands. Sometimes you can be sure that no player has the possible straight draw just because of the way the hand played out. If, for instance, there is a 6 on the flop and a 5 comes down on the turn, you can often be sure that no player would have stayed for the turn card with a 3-4, 4-7, 4-8, 7-8, or 8-9, because of both the high cards on board and the betting preflop and on the flop.

If you have the nut flush with no pair on board, and a player bets at you on the turn, you know that right now you have that player beat. If other players behind you have yet to act, you may be tempted to take a chance and just call here, hoping that the players behind you will also call, and that one or more will fill a straight on the river, or even make another flush if another of your suit comes down. These players would likely find it hard to lay down their hands on the river if they make the hand they are hoping for. The chance you take, however, is that the board may pair, giving someone with a set or two pair a chance to draw out on you.

As a matter of fact, I would raise here with my nut flush, and it would be a strong raise, at least the size of the pot. Any player who has a set will likely call, as will any player with a smaller flush. The straight and flush draws may go away, but you want to charge any player with two pair or a set as high a price as possible to draw to a full house. And if the board does not pair, then any sets or flushes in play are also likely to call your bet on the river when you know you have the nuts.

Actual Hand Example

Let me describe an actual hand that shows how slowplaying can backfire. I like this example because I won this hand. I've lost so many hands trying to slowplay in tournaments that I now know better. This is what happened to a player who tried slowplaying me late in a tournament.

I was in late position in an unraised pot with six players in for the flop. I had pocket 6s. This is a hand I would almost certainly throw away if I did not flop a set, as the likelihood of overcards to my pair coming down was so great.

The flop was 9-3-3.

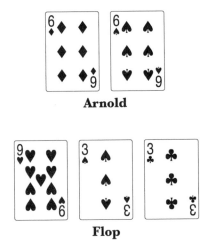

Arnold

Flop

The players in front of me checked, and there was only one player to act behind me, the player on the button. I bet. This was not a bluff, but a value bet based on my belief that I probably did have the best hand at this point. There was some chance that the player on the button who had yet to act had a 9, or that some player held a 3, but I felt my hand was the best hand at that point, so I would charge the overcards to see the turn.

The player on the button called my bet, as did two of the players who had checked in front of me. I suspected all held overcards.

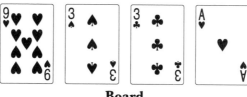

Board

The turn card was an ace, a card I had really hoped not to see. Both players in front of me checked. I decided to keep the lead here and bet. This was not really a bluff, despite the fact that the ace is a scare card. Unless the player yet to act had an ace, I probably still had the best hand at this point, and I did not want any overcards to get a free card here to try and beat me. My bet would probably be read by those at the table as a declaration that I had an ace. If I had been in an earlier position, I could not have made this bet with three players to act behind me. But with two players already checking, indicating neither had an ace, then the only ace in hand I had to fear was the player on the button. If he had no ace, then I would take the pot right here. If he raised, then my betting was done, and I would give up this pot to any action at all.

The button called. The other two players folded.

I assumed the button had an ace, but that he did not like his kicker enough to raise me. I would not bet again, and if he bet on the river, I would fold. I knew my 6s were no good.

To my delight, however, the river produced a 6, giving me 6s full of 3s. I felt that I probably had the best hand now, and that there was no reason to slowplay. The button player could not possibly fear that 6, so he would at least call my bet with his aces up, or even with a single ace with a bad kicker. There was just too much money in the pot for him to fold now. Because I put him on an ace with a bad kicker, I decided against an all-in bet, as that might scare him out of the pot, and I wanted to get more chips out of him if I could.

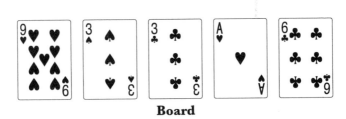

Board

I bet about half the size of the pot, and he raised.

I considered the possible hands he could beat me with. I did not believe he was slowplaying pocket aces or pocket 9s. The only other hand that could beat me was pocket 3s. I reraised, and he reraised me all-in!

Now, fearing he had either pocket aces or pocket 9s and a bigger full house, I still called. If that's what he had, he'd have to show it to me.

He showed down an A-9, just two pair, and I took down a huge pot.

What did he do wrong?

First, when the flop came down 9-3-3, he had my 6s beat with his 9s, and he should have raised. He had two pair, including top pair with an ace kicker. He should have raised me to see if I really had a hand or if I was just taking a shot. By calling, he was also taking a chance that an overcard to the 9—any T, J, Q, or K—might come down on the turn and give me a higher pair than his 9s. There was also a possibility that I might have been betting on the flop with a hand like A-K or A-Q, in which case he was giving me a card on the turn with another shot at beating his lowly pair. You just don't try to trap a player when all you have is top pair, and that pair is 9s.

When the ace came down on the turn, he now had aces and 9s—the top two pair—yet, he only called my bet again. He probably did believe I held an ace when I bet, but he also had to believe he had the best hand. Then, on the river—after I'd made my full house!—his aggressive raise and reraise showed that he had not just been playing cautiously by calling my bets, but that he actually had been slowplaying what he believed to be the best hand (and was, until the river!). Unfortunately, he let me stay too long. Had he raised on the turn, I would have folded my 6s in a heartbeat. He'd had two easy opportunities to push me out of that pot.

You make your money in hold'em by betting your strong hands aggressively. Betting builds the pots for your wins, charges players on draws a price to try to draw out on you, and folds players who won't pay the price. When you have a good hand, you rarely want to give free cards to others. The vast majority of the time, you should save slowplaying for the rare occasions when you have the nuts, and you truly believe that by letting other players make stronger hands you can squeeze more chips out of them. There are times in fast tournaments when it is worth the risk to slowplay with less than the nuts, but not often.

PLAYING THE RIVER

With five cards on the table, every possibility is now on the board. There will likely be many possible hands that can beat yours. But you can often eliminate many, or even most, of the possible hands that could be in play, simply based on how the betting has gone since the hand began.

After the river card is dealt, look at each player in the pot and evaluate how that card may have helped or hurt him based on what you guessed him to have on the turn. If you had put a player on a flush draw, for example, and the third card to the suit comes down, does he bet? Whether you are involved in the pot or not, follow the action and see if your assessments change.

Any time you feel you have a reasonable chance of winning the pot on the river, but you are unsure, then check and call any standard bet. If the betting is very aggressive with raising and reraising, in a pot with three or more players in it, I would fold top pair, and maybe two pair, depending on the dangers on the board. In multi-way pots, raises and reraises with four to a straight or flush on board always indicate that these hands have been made. I would usually fold a set only if there are four to a flush or four to a straight on board, though I would definitely call any standard bet with my set, especially against a single opponent. Many of these decisions depend on your chip position and your assessment of your opponents in any given hand.

If I truly believe my hand is the best hand, then I will definitely bet and raise on the river, even if I do not have the nuts. If I can jack up the money in the pot before I take it down, then I will do so. Chips are what this game is about, and you must have the guts to go for more chips if you think you can get them when you really believe you have the best hand.

MORE POSTFLOP THOUGHTS

Postflop card strategy depends on a combination of math and psychology. For the math end of it, you need to have a firm grasp on the concepts of "outs" and "odds," and how tournament structures affect these concepts. That's the next chapter. For the psychology part, I primarily use a method of player profiling that I've found to be useful for tough decisions. That's the chapter after next. Then, after these two chapters, we'll get to the last element of the rock-paper-scissors strategy—how to play your chips as a weapon in a fast tournaments.

7

CARD STRATEGY II: OUTS AND ODDS

"Pot odds" are a crucial component of any hold'em strategy, but as you will see in this chapter, tournament structures often alter the standard logic of pot odds. **Pot odds** are nothing more than a simple gauge for estimating your return on investment in a poker hand. If you are investing in a commodity, say soybeans, that continually returns seventy-five cents on the dollar, you've got to stop making that investment or you'll go broke. But if your soybean investments consistently return a buck-and-a-quarter for every dollar you put into them, you're going to be making a lot of money. It's the same in poker.

Like commodities, poker hands are high-risk investments with no guaranteed return. When the flop comes down with two spades, and you're sitting there with the A-K of spades, you may not have anything but an ace high hand right now, but if any spade comes down on the turn or river, you've got the nut flush. So, if one of your opponents bets, you must decide if a call is worth the investment. At the moment, all you've got is potential. You know from experience that most of the time your flush won't materialize. For your call to be profitable, the pots you win when you do make your flush have to pay you enough to cover all of the times your flush doesn't come and then some—for profit. If you don't make enough when you hit your flush to cover your prior losses, you'll lose money like all bad investors.

The nice thing about poker hand investments—and that can make them much more attractive than soybeans—is that you can actually figure out the long-run return on a nut flush draw. Compared to poker, commodity investing is a crapshoot. With a poker hand, you can mathematically calculate the exact probability of your flush or straight materializing and the amount you need to win, when you win. Once you know these two simple pieces of information, you can calculate whether or not the investment in this potential hand is a good one.

POT ODDS

Experienced hold'em players who already know how to keep track of the size of the pot and who already understand the concepts of "pot odds" and "outs"—and can use these concepts in making their betting and playing decisions at the tables—can skip to page 129 of this chapter. For everyone else, let me assure you: You must know this stuff if you intend to win! Most amateurs are clueless when it comes to outs and odds. Even if they've read a book or two (or two dozen!) on hold'em, they brush by the chapter on pot odds quickly because they don't like the math. Study this chapter and start taking their money. I don't care how good of a poker player you are, how well you can read your opponents, or how good you are at bluffing—some math you just can't ignore. I'll try my best to make it simple.

Pot odds are simply the ratio of the amount of money in the pot (potential return) to the cost of your call (potential investment). Here's the situation: You are in a pot with two other players. You are on the button with an A-4 suited, say spades, and the flop comes down Q-9-2, with only one of these cards a spade. Neither player bets on the flop. You bet, hoping to take the pot here, but both players call. On the turn, a king of spades comes down, making the board Q-8-2-K with two spades, and giving you four cards to the nut flush. The first player bets, and the second player raises all-in.

At this point, all you have is a nut flush draw, and you are certain that one, if not both, players in the pot currently have you beat. There is only one card to come, and if that card is not a spade, you assume you will not win this pot with nothing but an ace high. If an ace falls on the river, you will have top pair, but that hand may already be beat. If the all-in player has an A-K or A-Q, an ace on the river will cost you a lot of money. And he may already have two pair, or a set, in which case an ace on the river would again be of no help to you. What you really need here is a spade, and only a spade. So, is calling the all-in bet to try for the nut flush a good investment?

This is a math problem, pure and simple, and the first step in answering this question is to figure out the pot odds. Again, the pot odds are simply the ratio of the amount of money in the pot to the cost of the call. If the pot has $1,000 in it, and the bet to me is $100, then the pot is giving me odds of 10 to 1.

If a pot has $300 in it, and I must bet $50 to call, what are the pot odds?

If you immediately answered 6 to 1, then you probably did okay in school when you studied multiplication and division. If you set out to gamble professionally, you will be doing simple math like this constantly. Just about everything that pro gamblers ever bet on—from sports and horse racing to poker and blackjack—is based on the concept of odds.

Looking Deeper Into Pot Odds

Now, let's go back to our example and add some details. Let's say you are on the button with your A-4 of spades, and the two other players in the pot are the two blinds. And, let's say the blinds were $50-$100, and you raised to $300 before the flop, with both blinds calling your raise. This would put exactly $900 in the pot preflop. The flop comes down Q-9-2, rainbow, with one spade. When both blinds check, you bet $500—just over half the size of the pot—in an attempt to take down the pot right then. You figure your ace high may actually be the best hand, and you're also making the correct position move on the pot. To your dismay, however, both blinds call your $500 bet, making the pot $2,400.

Now, the king of spades hits on the turn, giving you four spades to the nut flush. The small blind player bets $1,000, and the big blind—who was short-stacked to start the hand—raises all-in, with $1,400. You've got about $7,000 in chips, but do you want to call this $1,400 bet on a flush draw? The pot at present has $4,900 in it.

What are the pot odds?

Well, $4,900 to $1,400 is about 3.5 to 1. And note that you always want to think in terms of the odds "to 1." The fact is, the odds can be expressed with perfect accuracy as 4,900 to 1,400, but you are going to be learning the odds of making various drawing hands as the odds "to 1." To easily compare the odds of making a hand to the pot odds, you need to be able to translate 4,900 to 1,400 as 3.5 to 1.

Technically, this is just a simple division problem. 4,900 to 1,400 is the same as 49 to 14. If I divide both numbers by 7, I get 7 to 2, which is the same as 3.5 to 1. And feel free to round numbers if necessary—you just need a rough estimate. If the pot contains something like 2,965, and the bet to you is be 950, don't worry about dividing 2,965 by 950. Just round these numbers to 3,000 and 1,000, and you'll know in an instant that the pot odds are roughly 3 to 1.

Getting back to our pot of $4,900 with the bet to you $1,400, or pot odds of 3.5 to 1, what do these numbers mean? Do you have the pot odds to call that $1,400 bet on a flush draw?

You could answer this question very quickly once you know a few simple facts that every hold'em player should know. There are three very common drawing hands that you will have to make decisions on time and again. These hands are four to a flush, four to a two-way straight, and four to a one-way straight. With one card to come, these are the odds against your making one of these hands:

Flush Draw:	4.2 to 1
Two-Way Straight Draw:	5 to 1
One-Way Straight Draw:	11 to 1

That answers the question pretty quickly. Since you need pot odds of better than 4 to 1 to draw to your flush, and this pot is giving you only about 3.5 to 1, it's a bad bet. You should fold. And even if you assume that the player who bet the $1,000 will call the extra $400—which would be a pretty good assumption—the pot odds still wouldn't be 4.2 to 1 for your call.

A Different Pot Odds Scenario

Now let's take the exact same hand with a different situation. Let's say there was an early bet of $300, with two callers to that bet before it got to you. And after you threw in your $300 on the button with your A-4 of spades, both blinds called, putting six players and $1,800 into this pot before the flop. And, let's say the same flop comes down, and the small blind leads out with a $300 bet—which, by the way, is a very small bet into an $1,800 pot. All four other players in front of you call the $300, putting $1,500 more into the pot, to make it $3,300. You throw in your $300 bet also, making the pot $3,600. You fear someone may be slowplaying a hand, and all you really have is an ace high with a poor kicker, but you're happy to be able to see the next card so cheap with such a big pot. That pot is just too big to throw in the towel at this point.

Now comes that king of spades, giving you the nut flush draw. And now, the small blind bets $1,000, and the big blind raises all in for his $1,400. The initial early raiser folds, but the two other players at the table call. With $3,600 + $1,000 + $1,400 + $1,400 + $1,400 = $8,800 in the pot, is it a good investment to call that $1,400 bet now?

Well, how quickly can you divide 88 by 14? It's enough to know that your pot odds are a little better than 6 to 1. Since you only need pot odds of better than 4.2 to 1 to call on a flush draw, this is a good bet on which you will profit in the long run. Same hand, same cards on the board, same size bet to call—but in this case the pot odds tell you to throw your $1,400 into the pot. When the payout will be this big, it's worth it to try for that nut flush.

Although you will lose this bet most of the time, in fact, roughly four times for every win, the fact that the pot is paying you so much more than 4.2 to 1 makes this exactly the kind of investment situation you're looking for when you're playing. But note this: whenever a situation leads you to believe that your hand is already beat, and your opponent will not fold to any bet you make, then you must revert to playing the math. The psychology of the game is out the window at this point. *You need cards to win.*

Know the Pot

You should always know the number of chips in the pot—and you should know this whether or not you are involved in the current hand. Obviously, when you are involved in the hand, you need to know the number of chips in the pot in order to make your betting decisions. You cannot make decisions based on the pot odds without knowing how much there is to win.

Even when you are not involved in a pot, however, you want to know if those who are involved in the pot are making good pot-odds decisions. If, for example, a player calls a bet on the flop or turn, and the hands involved are ultimately shown down, you want to know if the player who made the call was on a draw, and if he had the pot odds to call. You want to identify players who make "bad" calls based on the pot odds, because you may have opportunities to make money from these players later. You also want to identify which players seem to be making smart calls based on the pot odds. If you are later involved in a pot in which you believe one of these players is on a draw, you can "price him out" of the pot by making the pot odds unattractive to him.

So, always keep track of the number of chips in the pot. Chips get added to the pot slowly and the count only goes in one direction—up. Keeping track of the pot total becomes automatic after a while.

Start your pot count with the total of the blinds (and antes, if any), then add to this total as players bet, call, and raise. If you are diligent about tracking the pot total on every hand played, soon you won't even have to think about it anymore. The only trouble you'll ever have will be when some player pushes in some multi-colored mess of chips on an all-in bet.

When I am playing in a tournament, I could at any time tell you the exact number of chips in the pot whether or not I was involved in the hand. Not the approximate number of chips, but the exact number. This is an elementary skill you must develop if you are serious about winning tournaments.

In small buy-in tournaments, very few players always know how many chips are in the pot. I have actually seen players who must make a decision on whether or not to call a bet ask the dealer to spread out the chips on the table in a large pot so they could count them! I always feel like saying, "It's $13,450," just to keep the game going. Of course, I would never do this, because I see no reason to tell the whole table that I'm keeping track of the pot amount. Also, I feel no compulsion to help an opponent at the table, even if I'm not involved in that particular hand. This player will likely get only an approximate count, because it's not easy to count chips that are not stacked and organized by denomination. Since it is easy to count chips as they initially enter the pot, do it. You'll be a step ahead of 90% of your opponents in the small buy-in tournaments.

Although many of the players in the fast tournaments are simply amateurs who know little about poker, the inability to keep track of the pot can also be a sign of a player who learned poker on the Internet. In the online poker rooms, the total amount of the pot is always displayed on the screen, so players do not have to count chips as they go in.

If you keep a tally of the chips in the pot, you will occasionally notice players who make exact pot-sized bets, even in unusual amounts. For example, a player may bet $2,850 on the river into a pot that contains a small mountain of green and black chips that you know total exactly $2,850. This type of player will often have made other weirdly precise pot-sized bets, and similarly precise half-pot-sized bets as well. This is a tell, and you can use it. Whether his overall play seems strong or weak, you know he is paying a lot of attention to the game and is probably more dangerous than most of the players at your table. He is also a bit too tight and formulaic in his play, and probably scare-prone.

I would not advise you to make such precise bets. You want to know the number of chips in the pot in order to make your decisions, but you do not want to appear so ultra precise to other players who know the amount in the pot. If you want to make a pot-sized bet, and the pot has $2,850 in it, just toss in $3,000.

Other Uses for Pot Odds

Good poker players use pot odds for more than just deciding when to call a bet. Pot odds can also tell you when to lead out with a bet or raise a bet, and by how much. For example, if you have flopped a set, and there are two cards to a flush or straight on the board, you want to make your bet high enough that any player drawing to that flush or straight will not have the pot odds to call. If, for example, there is $1,000 in the pot, you can make the pot odds only 2 to 1 for any potential caller on a draw simply by betting the size of the pot ($1,000) yourself.

If a player on a draw does call when you raise in a situation like this, it's important that you know that he paid too much, even if he does draw out on you. Say, for example, that you had a set, and made a raise sized to make it incorrect for any flush draws or straight draws to call. But, one or more of these drawing hands calls anyway. Amateur players get very upset when this happens. But most pros care little about the results of any given hand. They will simply notice that this player paid too much for his draw, and they'll know that having this player at the table will be like having a mini-ATM machine at hand.

You will make lots of withdrawals from players who play without consciousness of the pot odds and pay too much when they have a drawing hand. In fact, as Sklansky points out in *Theory of Poker*, when you are playing your cards—as opposed to your position—you will earn the most in poker not from being dealt pocket aces, or flopping sets, but from players who make mistakes. And the biggest mistake, the most expensive mistake, the most frequent mistake you will profit from is other players paying too much to try and make hands.

THE CONCEPT OF OUTS

The odds against a potential winning hand getting one of the cards needed to become an actual winning hand always depend on the number of "outs" that hand has. An out is simply a card that would get you "out" of the jam you're currently in, facing a stronger hand when all you have is a draw.

With four cards to a nut flush, it's easy to count the outs. Since there are 13 cards in each suit, and you know that there are four cards in one suit between the board cards and the cards in your hand, there are exactly nine cards left that could make your flush. You have nine outs.

So, how do you figure the pot odds once you know how many outs you have? Simple. First subtract the number of outs you have from the total number of unseen cards. The number of unseen cards is always 47 after the flop, or 46 after the turn, because you start with 52 cards in the deck and subtract the cards you've actually seen on the board and in your own hand.

So, to calculate the odds against making a flush draw on the turn, you subtract your outs from the unseen cards:

$$46 - 9 = 37$$

And the odds against your drawing to the flush you need are simply the ratio of this total to your number of outs—in this case, 37 to 9, or just over 4.1 to 1 against you. So, if you get pot odds of 4.2 to 1 or more for your flush draw, you make the call.

Now let's say you have an open-end (or two-way) straight draw—say there's an A-5-6-J on the board and you have a 7-8. For your 5-6-7-8 straight draw, you have eight outs— the four 9s and the four 4s. If any one of these eight cards come down, you will fill your straight. This gives you $46 - 8 = 38$ non-outs to your 8 outs. Odds of 38 to 8 come to 4.75 to 1 against your making the straight. To keep things simple, and to make some profit, you're looking for odds of roughly 5 to 1 to make the call.

For an inside (or one-way) straight draw—with say an A-5-6-J on the board again, but a 7-9 in your hand, you have only four outs—the four 8s. The odds against your making this straight with the unseen cards are 42 to 4, or 10.5 to 1, so you need roughly 11 to 1 pot odds to make the call.

More on Outs

There are other more complex considerations that may bear on pot odds. For example, if you have a draw to a straight or flush that is *not* the nut straight or nut flush, you must consider the possibility that you will get one of your outs, but still get beaten by a bigger straight or flush. For example, if the board has an A-5-9-J, with the A, 5, and 9 all diamonds, and you have the jack of diamonds, making that diamond flush on the river could be dangerous. Any player holding a king or queen of diamonds will beat you.

You may also have a straight or flush draw with an overcard to the board, and believe that if the board pairs your overcard, this would also win the pot for you. That may be true, but I would advise caution in counting overcards among your outs. Too often, your overcard "out" comes down, but you still lose the hand to a stronger hand—two pair, a set, or a higher overpair.

Also, as a general rule, if any straight or flush draw is not using both of the cards in your hand—meaning there are three to the flush or straight on the board and you hold only one of the needed cards to complete the hand—*slow down*. Even if you get one of the needed outs for your straight, you may end up losing this pot to a higher straight, or splitting it with an equivalent straight.

For example, suppose you have an ace in hand when the board on the turn is K-Q-6-10. Even if the pot is now offering you the 11 to 1 needed pot odds to draw to this inside nut straight, you may not be the only ace at the table, especially if multiple players are in the pot. And if the jack shows up on the river to complete the straight, the only bettors remaining in a multiway pot will be the players with aces (and any dreamer who may be holding a 9 and just can't let it go). If you decide to call because the pot is paying you 11 to 1, you may make your nut straight, but you won't be paid full price for your call if any other player in the pot also has an ace. And even if you happen to be the only ace in play on this hand, over the long run you won't always be, so the call is a bad investment in the long run unless you're getting much better odds than 11 to 1, and that's a rare pot.

In a tournament, and especially in a fast tournament, you

might make this call despite insufficient pot odds because of what the potential big win might mean to your chances of advancing in the tournament (or because of the effect of potential rebuys on the pot odds—see the chapter on rebuys). If you are very short on chips, this hand might represent your best shot at a comeback, but with odds of 11 to 1 against your making it, you'd have to feel pretty certain that your survival chances without taking down this pot are slim to none. Risk/reward situations that would not occur in ring games do occasionally arise in tournaments because you're ultimately fighting for the tournament prize money, not just the chips in the pot.

In any case, if you play according to the fast strategies described in this book, you will avoid most situations where you are doomed if you don't make a bad call. In the above example, any player so short-stacked that he would need that pot to ensure his survival should not have entered that pot preflop with an ace in hand with anything but an all-in bet in the first place. Still, in a tournament, I might very well may make a call on a hand like this with a pot that paid anywhere near 11 to 1, even if I was not desperate for chips, if the call itself did not greatly hurt my chip position. In tournaments, a really big pot often has an implied value well above the dollar value of that pot. But again, we will discuss tournament-specific strategies in much greater detail later. For now, let's finish our discussion of pot odds.

POT ODDS WITH TWO CARDS TO COME

Once the flop has come down, and there are only two cards to come, you will frequently have to make a decision on a big bet or even an all-in bet. The pot odds required to call a bet when there are two cards to come are different from the pot odds required when there is only one card to come.

Assuming you understand the math on how to figure the odds with one card to come, figuring the odds with two cards to come is similar, but with a quirk to it. With two cards to come, and two shots at hitting one of your outs, you might assume that you could simply double the number of outs in your calculations, and just cut the pot odds you need for a call in half. But this is not quite accurate. The proper math requires that you subtract the times when you will hit an out on *both* the turn and the river. The chart below should be memorized by every hold'em player. You will use this information again and again in tournaments.

POT ODDS NEEDED TO CALL

# Outs	1 Card to Come	2 Cards to Come
15	2-1	0.9-1
12	3-1	1.2-1
9	4.2-1	1.9-1
8	5-1	2.2-1
4	11-1	5-1

NUMBER OF OUTS FOR COMMON DRAWS

15 Outs: a two-way straight draw *and* four to a flush (or a two-way straight flush draw)

12 Outs: a one-way straight draw *and* four to a flush

9 Outs: four to a flush

8 Outs: a two-way straight draw, *or* drawing to a full house or quads when you hold a set

4 Outs: a one-way straight draw, *or* drawing to a full house when you hold two pair

With an open-end straight flush draw, you have 15 outs. With two cards to come, the pot doesn't even have to be giving you even money to make this a good call. It's more likely that one of your outs will come down than not. But you don't have to be drawing to a straight flush to have 15 outs. So long as you have a two-way straight draw *and* four to a flush, you have 15 outs. If, for instance, you have Q-J spades in the hole, and the board shows a 10-4 spades and a king of diamonds, you have a two-way straight draw and four to a flush.

You could, of course, **backdoor** the straight flush—make a

THE POKER TOURNAMENT FORMULA

straight or flush with cards that appear on both the turn and river—by getting the right cards on the turn and river, but don't bother figuring out your pot odds on a hand that requires you to draw two cards to make the hand you need. The odds against such draws are just too high. Believe me, the pot won't contain enough chips unless you're down to the felt and pot-committed.

Note that if you have a set, you may occasionally want to know your pot odds for making a full house or quads. Usually, with a set, your hand is strong enough to call (or raise) just about any bet. But, if three or four to a straight or flush are on the board, and there is already a big bet and a raise in front of you, you may well feel your set is already beat. A set can turn into a full house or quads, however, and you have 8 outs to improve your hand to one of these stronger, and likely unbeatable, hands—the same number of outs as needed with a two-way straight draw.

With four to a flush and one card to come, you're looking for pot odds of 4.2 to 1 to justify calling. Those odds, however, are based on your having nine outs to make your flush. If you are up against an opponent who currently has a set or two pair and the card that gives you a flush also pairs the board, you have to be aware that there is a possibility your opponent has made a full house. If one of the cards on board is not in your flush suit, then you may have only eight outs, and you would need pot odds of 5 to 1 to justify a call. With two cards on board not in your suit, then you may have only seven outs, and you would need pot odds of 6 to 1 to justify a call.

Do you absolutely need to memorize the chart?

Yes. There is very little mathematical data you need to memorize for hold'em tournaments, but this chart is extremely important. You will use this information in every tournament you play. It's not that you will necessarily be in that many situations where you have to figure out the pot odds for your own calls. But you will constantly be watching the calls of every other player at the table to see which players make calls without sufficient pot odds. Many players do, and these are the players you want to get into pots with when you have a strong hand.

IMPLIED ODDS

One other thing that is important to consider—but only under special circumstances—is the concept of *implied odds*. **Implied odds** take into account your estimate of how much more money might get into the pot at the showdown if you throw in your bet. Estimating the implied odds is more of an art than a science. But there is a logic to it.

If you believe that one or more of the players involved in a hand can be counted on to call a bet you will make if your out comes down, then you can mentally add those chips to the pot when calculating the odds you're getting for your current bet. A player could be counted on to call if he has such a strong hand that he will be unable to lay down his hand to a bet. For instance, if the board shows a K-Q-J-10 at the turn, and this player bets, there is a very strong likelihood that he has an ace in hand for the nut straight. If two of those cards on board are suited, and you would make the nut flush on the river if your suit came down, you could mentally add to the pot the amount you believe this player will call if you bet on the river. He may not call an all-in bet with three to a suit on board, but with the nut straight, he would definitely call *something*. You could count on that.

You must be careful about these "guestimates." For instance, let's say you're holding an ace of hearts and three hearts are on the board. If a fourth heart comes down, you'll have the nut flush—but will you really be able to get any more chips out of any other players in the hand? Very few players would call any substantial bet with four to a suit on the table, unless possibly they were holding a high card in that suit themselves. This is not something you can count on. Even players with sets and straights will fold to a board this scary. In a case like this, don't count on any implied odds. There are none.

But there are many situations where you have to look beyond pot odds on a decision, because if you figure an opponent will put more chips into a pot and you can trap him if you hit your draw or speculative hand, then the implied odds may make an otherwise bad decision a good one.

WHEN POT ODDS DON'T MATTER IN TOURNAMENTS

In non-tournament hold'em games, pot odds are always the crucial factor when you are considering calling a bet when you have no made hand. In tournaments, however, there are situations where pot odds are not the critical factor.

I gave an example earlier of a player with an inside straight draw on the turn who was not getting sufficient pot odds (11 to 1) to call an all-in bet. In that example, the call might be correct if he is so short-stacked that this is his best shot at winning enough chips to have a legitimate chance at the prize money.

One factor that exists in tournaments that does not exist outside the tournament format is being "pot committed." A simple definition of **pot-committed** is a player who has half or more of his chips already in the pot on a hand. This is a bit of an oversimplification, but would usually be true. Essentially, you are pot-committed if abandoning those chips you already have in the pot would leave you in such a poor chip position that your chances of remaining competitive in the tournament would be pretty slim. In other words, you're pot-committed when, if you don't win this pot, you're probably dead anyway, so you might as well call. You're not really violating the math of the game when you do this. Even if you don't have the pot odds to throw your last chips into the pot on this hand, this may still be your best opportunity mathematically for advancing and making some money in this tournament. You've got to go for it.

Tournaments can also present situations where you have the pot odds to call, but calling may be ill-advised because you stand to advance in the tournament by letting your hand go. Say, for example, that late in a tournament you have four cards to a nut flush, and three players at your table are already all-in, including the chip leader who could knock them all out. The pot may be giving you 5 to 1, sufficient pot odds to call, but do you want to risk the whole tournament on a hand where you know you would be knocked out of the tournament 80% of the time and your current chip stack is strong enough that you have a very good shot at getting into the money without winning this pot? Some tournament players would definitely go for it, figuring that the payoff would be so big that it would set them up for a strong chance at finishing in one of the top money positions. Other players would choose to sit this one out and wait for a less risky hand to try to advance. Whether or not calling would be the best play here should be determined by exactly how well-stacked you are. If you are in second chip position in the whole tournament, and the tournament is already down to the last dozen players or so, then going up against the chip leader on a drawing hand, even with sufficient pot odds, is not the best play for making money. You've had a long hard fight getting to second place, and this late in the tournament you don't want to blow the whole thing on a long shot.

In tournaments, pot odds are generally overrated by many players, and this is especially true in the fast events. Once you're past the halfway point of a tournament, you'll often find that pot odds are less applicable than the odds of various other tournament factors: Will your opponent fold if you bet, raise, or check-raise him because he can't afford to risk his tournament life on this hand? And how does he perceive your situation? What are your chances of making it into the money if you don't win this pot? What are your opponent's chances? Since a tournament only has a payout at the end, and not at the conclusion of every pot as in a ring game, you have to remember that you are *always* going for a bigger win than the chips sitting in front of you in a single pot.

Whatever you do, however, do not start ignoring pot odds just because you're in a tournament. Don't start calling on high-risk draws without sufficient pot odds, or throwing good draws away when you do have the pot odds to call. You've got to weigh the various factors before making any decision that violates the pot odds.

How to Practice the Card Strategy

Use the same practice methods for learning card strategy that you used to learn position strategy. Use poker tournament simulation software, and finally use live tournament play.

The main difference from position strategy practice is that you will no longer be playing your hands in the dark. When you first start looking at your cards again, you will suddenly feel like you now have an unfair advantage over your opponents! You can actually see what you're betting on!

Because card strategy is so complex, and you must continue to apply position strategy as well, do not start practicing the chip strategy until you really have the other two strategies down cold. While you're working on acquiring these skills, read the following chapter on player types, as this type of stereotyping will help you in both your card play and position play when it comes to actually starting to get reads on your opponents.

8

PLAYER TYPES

Before we get into chip strategy, the final element of the rock-paper-scissors approach, I want to address the psychology of the game from my perspective as a math guy. Most of the "reads" I get on players do not come from any mind-reading ability on my part. When I first started playing poker, I studied Mike Caro's *Book of Tells*, and some of his suggestions have been helpful to me. Primarily, his revelation that "weak means strong" and "strong means weak" has been of inestimable value.

In one of the first tournaments I played, in a pot I wasn't even involved in, a flop came down with two queens. The under-the-gun player said in a wimpy voice, "Well, I'll just try a little probe bet here," and he bet the minimum allowed. Thinking immediately of Caro's weak-means-strong dictum, I knew beyond any shadow of a doubt that this player had a queen in hand. I knew it. He ended up taking all of the chips of his opponent who had entered the pot with pocket kings, and who pushed all-in in reaction to that "probe bet."

But I think many of the tells Caro discusses work better with players who are more knowledgeable poker players than I've found in fast tournaments. Players who are not good at reading the board often *feel* strong when they're weak, and vice versa. In the fast tournaments, you will continually see players call all-in bets with hands that indicate they have no ability whatsoever to read the board. With four to a flush on board, they'll call an all-in with top pair. How do you get a read on a player who doesn't know the value of his own hand?

At the same time, I don't believe any player can consistently make money in tournaments without some ability to read other players at the table. There will be times when you must lay down very good hands simply because you *know* that your opponent has you beat. And there will be times when you will call all-in raises with hands that are far from the nuts simply because you *know* the raiser is bluffing. At times, there will be a logical basis for your reads derived from the way the hand has played out and your knowledge of how your opponent plays in general. But at other times, you must simply make gut-level decisions based on your feeling for the situation. And your ability to make these decisions correctly will contribute greatly to your success.

A lot of books on poker have methods of classifying opponents at the table. Phil Helmuth suggests animal classifications—mice and jackals and lions—in which mice are timid, jackals are sneaky, lions are aggressive, and so on. The first author I'm aware of who provided an animal classification system for opponents was limit tournament pro Ken Buntjer, though he suggested different animals—sheep, donkeys, and alligators.

I liked the animal approach because it's somewhat mathematical in its approach to psychology. You classify a person based on his past history of play—or at least, what you've seen of it—then you assume he will stay true to his type.

So, I tried fitting fast tournament players to the animal stereotypes suggested by these books, but I ran into a problem because so many players didn't seem to fit. I tried coming up with my own animal types based on the players I was actually seeing—rats, roaches, weasels, buzzards, hyenas, and slugs. These were apparently not the players that Phil Helmuth was battling in the major tournaments. Whereas Helmuth saw himself as an eagle among the elephants, lions and jackals, I envisioned myself as an exterminator down in the no-limit hold'em sewer. Unfortunately, the system didn't seem to help me play my hands.

The most useful player classification system that I ever heard of for fast no-limit hold'em tournaments—and which I quickly adopted—came from my blackjack playing partner, Radar, who had started experimenting with poker around the same time that I was starting to play the small buy-in tournaments. Radar had categorized four player types that were common in the low-limit ring games. These categories were based on both the players' social characteristics and literal descriptions of their play—ace masters, flush masters, cagey codgers, and canasta ladies. As soon as I heard Radar's descriptions, I realized I was seeing the same players in the fast tournaments.

I ended up expanding on Radar's player classification system and still use it to this day in fast tournaments. The character types I run into repeatedly are: ace masters, flush masters, pair masters, cagey codgers, canasta ladies, boat people, ball-cap kids, show'n'tellers, wimps, and oafs. If you can learn to recognize these types of players at your tables, you will improve your results immensely. I estimate that 70% or more of all the opponents you'll face in the small buy-in tournaments will be one of these types. The more dangerous players are the ones who can't be characterized so simply. So, let's look at the most common types you'll encounter in every small buy-in tournament.

ACE MASTERS

An **ace master** will play any ace and will even call preflop raises if there is an ace in his hand, no matter how bad his kicker. This type of player will greatly contribute to your overall profits. An ace master will often call to the river if an ace has not yet appeared on the board, no matter how scary the board may look to a more skillful player. And if that ace lands, he will call any bets and raises in the hope that his pair of aces will hold up. An ace is like a magic talisman to this guy. You will identify these players by noticing the hands they show down, such as A-7 off-suit, and realizing that they actually entered the pot in early position, or called a raise from a middle position, with that hand, when they were far too short on chips to be messing around with calls on a hand like that.

FLUSH MASTERS

Another common type of fast-tournament player is the **flush master**. A flush master will play any two suited cards. You will identify these players when they win (or lose) pots by showing down very weird flushes. A classic flush master will enter a pot with any two suited cards from any position, no matter how bad those cards are. They will sometimes show down a suited 8-3 or a suited 10-2, for example, after entering the pot from early position. Flush masters live for flushes. Flush masters will also stay in a pot, calling all raises, if two of their suit are on the table. They are undying optimists when it comes to making flushes.

A more discerning flush master is the one who plays suited cards only when one of them is a high card, J, Q, K, or A. These flush masters often make top pair, then get beaten by a player with a better kicker. In some sessions, you will see these types of showdowns over and over again, but they never learn.

MORE ON ACE MASTERS AND FLUSH MASTERS

Both flush masters and ace masters will sometimes win pots with very unusual two-pair hands. For example, a flush master may enter a pot with a suited J-4, and win the pot by making jacks and fours. This will drive you crazy when you raise preflop with A-J, and you realize he called your raise with that hand. But, ultimately, he won't make two pair often enough to justify the expense of all his calls, and you'll make a lot more money from these players than you'll ever lose to them.

Neither ace masters nor flush masters ever bluff. This is why you want to identify these players at your tables. If an ace master bets when an ace hits the board, just throw away your kings. Game over. It will be frustrating when this ace hits on the river, since you will have been the one building the pot with your aggressive raises, but again, you'll get a lot more from these players in the long run than they'll get from you, and if they didn't draw out occasionally, they wouldn't keep playing.

This, in fact, is why you want to bet aggressively into these players. Make them pay to draw out on you. Both ace masters and flush masters tend to hate aggressive players. They want to draw for free. Also, many ace masters are also flush masters. If you give one of these players a suited ace for a starting hand, he is in heaven.

Both ace masters and flush masters tend to be calling stations.

They rarely bet aggressively, even if they hit their ace or flush, because they usually have a bad kicker with their ace, or a poor flush, far from the nuts. They always know they don't have the best possible hand, but neither can they lay their hand down. They simply call.

And, because these players play so many poor starting hands, when they are actually dealt a premium hand, they will overplay it. An ace/flush master who is dealt an A-K suited will fall deeply in love with his hand. This is one hand where he will raise before the flop, and will often bet on the flop, and call any bet, no matter what cards hit the board. He will also often call to the river no matter what cards are on the table. There can be four cards to an open-end straight on board, with no connection to his A-K, and he will play his hand to the death.

PAIR MASTERS

Some players simply cannot lay down a pocket pair. If a **pair master** is dealt, say, pocket jacks, he will often be unable to lay them down, even if a king comes down on the flop and two other players are betting and raising. He will play those jacks to the bitter end. Pair masters remember all the hands they've seen players win by bluffing, or by simply having an ace high, or by making bottom pair with an ace kicker, and so on, so they cannot lay down an actual made pair as long as there is any other card on the table of a lower denomination. Because pair masters are also often ace masters, they may sometimes fold if an ace hits the table because they assume that there is a player with an ace in hand if there is any betting at all. Some pair masters are also flush masters, and they can be scared off by three or four to a suit they don't have. But nothing else scares them.

Sometimes even with an ace on the board, pair masters stay in pots until the river, calling raises in hopes that their pocket pair will turn into a magical invisible winning set. Sometimes it does, and this will drive you nuts, as you wonder how he could possibly have stayed in the pot calling your raises with his lowly pocket 6s.

Pair masters, like ace masters and flush masters, have no sense of probabilities or pot odds. They are just eternal optimists who play too many hands, stay in hands too long, and slowly give away their chips.

Pair masters are dangerous when they suddenly start betting with maximum aggression, whether on the flop, turn or river. This aggression inevitably means that they have hit their set. If you can't beat a set, get out of the way.

CAGEY CODGERS

The typical **cagey codger** is gray-haired or bald, 60 to 80+ years of age. If he's got a cap on, it says "VFW" or perhaps sports the name of the ship he served on in the Navy. But don't assume that just because a player fits that physical description that he falls into the category of cagey codger. Quite frankly, I fit the physical description pretty well myself and I'm not one. In fact, as I use the term, there are also female cagey codgers and cagey codgers in their 20s and 30s. It's the *style of play* that makes a player a cagey codger. The fact is, I'm just profiling. When I see an old guy at the table, I immediately think "possible cagey codger" and I'll play him this way until he proves otherwise.

The stereotypical cagey codger has been playing poker for quite a few years and takes pride in his game. He is retired and pretty much spends his days camped at the low-limit poker tables. The best get into $6/$12 and $10/$20 limit games to supplement their retirement incomes. The second tier gets into the lower-limit games, primarily to socialize with other retirees, and hoping to hit the bad beat jackpot. Cagey codgers often follow the bad beat jackpots around town, and they have their own network of information on these jackpots. If you play in limit games with a lot of cagey codgers, they tend to take turns being sheriff.

In the low-limit ring games, cagey codgers like to see a lot of flops cheap, so they hate it when some aggressive kid shows up at their table and starts raising preflop. If the kid continues with this aggression after the flop, it really gets to them. They don't mind a preflop raise if a player's got a high pocket pair or big slick, but these aggressive kids raise with any damn thing, chasing them out of pots and making the game more expensive, and ruining everyone's chances of hitting that bad beat jackpot that's the game's prime attraction.

In the no-limit hold'em tournaments, cagey codgers are fish out of water. Some are attracted by the prize pool in the same way that they are attracted by bad beat jackpots. The fact that a player can buy in for $40 and have a legitimate shot at thousands is the main draw. A true cagey codger rarely makes a rebuy or add-on in tournaments that allow these extra chip purchases. The way he sees it, if the cards come his way, he'll make money. If not, he'll get off cheap.

But even the best cagey codgers don't really like the aggression of no-limit tournaments. Since it's too expensive to play the sheriff in these tournaments, they tend to overly tighten up their play, refusing to get involved without at least a pocket pair or strong ace. Their specialty is to lie in wait for the chance to slowplay a set or nut flush, which they inevitably use to kick some aggressive kid's butt.

Any time a cagey codger is in a pot, especially if he is calling bets and raises, you've got to be careful. Cagey codgers only occasionally make a final table because they generally play too tight. But they are really tricky when they have a hand. They will rarely raise until the river, and they look more like calling stations when they have the nuts. They usually get any aggressor to move in on them, so they don't even have to raise. They absolutely love check-raising, and they are prone to betting a small amount at the river if they have to act first, in an effort to look weak and get an opponent to go over the top.

Cagey codgers never bluff. They are also very good at reading the board, and they can lay down top pair or an overpair when the board looks too dangerous. But they will bet or call for value when they think they've got a legitimate shot at winning the pot. Be very careful if considering a bluff at a cagey codger.

There are quite a few cagey codgers in the small buy-in tournaments in Las Vegas. You will likely run into two or three at your tables in a single tournament if you last a few hours. And don't be surprised if you run into some younger players who employ this same tight, tricky, slowplay style. Because they are both common and dangerous, you should try to identify them as quickly as you can. If they stay in a pot, they have something, and usually something pretty strong.

So, play very carefully if a cagey codger is in the pot. Since they don't bluff and they don't take shots, they're easy to deal with if you stay aware of them.

CANASTA LADIES

The stereotypical **canasta lady** looks like my Great Aunt Peggy back in the '50s with flamboyant dyed hair, dangling earrings, and lots of make-up built around some very red lipstick. My Aunt Peggy actually played canasta with my mother and other aunts. She grew up in an era without television—or money—when people's primary form of entertainment was cards.

Canasta ladies, like cagey codgers, haunt the low limit ring games, stalking that elusive bad beat jackpot. In the $2-$4 games, canasta ladies play every hand. But in tournaments, canasta ladies are even tighter players than cagey codgers. They play very few hands. They primarily differ from cagey codgers in that when they play, they are not tricky at all. Like cagey codgers, canasta ladies come in all shapes, sizes, age groups and sexes.

A canasta lady will immediately be aggressive with any premium hand. She won't slowplay you and check-raise you as a cagey codger will. If she does enter a pot with a raise, watch out. It's aces, kings, or A-K. Anytime a canasta lady is betting, get out of her way if you don't have the nuts or a very powerful hand yourself. If a canasta lady makes a final table, it's a result of her having been dealt exceptionally good hands at tables where the other players were too dumb to get out of the way. Like cagey codgers, canasta ladies don't bluff. I don't know how many times I've watched some aggressive kid trying to bully a canasta lady out of a pot, only to have his all-in bluff called on the river. You just don't mess with canasta ladies.

BOAT PEOPLE
(AND I USE THIS TERM WITH ALL DUE
RESPECT)

Years ago, I first heard the term "boat people" in reference to Cuban refugees who had braved the shark-infested waters between Havana and Miami on homemade rafts, often constructed of truck tire inner tubes and scraps of wood. Since then, similar fearless and determined people have launched themselves into the world from a number of other countries and life situations, including poverty, persecution, and war. These are people who were willing to risk their lives to achieve their goals, who have faced down unimaginable peril. If one of them winds up at your tournament table, you should know he or she is not going to be afraid of mere cards.

Boat people are smart, aggressive and absolutely fearless players. They can be ruthless and treacherous, and with a lot of chips, unstoppable. They can run over a table, steal blinds and pots from any position, and have such an unwavering attitude of aggression that other players back down despite knowing what's going on. Having read Nolan Dalla's biography of Stu Ungar (*One of a Kind*, Atria Books), I would classify Stu Ungar as a member of the "boat people" group. Although he was a New Yorker, he overcame childhood hardships far beyond what most poker room inhabitants have ever had to face. The inordinate real life hardships that boat people have overcome allow them to sense fear like a pit bull. You can forget about rattling them with a check-raise.

Boat people may or may not be immigrants who escaped from war zones, but all players in this group have a fearless attitude that gets them to many final tables on nerve alone. They will not hesitate to raise you all-in if they think you are bluffing, even when they are bluffing. And because they play both their premium hands and their bluffs with similar aggression, they are not easy to read.

If you have a tight image at a table, you can bluff a boat person out of a pot, but it will take an all-in bet to do it. If you have shown down any marginal hands, however, they will never trust you, and this is not the player with whom you want to get involved in a game of chicken.

SHOW'N'TELLERS

These players are a sheer joy to have at your table, and there are lots of them in the fast poker tournaments. **Show'n'tellers** continually show their hands when they don't have to. If they bet and get no callers, they show the hand they bet with. If they call a player on the river, and he turns over the winning hand, they don't just muck their cards—they toss them onto the table face up. Not only that, but when they can't show their cards because they're folding while other hands are still live, they'll often discuss the cards they folded when the action is over!

Some show'n'tellers are simply rookies who don't quite get the concept of deception in poker. Most, however, are experienced players who simply feel compelled to justify their play to other players at the table. They are more concerned with being seen as smart than they are with actually winning.

If you get two show'n'tellers at your table, it can get very amusing. They love finding each other so they can discuss their hands and strategies with a willing participant, and they love dropping all the poker lingo they know. "I had so many outs." "The implied odds were tremendous." "I had him dominated." And they love to talk about the hands they "put you on."

At my first table in one of the Mirage Tuesday night tournaments last year, I had the most perfect specimen of show'n'teller I had ever encountered. For an hour, he never stopped talking about his hands, his bets, his folds, his outs. Every player at the table knew every hand he was dealt, whether he played it or not. At every showdown, whether he was in the hand or not, he would tell the players who showed their cards what he had "put them on,"—always, of course, *after* they had exposed their hands. In his perfection, he made Phil Helmuth and Daniel Negreanu look like rank amateurs when it came to reading players' hands.

Here's how he went out of the tournament: He was on the button and the table folded around to him. He made a standard raise, about three times the big blind. The small blind folded, but the big blind pushed all-in.

With no hesitation whatsoever, he said, "I call," and turned up his hand, pocket 8s. The big blind turned over pocket kings.

And with a straight face, no intended irony or humor, Mr. Show'n'Tell says: "I put you on kings."

BALL-CAP KIDS

The typical **ball-cap kid** is in his 20s or 30s and wears a ball-cap that has the logo of one of the popular online poker sites—Ultimate Bet, Full Tilt, whatever. The cap may be worn with the brim low on the brow to hide the eyes, or backwards—hip-hop style. The kid also often wears wraparound shades.

Lots of poker players are young guys who wear caps and dark glasses. There are two signs of a true ball-cap kid. One: He always enters every pot with a raise. And two: He bets by flinging his chips into the pot. There are lots of ball-cap kids in the limit games. In these games, when they toss in their raises, they often throw in one chip too many, then have to pull it back. The effect they are trying for is to look like their hand is so strong, the amount of the bet is meaningless.

Ball-cap kids are smart players, and many have read the major authors. They have all noted Mike Caro's general advice that players who put chips into the pot neatly and precisely are more likely to have weak hands, while players who splash their bets in haphazardly are more likely to have strong hands. Ball-cap kids always want to look strong, not only in poker but in life, so they splash.

Ball-cap kids play with aggression and they like to bluff. They understand position play and use it. Many have logged more hours in the Internet poker rooms than in live games. The good ones make a lot of final tables. You always have to be careful if a ball-cap kid is in a pot. As they usually enter with a raise, and always play with aggression, they are not easy to read.

The less-skillful ball-cap kids look the same as the talented ones—very aggressive in position—but they are poor at reading their opponents, probably because they haven't played much against live opponents. They frequently bust out of tournaments by taking shots at some of the easiest players to read—ace masters, cagey codgers, or canasta ladies. They just don't know when to turn off the aggression. They always read checking and calling as weakness, no matter who is doing it.

You can make a lot of money from the ball-cap kids when you have a strong hand simply by adopting the cagey codgers' slowplay style. Just be careful. They will often raise preflop with trash hands, and if the flop hits them, you could be in trouble. They are dangerous when they have a lot of chips. Short-stacked, they have little patience and will quickly take a shot with nearly anything.

WIMPS

A **wimp** generally exits a tournament by watching his chip stack get ground down by the blinds. A wimp is the most pathetic player in any no-limit hold'em tournament, the player who gets blinded off while waiting for a hand. He epitomizes the term *dead money*. His chips have no life to them at all. They just sit there in front of him getting eaten away slowly. Wimps can be counted on to do this in almost every tournament they enter.

The small buy-in tournaments are heavily infested with wimps. These players have absolutely zero chance of ever making it into the money other than from inordinately lucky cards. Wimps may be the single most common type of player you will find in the small buy-in tournaments. Wimps are the reason that the ball-cap kids and the boat people generally make a lot of chips in the early stages of the tournaments. Wimps just give their money away to aggressive players. They do not understand that in a no-limit tournament, players must check their fear at the door. This is not a card game, but a game of courage and aggression. The wimps don't get it.

Let me give some specific examples of how you might play various hands if you were the typical wimp.

1. You have K-Q suited. There's an early raise and you call from the button. The flop comes down Q-10-5 rainbow. The early raiser makes a large bet. To call him would commit you to the pot. You will either have to fold or go all in. You fold.

You wimp! Wimps like to brag about their "great laydowns." They justify their wimpy play by saying things like, "I put him on a set of 10s," or, "I knew from his bet he had me out-kicked." Wimps always put aggressive bettors on whatever they're afraid of.

2. You're in middle position with pocket 10s. With no callers in front of you, you make a normal raise, three times the big blind. You get three callers to your raise—the player to your immediate left, the button, and the big blind.

The flop comes down with three deuces, giving you a full boat, deuces full of 10s. The big blind checks. With two players to act behind you, you check also.

Wimp! Only a wimp would check this hand! Why would you check? Are you afraid that one of the callers to your preflop raise is holding a deuce? Unlikely. Are you slowplaying your full house, hoping one of these other players will take a stab at it so you can check-raise him? Bad idea. With three callers to your raise, and no reraise, it's unlikely that there is any pair bigger than 10s in the hands of your opponents, but a very great likelihood that there is an assortment of unpaired cards in their hands higher than your 10s, and you're taking a chance here on giving three players with likely high cards a free card on the turn? So, how are you going to play your hand if an ace, king, queen or jack falls on the turn? Now are you going to bet?

Wimps are forever "slowplaying"—and not because they have the nuts and want to give other players a chance to catch up in the hand. Wimps slowplay dangerous hands simply because they are afraid to bet.

3. You're in the big blind with Q-3 offsuit, not a hand you would normally play, but with two callers and no raiser, you get to see the flop. The flop comes down Q-9-7. You made top pair, but you hate your kicker. You check.

Wimp! You have to bet this flop. Granted, you would not normally enter a pot preflop with Q-3, but there you are and you paired the queen, so bet! By not betting, you are very likely giving up a pot when you have the best hand. What will you do if the player on the button bets here? Will you fold? He may be betting because he has second pair with an ace kicker. He may be betting just to claim the pot since no else seems interested in it. You have no idea where you stand in this hand if you do not bet.

If the button does bet out, the true wimp often realizes at this point that the button player may just be taking a shot, so he doesn't fold, *he calls*, thinking maybe he does have the best hand. On the turn, the wimp checks again, the button bets, and the wimp calls. On the river, a king comes down, the wimp checks, the button pushes all in, and the wimp folds. Now it really does look too dangerous to call.

4. One last example. Let's set up the situation precisely. The blinds are $50-$100, and you are in the big blind. You have $1,400. The table folds around to the button, and the button raises the bet to $400, a fairly standard raise. The player on the button is a very aggressive player who has been stealing your blinds consistently. The small blind folds. You look down at your hole cards to find pocket queens. You call the extra $300.

Wimp!

You have only one play in this situation when you are this short-stacked. You push all-in. By calling, you'll only have $1,000 left. How are you going to play your queens if an ace or king hit the table on the flop? Bet and pray? Check and fold? Why are you going to give the button player three cards to see if he can beat your queens? When you are this short-stacked, you push all-in and take this pot right now. There is $550 in there and you need those chips. If the button player actually has a strong enough hand to call your all-in bet, so be it. Maybe you'll actually double through him. But you must make him pay to try and beat you.

If you ever find yourself dreading the approaching blinds because they will take away so many of your precious chips, you've already waited too long for a playable hand. You've had a lot of playable hands if your chip stack is this short. Long before this point, you should have been looking for a shot to take. Before those blinds get around to you again, make a decision to go all-in. If you find yourself under the gun, and you still have not made your play at the pot, the time is now. The cards you play are of no importance. 3-2 offsuit? Possible straight. Go for it. If you lose, you lose. But make a determination that you will never allow yourself to be in this position again. You must keep your chips alive on the table at all times. If this happens to you again and again, you may not have the heart for this game.

Wimps are forever finding reasons to not bet. If they bet, it's a weak bet, and if they're raised, they fold. There's always a better possible hand than what they have. They check, call, and fold. In the College of No-Limit Hold'em, wimps major in slowplaying dangerous flops, minor in great laydowns, and as their elective courses, they take Checking 101 and Advanced Folding. They are forever writing their thesis on "Bad Beats: The Story of My Life."

OAFS

An oaf can be any age, any sex, and any nationality. An **oaf** is simply a player—in Las Vegas, most often a tourist—who has decided to enter the tournament despite knowing virtually nothing about how to play poker. Oafs also frequently show up in the limit games on weekends, usually the lower limit games. Most are simply looking for fun after trying the casino's blackjack, three-card poker and slots.

Oafs are usually identifiable within the first 15 to 20 minutes of a tournament. They innocently reveal their ignorance by asking very elementary questions about how the blinds work. Or they may bet out of turn, or ask a question about the hand rankings, or make improper (usually too small) bets or raises. Simple things.

Many times, oafs get blinded off without ever playing a hand, afraid of getting involved in a pot because they might make mistakes. Sometimes an oaf will get involved in a pot for no reason, just trying to look like he knows what he's doing. Sometimes, oafs bet aggressively, especially if drunk. I have seen aggressive oafs make a lot of money by betting aggressively before other players at the table were aware they were oafs.

I once watched an aggressive oaf become the chip leader at my table in the first hour of play by pushing all of his chips into the pot on the river on every pot he was involved in—and he entered a lot of pots. He would call before the flop, on the flop, and on the turn, then move all-in on the river and scare off other players who were clearly making some agonizing laydowns. I actually believed I was watching the reincarnation of Stu Ungar. I had no idea how he could possibly read every opponent he was facing so accurately that he knew he could drive them out of pot after pot like that. I did know that he could not possibly have made that many great hands himself. Then, toward the end of the first hour, a woman pushed all of her chips into the pot when there were four to a flush on the board, and no pair showing. The oaf called her all-in bet. He had no card in that suit.

That was when the table discovered the player was an oaf. The dealer had to explain to him why the woman had won this pot. He didn't know what a flush was! He had a card in his hand that paired a high card on the board, so he thought he should win. He did not speak English very well, and there was a five-minute comedy as the dealer tried to explain the game of poker to the chip leader at the table.

Most of the time, however, oafs do not fare so well. Their mistakes and misunderstandings give them away early. Just about every player has mistakenly bet out of turn, or revealed his cards when he thought the betting was over, usually through minor inattention to the game. This is not the sign of an oaf. An oaf must have his error explained to him, in detail, usually by the dealer, because he doesn't realize he did something wrong.

Oafs almost never make it to a final table, though I have seen players who were close to being oafs make it into the money. It's amazing how lucky some players can be in a tournament that lasts only a few hours. Most oafs, however, do little else at a table but contribute to pots they have no chance of winning. Having a true oaf at your table is a gift from God.

PUT EACH PLAYER ON A HAND

To build your player reading skills, put every player involved in a pot on his or her most likely hand. I do this by using whatever stereotype I have for each player, based on my observation of that player's prior play. As the cards come down and the play continues,

I adjust my reads to correspond with their actions. Do this for every pot, whether you are involved in the pot or not.

You will get better at this with experience. You will know you are becoming a dangerous player when you virtually always know which player will win the pot before the showdown. You will also learn to read some of the more difficult to read hands, like sets. You will often be surprised by sets at first, but after a while, you'll be able to feel it when a player has a set. If he's a good player, you won't feel it until his check-raise.

The players who never seem to improve are the players who simply play their two cards and hope for lucky hands. The players who make money are the players who pay the least attention to their own two cards, and the most to figuring out everybody else's.

BEWARE OF INITIAL IMPRESSIONS

I must also emphasize that although player profiling often starts out as a function of a player's physical characteristics, you must be very careful about applying any stereotype strictly on the basis of looks. The actual play you witness as the tournament progresses is far more revealing than any player's age, sex, nationality, or style of dress.

In one of the first tournaments I played, there was a white-haired gentleman at my table that I immediately categorized as a potential cagey codger. Within the first thirty minutes of play, however, he made a couple of very aggressive position plays from the button that led me to believe he was more of a ball-cap kid than a cagey codger. This reassessment turned out to be much closer to his type, but I had to continue to adjust my assessment in this tournament—as well as many other later tournaments—as he proved to be a highly skilled and dangerous player with a lot of tricky moves.

I've seen presumed ball-cap kids turn out to be wimps, canasta ladies turn out to be oafs, and conservatively-dressed businessmen turn out to be boat people. Profiling still works well for me, but I will adjust my read on any player very quickly if evidence refutes my initial impression. Again, you should really never stop reassessing your opponents. You can learn something about your opponents on just about every round if you keep your eyes open.

9

THE CHIP STRATEGY

I've already described the overall rock-paper-scissors power relationship of chips, cards and position, and discussed the strategies for two of these three elements—position and cards—at length. Now let's look at how the size of your chip stack affects optimal betting and playing strategy.

Both the basic position strategy provided in Chapter 6 and the card playing strategies provided in Chapter 7 assume that you have a "competitive" amount of chips, a stack that gives you enough chips to play and bet comfortably given the current blind level. But let's put numbers on this factor, because there are two common beliefs among no-limit hold'em tournament players that are completely wrong when it comes to fast tournament chip strategy. These false beliefs, which players have gotten from some of the popular poker books, are:

1. The early stages of a tournament are about survival.

2. Provided your chip stack is equal to at least 10 big blinds, you are not short-stacked, and may continue to wait patiently for a better-than-marginal hand.

In the fast tournaments, it is greatly to your advantage that so many players share these beliefs. But to achieve success in the fast tournaments yourself, you must replace these false beliefs with the following fast-tournament truths:

1. The early stages of a fast tournament, when most of your competitors are playing more carefully, are about chip acquisition, not survival.

2. A "competitive" amount of chips in a fast tournament is a stack of between 30 and 50 times the size of the big blind (and more if the antes have kicked in, as we'll see later). You are short-stacked when your chip stack goes below the cost of 30 big blinds. If you get down to a stack that equals the cost of only 10 big blinds, then you are desperate and on the brink of extinction.

Many fast tournaments have blind structures so fast that players start out with fewer chips than the cost of 30 big blinds. In a tournament like this, even though all players are in the same boat, you are still short-stacked, though, again, most players won't know it. This chapter will discuss how to alter your strategy to accommodate this condition, as well as others.

In a fast tournament where players start out with chip stacks equal to the cost of 30 or more big blinds, you may find yourself short on chips as the tournament progresses—even if you are keeping pace with the "average" chip stacks of most of your competitors—due simply to the rising blinds. All fast tournaments, in fact, get to a point where the "average" chip stack is short, even if it didn't start out that way.

Some fast tournaments provide players with starting chip stacks in excess of 50 big blinds. In a case like this, you may again have a chip stack that is not substantially larger or smaller than most of your competitors' stacks, but you are still long on chips given the starting cost of the blinds. More commonly in fast tournaments, you become long on chips by winning one or more substantial pots. In this case, you will usually be ahead of most of your competitors at your table.

Let's look at how the various chip positions affect fast tournament strategy overall.

THE NECESSITY OF BUILDING YOUR STACK EARLY

The reason the requirements for a competitive chip stack are so much higher in fast tournaments than in slow ones is because of the speed at which the blinds are rising. Most of the players in the fast tournaments have no handle on how quickly a big stack can become a small stack, and how often over the course of one of these tournaments your big stack will become a small stack, even if you suffer no major loss. Let me give an example.

The blinds were $50-$100 and I had just won $1,500 in chips on a hand where I made a standard raise under the gun before the flop, then called an all-in bet with my A-A, and my aces held up against A-K suited. This hand gave me a total of $3,300 in chips—a chip stack equal to 33 big blinds. I was feeling pretty good about my chip position. Only two players at the table had a bigger chip stack.

In this tournament, blind levels lasted 15 minutes, and one hand later, as I went into the blinds, they went up to $75-$150, so I was very glad to have made that double-up when I did. I gave up my $150 big blind to an early raiser, but called the extra $75 in the small blind in an unraised pot with an 8-9 suited. Unfortunately, the flop didn't hit me at all, so I lost a total of $300 in chips just going through the blinds, leaving me with $3,000 even.

A few rounds later, I called a $300 mini-raise with pocket 6s and three other callers in the pot, but unfortunately made no set and had to fold this hand to aggressive betting on the flop of high cards. I now had $2,700 in chips, and had no playable hand through the rest of this round. The blinds went up again just before they got to me—up to $100-$200—and I had no playable hand in the blinds, which cost me $300. This put my chip stack at $2,400—exactly 12 big blinds.

Twenty minutes—or exactly 12 hands—earlier, I had a chip stack equal to 33 big blinds. Now I had only 12. During this 20-minute period, I had simply gone through the blinds twice, completed the small blind once, and called one mini-raise. I had never really gotten deeply involved in any pot. Yet, I had gone from having the third biggest chip stack on the table to having the second shortest chip stack on the table that fast.

The next time the blinds got around to me they would be $150-$300, and if I didn't make some chips by the time I had to pay them, I'd be down to only $1,950 in chips, a desperate chip position in light of those rising blinds. So, twenty minutes after having 33 big blinds in my stack, I was contemplating the desperate position I'd be in if I didn't make some chips within the next few hands.

This is how it goes in these fast tournaments. There is rarely much breathing room, and being short-stacked an hour into the event, when everyone else has finally realized they're short-stacked, is often the kiss of death. In fast tournaments, desperation play is a continuous factor after the first hour of play. Waiting to worry about your chip position until your chip stack is down to ten big blinds is too late. Often when you are down to 10 big blinds, there will be players at your table with 40 to 50 big blinds, and more than half the table will be able to put you out of the tournament if you lose an all-in bet. And the players with those big stacks will likely call you down if they have any reasonable hand, especially if your chip stack goes down to only 6 to 7 big blinds.

In the fast tournaments that are the focus of this book, you must always play faster than would be optimal in long, slow tournaments. The position basic strategy I recommend, as well as my starting hand recommendations, are specifically designed for fast blind structures. But these recommendations assume that your chip stack is more than 30 times the size of the current big blind. If you have fewer chips than this, then you are short-stacked for a fast tournament, and your optimal strategy gets even faster. Before looking at precisely how you should alter your strategy plays based on your chip stack, let's first define three levels of being "short on chips."

If your chip stack contains a quantity of chips equal to the cost of:

21 to 30 big blinds:	you are SHORT
11 to 20 big blinds:	you are VERY SHORT
10 or fewer big blinds:	you are DESPERATE

It's not hard to keep these definitions straight. Just think 30-20-10. With 30 or fewer big blinds in your stack, you're short. 20 or fewer, very short. 10 or fewer, desperate. 30-20-10. Piece of cake. Now let's look at the chip basic strategy.

THE BASIC CHIP STRATEGY

Again, it's very much in your favor that most of the players in fast tournaments underestimate the chips necessary to remain competitive. Even more in your favor is the fact that most of the players in these tournaments also have a topsy-turvy view of how to employ their chips as a weapon in a tournament. If they have a lot of chips, they feel they can routinely call all-ins with marginal hands. When they are short-stacked, on the other hand, they tighten up. They wait patiently for premium cards so that they can enter pots with a more solid chance at a win—and they'll back out of dangerous situations quickly. All of this seems logical and sensible.

In fact, the more chips you have, the more careful you should be about entering situations that could make a big dent in your stack. The shorter your chip stack, the more aggressively you should play and the more shots you should take in an attempt to steal.

Players become more conservative in their play as their chip stack diminishes because their chips become so precious to them. But your short stack is not "precious." What's precious is that big mountain of chips that some player across the table from you is sitting behind. You think that by getting more selective in the hands you play that you're enhancing your chances of surviving until you finally get the miracle cards that are overdue. The fact is, you have to move fast if you intend to survive.

It's important to realize when you think about chips as a weapon that you do not need a mountain of chips to use your chips in this way. Ironically, the shorter your chip stack is—up to a point—the more you will use it as a weapon. It's only when your chip stack becomes too short to scare your opponents that it ceases to be a weapon. At that point, you have no weapons unless you happen to be dealt superior cards. Your continuation in the tournament becomes a matter of pure luck. This is why one of your primary concerns in any tournament should be keeping your chip stack healthy enough to be a threat to your opponents. The only way you can maintain a healthy chip stack is by keeping your chips alive in the game. You must get them into pots in the early stages of stack shrinkage, or their power as a weapon is neutralized. Rock breaks scissors. Pebble breaks nothing.

MASTERING THE COMPLEXITIES OF CHIP STRATEGY

Again, with more than the cost of 30 big blinds in your chip stack, you have a competitive chip stack and should stick to the position basic strategy and starting hand selections outlined in Chapters 6 and 7. These strategies are already much faster than you would use in a slow tournament structure. But when your chip stack contains fewer than 30 big blinds, you have to crank up your speed even more. In any fast tournament, you will inevitably be short on chips at various points in the tournament, and the faster the tournament, the more often and more drastically you will have to adjust your position and card strategies based on the size of your chip stack.

I've already defined three levels of short stacks—short, very short, and desperate—and given you the 30-20-10 memory aid to help you to quickly identify your chip status. Now let's get into the specific strategies for each of these three levels of short. These strategies are comprised of three major components:

1. Hand selection

2. Bet sizing

3. Bet timing

Let's look at each of these factors separately.

Hand Selection

David Sklansky in his tournament book and, more recently, Dan Harrington in *Harrington on Hold'em, Vol. II*, point out that in tournaments the shorter your stack the looser your starting hand requirements and the more aggressively you must play. In this chapter, I'll tailer these ideas to fast tournaments. For example, with a competitive chip stack, you would throw away an A-10 off suit from early position. But with a short stack, you would raise with this hand. If very short, you would push all in on any ace. And if your stack fits the desperate category, you would even call an all-in bet with any ace.

Bet Sizing

The shorter your stack, and the faster you must play, the more often you must raise, and the more of your chips you must bet when you raise. If you are desperate, with a chip stack totaling 10 or fewer big blinds, the only bet you will ever make is all-in. And most of your bets when you're very short, with a chip stack totaling 10 to 20 big blinds, would also be all-in. The shorter your chip stack, the more of a threat your pot-entering bet must present to your opponents. That's because betting all of your chips may scare away an opponent where a lesser bet may not. For example, let's say the blinds are $75 and $150, and you are on the button with $2,500 in chips. A player in middle position raises the bet to $500, a standard raise, and he is called by the player to his immediate left, making the pot $1,225 with the blinds. On the button, you find pocket jacks. Your $2,500 is only about 16 times the size of the big blind, so you are very short stacked. To call here would be a huge mistake, because your $500 call would make the pot $1,725, and leave you with only $2,000. In this situation, the only play you should consider is an all-in bet. You need the $1,225 that is in the pot right now, and your best shot at getting it is by chasing both players out before the flop. That $2,500 is a very serious bet when they have only committed $500 each. Take this pot *now*.

Bet Timing

The faster you must play, the earlier in a hand you must get your money into the pot. If you are very short or desperate, you must get all of your chips into the pot before the flop, and if you are desperate, you would even do this from under the gun. Let's look at more precise strategies for when you are short, very short, or desperate.

THE SHORT STRATEGY

When you are short (21 to 30 big blinds), you still have enough chips to scare anyone in most pots before the flop, assuming only limpers have entered or even a player who made a standard raise of three to four times the size of the big blind. But on later streets, especially with multiple players in the pot, the pot may grow to a size where your remaining chips would be insufficient to scare any player with a decent hand out of the pot, and you may not even be able to raise a sufficient amount to ruin the pot odds for a player on a strong draw.

So let's look at how card strategy changes when you are short.

Competitive Chip Stack (31-50 Big Blinds)

Early Position

If first in, raise with all pocket pairs from 7-7 to A-A, and A-K, A-Q, A-J. If not first in, raise any limper or reraise with J-J to A-A, as well as A-K. Call any standard raise with 7-7 to 10-10, as well as with A-Q and A-J. Otherwise fold.

Middle Position

If first in, raise with all pocket pairs from 7-7 to A-A, and A-K, A-Q, A-J, K-Qs, Q-Js, J-10s. If not first in, raise any limper or reraise with J-J to A-A, as well as A-K. Call any standard raise with 7-7 to 10-10, as well as with A-Q, A-J, K-Qs, Q-Js, J-10s. Otherwise fold.

Late Position

If first in, raise with any two cards. If not first in, raise any limper or reraise with J-J to A-A, as well as A-K. Call any standard raise with 2-2 to 10-10, as well as with A-Q, A-J, A-10, A-9s, K-Qs, Q-Js, J-10s, 10-9s, 9-8s. If not first in but on the button, raise any limper or reraise with J-J to A-A, as well as A-K. Limp in or call any standard raise with any two cards. Otherwise fold.

Short Chip Stack (21-30 Big Blinds)

Early Position

If first in, raise with all pocket pairs from 7-7 to Q-Q, and A-K, A-Q, A-J, but limp in with K-K or A-A, and reraise all-in if any player goes over the top of you. If not first in, raise or reraise all-in with 7-7 to A-A, as well as A-K, A-Q, and A-J. Otherwise fold.

Middle Position

If first in and your chip stack is between 25 to 30 big blinds, raise with all pocket pairs from 7-7 to Q-Q, and A-K, A-Q, A-J, but limp in with K-K or A-A (and reraise all-in if any player goes over the top of you). If first in and your chip stack is between 21 to 24 big blinds (on the shorter side of short), raise all-in with 7-7 to A-A, and A-K, A-Q, A-J, K-Qs, Q-Js, and J-10s. If not first in, raise or reraise all-in with 7-7 to A-A, as well as A-K, A-Q, A-J. Otherwise fold.

Late Position

If first in and your chip stack is between 25 to 30 big blinds, raise with all pocket pairs from 2-2 to Q-Q, and A-K, A-Q, A-J, A-10, and A-9s, but limp in with K-K or A-A (and reraise all-in if any player goes over the top of you). If first in and your chip stack is between 21 to 24 big blinds (on the shorter side of short), raise all-in with 2-2 to A-A, and A-K, A-Q, A-J, K-Qs, Q-Js, and J-10s. Otherwise, make your *standard* late position raise *if first in* with *any two cards*. If not first in, raise or reraise *all-in* with 7-7 to A-A, as well as A-K, A-Q, A-J. *Call* a standard raise from the button if you do not have one of the raising hands listed above, but you have an ace. Otherwise fold.

THE VERY SHORT STRATEGY

If your chip stack will only cover the cost of 11 to 20 big blinds in any fast tournament, you must face the fact that you are not all that far from the exit door. But you still have enough chips to scare any player who does not have a really big chip stack or a really strong hand. Two things are important when you are this short on chips. One is that unless you have an all-in raising hand as defined below, do not enter any pot unless you are the first in. And second, any bet when you are this short will always be all-in. You want to take the first shot when you are this short on chips, because this is your best shot at stealing the blinds and antes, and if you push all-in, you will usually limit your competition to a single player if you are called.

Very Short Chip Stack (11-20 Big Blinds)

Any Position

Raise or reraise all-in with 7-7 to A-A, A-K, A-Q, A-J, K-Q, K-J, K-10, and Q-J.

Late Position

If first in, raise all-in with any two cards.

The strategy is to go all-in on any of these hands regardless of any action in front of you. When you're this short on chips, you must take risks because the risk of tournament death is greater if you don't play than if you do. These are stronger than average hands and by pushing all-in, you won't have any difficult postflop decisions.

THE DESPERATE STRATEGY

With a chip stack totaling only 10 or fewer big blinds, you must make a stand before you are blinded off. With a chip stack totaling 5 to 10 big blinds, you may still be able to steal a pot with an all-in bet, but that's not guaranteed. With fewer chips than this, you'd need a table full of wimps to get away with a steal if any other player has already entered the pot.

Desperate Chip Stack
(10 or Fewer Big Blinds)

Any Position

You have only one play—all-in before the flop. And you must make an all-in move before the blinds hit you. Being first into the pot is important unless you have a strong starting hand—defined as any hand containing an ace or king, any two cards both valued at ten or higher, any pocket pair, or suited connectors down to 8-7—in which case you will play your hand all-in from any position against any number of opponents. If first in, you should also make your all-in move with any hand of Q-9, Q-8, Q-7, J-9, J-8, or 10-9. If one of these hands does not appear before the blinds come around to you again, then make your all-in move with any two cards from under the gun.

At this point, you do not want to go through the blinds even one more time without making a play to get some more chips. You must make an all-in move before the big blind hits you, and the cards you play are close to irrelevant. Being first into the pot is important unless you have a strong enough starting hand as defined above, in which case the more opponents the better, because you really want to win a big pot if possible. A small pot, even a double up, won't help you much now.

When you are desperate, having one or more limpers in the pot in front of you is an excellent opportunity for you to pick up more than just the blinds and antes. Ignore any fears you might have about limpers being dangerous. If any of the limpers call your all-in bet, you've got a shot at climbing back to a competitive stack. Let the cards decide.

Again, never call a bet with fewer than all of your chips when you are very short-stacked or desperate. Push all-in. That's your only play.

Position is meaningless when you have no chips to back up a position play. If a player calls your all-in, you're not in big trouble unless he has a pocket pair higher than both of your cards, or unless one of his cards matches one of yours but he has a better kicker, in which case your cards are dominated by his, since you must draw out to beat him and you only have three outs—the three cards that would pair your kicker. If all he has is overcards, he's a favorite in the hand, but not that big of a favorite. All you have to do is pair one of your cards when he doesn't and you're back in chips. You will see this happen all the time in tournaments. A desperate player's J-3 beats an A-K because a 3 comes down on the flop and no ace or king shows up by the river.

FAST PLAY FINE POINTS FOR SHORT TO DESPERATE STACKS

I want to explain a bit more of the logic behind these fast play decisions when your chip stack is less than competitive. You'll note from the above strategies that if your chip stack totals less than the cost of 20 big blinds, then almost all of your play will be preflop.

The idea is to get all of your chips into the pot before the flop to cut off other players' options. Potential opponents will be on notice that they can either call your all-in bet and hope that their two cards hold up against your two cards through the flop, turn, and river, or they can get out of your way. Put *them* to the tough decision.

In making any dangerous all-in move, it's best to be the first player into the pot, or at least the first raiser into the pot. If the pot is raised in front of you, you need a legitimate hand to push in yourself. Still, as long as you have a stack size between 15 and 20 big blinds, you have enough chips to make a substantial reraise when you push in on a player who has raised in front of you, assuming he made a normal raise of 3-4 times the size of the big blind.

If the raiser has made a bigger bet than this, or if your chip stack is smaller than 15 big blinds, it becomes more likely that your opponent will call you. In this situation, it's a good idea to consider your relative chip positions, as well as your read on, or knowledge of, this player. If the raiser is a loose aggressive player who is as likely to be raising with 7-6 suited as with a high pocket pair, then make your move. If he's a rock who plays few hands, then unless you've got one of the best hands yourself, let this one go.

Here's the scoop on "rocks" in the fast no-limit hold'em tournaments. It's not easy to get them off a premium starting hand preflop, especially if you are short-stacked. They will call any raise, including all-ins, with any high pocket pair from jacks up, as well as with A-K. With medium pairs, or A-Q, A-J, or A-10, their call will depend on how badly they need chips themselves or how badly you can hurt them if, say, their chip position is better than yours but nothing to write home about. After the flop, however, rocks often get terrified if any overcards are on the board, or if three to a suit they don't have come down. Their pocket queens shrink up fast when the ace hits the table.

The most important thing to remember when you're desperate is that you cannot allow any player to make a move on you. This is why your only bet is all-in. Do not just make a normal raise, and never limp into a pot, if you are desperate for chips, unless you've got aces or kings and you're trying to get other players to go over the top of you. When you are in any desperate chip position, aggressive players with big chip stacks will be waiting for you to limp in or make a weak raise. Don't give them a chance to take a shot if you're not prepared to call an all-in bet.

The short-stack fast play strategies discussed here should not be considered carved in stone. Think of these strategies as the optimal way to play against generic opponents. In real world tournaments, I often violate these strategies based on my reads of players I'm actually facing. I always play the whole situation. Think of these strategies as a basic guide to the appropriate speed and aggression called for based on your cards, chips, and position. But if you are new to tournament play, and lack the experience to make difficult judgment calls, you won't go too far wrong following these strategies to the letter. These strategies work.

What happens in fast tournaments is that your chip position will continually move from competitive to long to short, back to competitive to desperate to very short, etc. It never lets up. A new blind level or a single pot won or lost will more often than not move you into a new level. You must adjust your speed of play continually, sometimes round by round, as you go in and out of these different chip positions.

Here's a convenient chart of the complete strategy for cards, chip stack, and position. In using this chart, remember that in Skill Level 2 and 3 tournaments, you can pretty much follow it to the letter. In tournaments with higher Skill Levels, however, you must be much more aware of your opponents.

COMPLETE FAST TOURNAMENT STRATEGY FOR PLAYING CARDS, POSITION, AND CHIP STACK

Competitive Chip Stack (31-50 Big Blinds)
Early Position
If first in, raise with all pairs from 7-7 to A-A, and A-K, A-Q, A-J. If not first in, raise any limper or reraise with J-J to A-A, as well

as A-K. Call any standard raise with 7-7 to 10-10, as well as with A-Q and A-J. Otherwise fold.

Middle Position

If first in, raise with all pairs from 7-7 to A-A, and A-K, A-Q, A-J, K-Qs, Q-Js, J-10s. If not first in, raise any limper or reraise with J-J to A-A, as well as A-K. Call any standard raise with 7-7 to 10-10, as well as with A-Q, A-J, K-Qs, Q-Js, J-10s. Otherwise fold.

Late Position

If first in, raise with any two cards. If not first in, raise any limper or reraise with J-J to A-A, as well as A-K. Call any standard raise with 2-2 to 10-10, as well as with A-Q, A-J, A-10, A-9s, K-Qs, Q-Js, J-10s, 10-9s, 9-8s. If not first in but on the button, raise any limper or reraise with J-J to A-A, as well as A-K. Limp in or call any standard raise with any two cards. Otherwise fold.

Short Chip Stack (21-30 Big Blinds)

Early Position

If first in, raise with all pairs from 7-7 to Q-Q, and A-K, A-Q, A-J, but limp in with K-K or A-A and reraise all-in if any player goes over the top of you. If not first in, raise or reraise all-in with 7-7 to A-A, as well as A-K, A-Q, and A-J. Otherwise fold.

Middle Position

If first in and your chip stack is between 25-30 big blinds, raise with all pairs from 7-7 to Q-Q, and A-K, A-Q, A-J, but limp in with K-K or A-A, and reraise all-in if any player goes over the top of you. If first in and your chip stack is between 21-24 big blinds, raise all-in with 7-7 to A-A, and A-K, A-Q, A-J, K-Qs, Q-Js, and J-10s. If not first in, raise or reraise all-in with 7-7 to A-A, as well as A-K, A-Q, A-J. Otherwise fold.

Late Position

If first in and your chip stack is between 25-30 big blinds, raise with all pairs from 2-2 to Q-Q, and A-K, A-Q, A-J, A-10, and A-9s, but limp in with K-K or A-A, and reraise all-in if any player goes over the top of you. If first in and your chip stack is between 21-24 big blinds, raise all-in with 2-2 to A-A, and A-K, A-Q, A-J, K-Qs, Q-Js, and J-10s. Otherwise, make your standard late position raise if first in with any two cards. If not first in, raise or reraise all-in with 7-7 to A-A, as well as A-K, A-Q, A-J. Call a standard raise from the button if you do not have one of the raising hands listed above, but you have an ace. Otherwise fold.

Very Short Chip Stack (11-20 Big Blinds)
Any Position
Raise or reraise all-in with 7-7 to A-A, A-K, A-Q, A-J, K-Q, K-J, K-10, and Q-J.

Late Position
If first in, raise all-in with any two cards.

Desperate Chip Stack (10 or Fewer Big Blinds)
Any Position
You have only one play—all-in before the flop. You must make an all-in move before the blinds hit you. Push all-in from any position against any number of opponents with any hand containing an ace or king, any two cards valued at ten or higher, any pair, or suited connectors down to 8-7s. If first in, you should also make your all-in move with any hand of Q-9, Q-8, Q-7, J-9, J-8, or 10-9. If none of these hands appears before the blinds come around to you again, then make your all-in move with any two cards from under the gun.

WHEN THE ANTES KICK IN
Most no-limit hold'em tournaments require preflop antes in addition to the blind bets after a certain number of blind levels. All hold'em tournaments start out with blinds only, but typically the antes will kick in somewhere between the third and ninth blind level.

When the antes kick in, the price of sitting and waiting for a hand gets a lot more expensive. No player can help but notice that the preflop pot is now substantially bigger and the value of stealing before the flop has increased. When the pot gets bigger preflop, however, the difficulty of stealing the blinds also goes up.

You must adjust your chip strategy when the antes kick in. The easiest way to do this is to adjust your definitions of competitive, short, very short, and desperate. Instead of using the 30-20-10 standard, after the antes kick in use 40-30-20. That is to say, you need a chip stack that's greater than 40 times the big blind to be competitive. With a chip stack that's 31-40 times the big blind, you're short. With 21-30 times the big blind, you're very short, and with 20 or fewer big blinds, you're desperate, and should play accordingly.

WHAT IF YOU'RE LONG ON CHIPS?

So far, we've only looked at how to play a chip stack equal to the cost of 50 big blinds or less. There are two ways that players may attain a fat chip situation. Some fast tournaments actually provide players with starting chips in excess of 50 big blinds, though this universal long-chipped state will never last long. The other and more common route to finding yourself long on chips is winning one or two substantial pots. And, believe it or not, if you use the aggressive fast-play strategies described in this book, you will often have a chip stack totaling more than the cost of 50 big blinds.

Let's look at both of these long-on-chip situations.

WHEN EVERYBODY'S LONG ON CHIPS

If you are in a tournament that provides in excess of 50 big blinds to all players for their starting chips, this is not the same situation as having a chip stack in excess of 50 big blinds while most of your competitors have substantially smaller stacks.

When all players receive a big chip stack, you have no "scare advantage" over your opponents. They are just as threatening to you as you are to them. In a fast tournament, however, this state of mass comfort will not last long. Depending on the exact amount of starting chips provided, the starting blind level, and the frequency with which the blinds go up, this fat chip condition may last anywhere from two to four blind levels, but that's it. Then this tournament will play out like any other fast tournament.

In this type of tournament, your best strategy is to play looser than you normally would at the start, meaning you should see more flops whenever it's cheap to do so. For example, if you have $2,000 in chips, and the blinds are $10 and $20, it would be correct for you to call any standard raise (bets of $60-$80) with many marginal hands—any two high cards, any pair, and suited connectors down to 8-7. (Reraise according to the strategy for competitive stacks.) You have sufficient chips at this point to see more flops in an effort to hit a nice score on an unlikely big hand. You want to earn some chips before the blind increases over the next hour or so speed up the whole tournament.

In this type of tournament, don't make the mistake of thinking that you are in the "survival" portion of a slow tournament where you can be very selective about the hands you play. There is no survival period in a fast tournament, even when you start out with a wealth of chips. You don't have 60-minute blind levels. You have 60 minutes to make some money or you will be short stacked. This is the time to be aggressive against all those survivalists. Play loose, get into more pots, and take position shots as appropriate. Be brave. If you lose chips on aggression plays, no problem. Now you can get even more aggressive with your shorter stack.

This advice may seem at odds with my advice at the beginning of this chapter, that you should play more aggressively in fast tournaments when you're short-stacked and be more protective of your chips when you have a lot of them. That advice is based on your having a big stack in relation to lesser-chipped opponents. If a fast tournament starts out with all players having big chip stacks, then you want to take more risks while the relative cost to you is small.

YOU'RE LONG, THEY'RE SHORT

Now we're talking! You have already won a substantial number of chips, and you're facing opponents who have not been so fortunate. The size of your chip stack will instill fear into any player who goes up against you with anything less than a powerful hand.

So, being over-chipped in relation to the blinds and the other stacks on your table is a big plus. Now how do you play a big chip stack? When you have a strong hand, you want to play with all due aggression. But remember, though chips beat position, they do not beat cards. You have to slow down if you believe you are facing a player with a hand so good he can't or won't lay it down. How can you judge when this is happening?

Players who like their hands simply will not go away when you bet. Most position players will not stay in pots or take shots at you if you are betting with any aggression at all. They will get out of your way quickly. In fact, since chips beat position, you can actually take position-type shots from any position at the table. You can steal the blinds from any position, even under the gun. If you get any preflop callers, your bet on the flop will usually dispel them. When you have a lot of chips, these types of shots are relatively cheap compared to your total chip stack. If you have a chip stack of $6,000, and you throw in a preflop bet of $400 when the blinds are $50 and $100, you can get away from your hand without severe damage to your chip stack. However, that $400 bet will be very threatening to any opponent who has only $2,000 in chips. You're betting less than 7% of your chip stack, but he must put 20% of his chip stack at risk to call your bet.

You can't make plays like this so often that it becomes obvious that you are just battering the table with your chip stack. Players in fast tournaments will start calling you down, or more likely pushing all-in on you, with legitimate hands. This is especially true if there are players at your table who are very short-stacked.

So, be selective in picking the spots to make your moves. Also, if you're making a chip shot, do so with cards that have some decent possibility of making something on the flop. I wouldn't raise from early position with 3-2 offsuit, but I might raise with 3-3, or 6-7 suited, even though these would not be good early raising hands with a standard competitive chip stack.

I'm not going to provide a precise strategy for hands to raise with or shots to take when you're sitting behind a big stack. If you have chips, and you play them with aggression, you will usually keep making more chips. Same old story. The rich get richer. But since you have to be careful of bumping into players who have monster hands, be aware that chip shots are usually best made in combination with position.

Here are three basic guidelines on using your chips as a weapon:

1. Never jeopardize any substantial number of your chips when the board is truly dangerous.

If you've got top pair, or two pair, but the board shows three or four to a straight or flush, make a standard raise but do not try to put a player all-in if he's got enough chips to hurt you. With a standard raise, he has to worry that you've got that straight or flush, and that you're trying to extract more chips from him. And throw your hand away if he pushes all-in and calling his all-in raise would take a big chunk out of you. Let the little stack have the chips. It's more important that you retain your chip lead and that you don't double him up. If he's gutsy enough to take a shot at you when the board is that dangerous, he deserves this pot.

2. Be wary of any players who call your bets postflop.

They may not be on draws. They could be slowplaying a monster. When someone has the nuts, you're the guy he really wants in the pot. If you keep betting, the position shooters will go away. The nuts don't go away. If you've got the big chip stack, and a legitimate hand, don't hesitate to toss it away if some player is calling your bets, then takes a big shot at you when you check or make a standard bet on the next round. And you may want to give up the lead in betting if you sense danger, based on your read on your opponent. Don't hesitate to get out of the pot while the cost to you is still small. You want to make the easy money when you have a big chip stack—and there's a lot of easy money—not take dangerous chances.

3. Be even more careful if multiple players are in the pot.

If someone pushes all-in when three or more players are in the pot, get out of the way if he's got enough chips to damage you. Example: you raise in early position before the flop with A-K suited (hearts) and you get two callers, each of whom has about half as many chips as you. The flop comes down K-J-10, with two spades. You lead out with a bet the size of the pot, and the next player to act pushes all-in. The other player folds. Your move: fold. You may have the best hand, but there are just too many ways you could already be beaten, let alone ways that you can be beaten on the turn and river. You do not want to endanger half of your chips on this hand. If this player had substantially fewer chips than you, then calling would be the right play. He may be holding a K-Q or Q-J, or even pocket queens, and pushing in on his top or second pair with a straight draw. He may have two spades, including the ace, and a nut flush draw. But there are too many other deadly possibilities. He may have flopped two pair or even a set. He may have A-Q and the nut straight. If this player has half as many chips as you, he can seriously damage your stack if you call and he wins.

This is why it's actually more difficult to play a big chip stack than a small one. You have to make judgment calls more often. If you had been short-stacked, you probably would have pushed all-in preflop with your A-K suited. Decision over. And with a modest stack, you would have pushed all-in on the flop, despite the dangers. Top pair, ace kicker, need chips—you just take your shot and pray. With a big chip lead on your opponents, however, you must play with both more aggression and more caution. It's a difficult balancing act.

PLAYING AGAINST A BIG STACK

Generally, the rule in no-limit hold'em tournaments is to avoid going up against players who have big chip stacks—that is, either more chips than you have or enough chips to cripple you with an all-in bet. This general rule is especially true when you have no hand to speak of and you are only playing position. Chips beat position (rock breaks scissors). Some players—especially the inexperienced players so abundant in fast tournaments—seem oblivious to their opponents' chip stacks, but the better players keep well aware of their competition's ammunition, and so should you.

When you have a substantial number of chips yourself, however, there are exceptions to the rule. Even if you are not the chip leader at your table, you will occasionally find opportunities for stealing a lot of chips from opponents who have more chips than you. The big stacks know how scary they are and you can use this fact against them, even when you're out of position. If you have anywhere near two-thirds of an opponent's big stack, you will be a player that he will not want to get involved with unless he has a very premium hand. Bullies prefer to pick on the weak.

When a player with a lot of chips makes a standard raise, he does not expect a call. He's knows that everyone at the table is afraid of his power to end their tournaments. The medium pairs and suited connectors and A-J suited hands will all fold preflop to this player's raise, although any of them may call the same raise with the same hand and same position against an opponent who is not quite so scary. This is something that you will discover pretty quickly when you have a chip stack that is substantially larger than most of the stacks on your table. Stealing pots becomes easy. You can raise with more modest hands from earlier positions. If you get a call, you can pretty much assume the caller has a premium starting hand, and play your cards after the flop accordingly.

So, whether you are in position or out of position with a big-stacked player, if he is a smart player, he will be nervous that you are in the pot at all. If you have position on him, it will unnerve him if you call his preflop raise. If he makes a standard bet on the flop, about half the size of the pot, it will unnerve him even more if you just call again, especially if you do so without much thought.

Even if he has position on you and calls your raise preflop, you can scare him by checking on the flop, then calling when he bets. Believe me, unless he has a monster hand, this will slow him down. For one thing, players with large chip stacks often call standard raises with mediocre hands, and often fold an opponent with any bet on the flop, knowing that they can get away from their hands cheaply, for a small percentage of their chips, if their opponent makes a really strong hand. The idea here, whether you are in or out of position against him, is to make him fear that you are slowplaying a monster. He's the big chip stack at your table, and you either called his preflop raise, then called his bet on the flop, or you raised him preflop, then check-called his bet on the flop. Do you have aces? Did you flop a set? Are you on a draw? How can you want to stay involved with him when he has the chips to destroy you?

What usually happens on the turn when he has position on you is that when you check, he will check. Then you can push all in on the river and take the pot. What's better, however, is for him to bet on the turn when you check, so you can check-raise him all-in right there. The reason you don't just call here is that you don't want to give him a chance to make a strong hand with the river card. Also, if his bet on the turn is a really big bet that would pot-commit you, you can still get away from your hand pretty cheaply. If his bet is that big, he probably does believe he has you beat, and he won't go away.

When you have position on him, he will often give up the lead in betting on the turn, and when he checks, you push all-in. If, however, he makes a sizable bet, you'll have to get away from your hand. If he makes a more standard bet on the turn, you've got a judgment call. Will he give up this pot if you push all-in on him?

There are many variations on this play that you can use to attack big chip stacks postflop. None of these would be basic strategy plays, but once you've got the basic strategies for cards, chips, and position down, it's time to start adding plays like these to your arsenal. These plays work best when you have a pretty good read on the type of opponent you are facing, even if you are unsure about his cards. Is this a player who would enter the pot with just about any hand, simply because he has a big stack? Is this a player who will bet just to keep the lead even if the flop presents dangers? Does this player see you as a solid player because you have shown down only strong cards? All of these factors and more should play into your decision to try an advanced move like this.

MOVING FROM FAST TOURNAMENTS TO SLOWER TOURNAMENTS

If you get used to playing in fast tournaments with similar patience factors, it will be disorienting when you first play in a tournament with a slower blind structure and a higher patience factor. The first time I played in Bellagio's $540 tournament, it was very disconcerting to play with 40-minute blind levels. I was used to thinking in terms of having to make my moves fast, before the blinds came around again.

In the Bellagio tournament, you go through the blinds at least twice at every level, and sometimes three times. You are not as frantic for chips, and neither are your opponents. Everyone at the table can and does wait to play more premium hands and situations, and because there are fewer all-in bets before the flop, postflop play gets much trickier. The more skilled players have more time to study their opponents and learn how to manipulate them.

In Dan Harrington's *Harrington on Hold'Em II*, the author describes the times when the blind levels are changing in long slow tournaments as "inflection points." In fast tournaments, with their much smaller starting chip allotments and much shorter blind levels, the entire tournament is essentially a constant "inflection point," especially after the halfway point when any average chip stack is short.

If you intend to advance from the fast tournaments to slower tournaments, Harrington's book, as well as the others in this book's bibliography, are all required reading. Also, David Sklansky's *Theory of Poker* should be studied for a general understanding of the mathematics behind poker logic. Slow tournaments are simply not the same animal as fast tournaments, and no one book could ever be all you'd need for these much tougher games.

10

REBUYS AND ADD-ONS

Many of the small buy-in tournaments allow players to purchase chips over and above the initial buy-in amount. And many of the players in these rebuy tournaments are clueless as to when and whether to rebuy.

Although I will discuss the various rebuy formats that are popular in poker rooms today, I think it best to start with an overview of the logic behind rebuy strategies, so that you can make good rebuy investment decisions no matter what format you encounter.

THE PRINCIPLE OF RETURN ON INVESTMENT

Again, the general principle that should guide your decision on whether to voluntarily purchase extra chips in a tournament is the same principle that should govern every skilled gambler's decision on whether to make any bet: you make the bet if there will be a positive return on your investment. A rebuy, like a tournament buy-in, is nothing more nor less than a bet. You are simply placing a specific amount of money at risk, in expectation that the return will be greater than the amount wagered. If rebuying will increase your payouts from the tournaments you enter more than the cost of the rebuys, then the rebuys are worth the gamble.

It's easy to make a statement like: if you have more chips in a tournament, you'll win more. But, since these extra chips have a cost, then even if the statement is true, the question is whether the amount of increase in win is worth the price being paid for it. Furthermore, do extra chips always mean increased wins? Are there some players who play so badly that no amount of chips can increase their win percentage? Are there some players who play so skillfully that they don't need extra chips?

Lots of players have opinions on these things, but can we mathematically prove that more chips mean more wins? Can we calculate how much we should be willing to pay for more chips before the price exceeds the value?

THE LOGIC OF REBUYS

To clarify the logic behind good rebuy decisions, let's simplify the problem by analyzing a coin-flipping tournament instead of a poker tournament. And let's make it the simplest coin-flipping tournament imaginable.

In this coin-flipping tournament, there are two players. Each player buys in for $100, for which he receives a single $100 chip. Each player places his single chip as an all-in bet. The dealer flips the coin, and one player calls "heads" or "tails" in the air. If the player calls correctly, he wins the other player's chip, busting him out, and the tournament is over. The next tournament goes just like the first one, except that the other player gets to call heads or tails this time.

Neither player has an advantage in this tournament. Assuming an honest coin and an honest dealer, calling the coin is no advantage. The players may go through various lucky streaks, but in the long run, they would break even on this game.

Now, let's say that a voluntary rebuy option is offered. For another $100, each player may purchase an extra $100 chip. The tournament will run exactly the same, with a player winning the tournament by busting out his competitor. Player A decides to always make the rebuy. Player B decides to never make it. So, in essence, this is a tournament where Player A starts with two $100 chips and Player B starts with only one.

Will Player A's rebuy lead to more wins? Absolutely. In fact, it can be shown mathematically that he will win exactly twice as often as Player B. Therefore, the rebuy in this tournament has increased Player A's win percentage substantially.

I'll spare you the math here, as I'm trying to explain the logic rather than the statistical notation. But what essentially is happening when Player A starts out with two $100 chips versus Player B's single $100 chip, is that Player A can win the tournament on a single correct call, whereas Player B is required to make two correct calls. If Player B makes the first correct call, but fails to make the second, then he is back where he started, again having to make two consecutive correct calls to win. If you work it out on paper, or try it with coins, you'll see that in the long run Player A will win exactly twice as often as Player B.

But, will Player A win more money? No. The two-thirds of the time that Player A wins the tournament, he will win Player B's $100 buy-in. But the 1/3 of the time that Player B wins the tournament (with two correct calls), he will win both Player A's buy-in and rebuy, for a total of $200. In the long run, alas, they will still break even in these coin-flip tournaments. The major difference will be that the average tournament will last longer because it will not always be decided with a single coin flip. More chips will be in action (the average amount wagered per tournament will be $200 each instead of $100 each), but the overall breakeven result will not change.

For the sake of simplicity, this analysis includes no house commission, although any real tournament would charge players a fee to enter. If you assumed in the above hypothetical tournament that the players each had to pay $109 to enter, with $9 going to the house and $100 going into the prize pool—then this would not be a break-even tournament for the players. In fact, each player would lose $9 per tournament, though this loss would be to the house, not to each other. (In order to succeed in tournaments, a player must have sufficient skill not only to beat his opponents but to overcome the house commission, and this would apply to poker tournaments as well as coin-flipping tournaments.)

In any case, since the rebuy strategy in this coin-flip tournament makes no difference to either player's break-even result, does this example tell you that rebuys are worthless? Not at all. We've just begun with this analysis. Let's take it further.

When Rebuys Pay

Let's now say that a single $100 chip rebuy is allowed, but this time the rebuy chip is discounted, and may be purchased for only $50. Now, let's see what happens when Player A makes the rebuy, but Player B does not.

First, note that this discounted rebuy format doesn't change the tournament itself, but only alters the prize pool, because although Player A has $200 in chips, he has put only $150 into the prize pool. If Player B wins the tournament, he will win only $150 in cash. You can probably guess what will happen here, based on our prior example. Because Player A has twice the chip stack of Player B, he will win $100 twice as often as Player B will win $150. Or, put more simply: For every $200 that Player A wins, Player B will win only $150, giving Player A a profit of $50 every three tournaments.

So, even though Player A is spending more to get his wins, the extra investment is paying off. Player B, by trying to save money, is losing in the long run. What's happening here is that by purchasing the discounted rebuy chips, Player A is lowering his average cost per chip from $100 to $75. With this strategy, Player A is able to profit from playing a break-even coin-flip game.

This coin-flip example indicates that if rebuy chips are discounted, there is an advantage to purchasing them—even if you are just playing a break-even game—provided you have an opponent who does not make the rebuy. Furthermore, if you carried out this example to demonstrate the effects of Player A making multiple rebuys, you would see that each succeeding rebuy at a discount would further lower the cost per chip, and give Player A a greater advantage (and profit) over Player B, assuming Player B made no rebuys or voluntarily limited himself to fewer rebuys than Player A.

Player B's only defense against Player A's rebuy strategy, when rebuys are discounted, would be for him to make the same number of rebuys as Player A. Otherwise, Player A will beat him in the long run, even though neither player has any advantage over the other in the coin-flipping game itself.

Now, because you intend to play poker tournaments, where skill is involved, let's look at how skill will affect return on a rebuy investment.

Let's say Player A is a skillful coin-caller, who actually has the talent to call heads or tails correctly 60% of the time, instead of the expected 50%. (Don't ask me how he can do this. We're just bending this coin-flipping tournament into something that more closely resembles poker. Some poker players have talent. Others don't.)

Now, if neither player makes a rebuy, Player A will have a long run 10% advantage over Player B. Player A will win six out of his ten calls, while Player B will win only five out of his ten calls. So, for every twenty tournaments, Player A will win eleven and Player B will win nine. That means Player A will come out $200 ahead for every $2,000 of his action (or every twenty $100 tournaments), which is a 10% win rate. Or, simply put, Player A will be winning, on average, $10 for every $100 tournament he enters.

Now, with Player A having this 10% advantage, consider what happens if Player A makes a $100 rebuy and Player B does not. And we'll assume here that he again pays full price, $100, for his rebuy chip. Player A will still win at the rate of 10%, but his rebuy strategy will again force Player B to win two consecutive calls in order to win a tournament, again stretching the average tournament out longer, so that Player A will earn a 10% profit on a greater amount of action per tournament. Once more, I'll spare you the math, but on average, if Player A makes that $100 rebuy, each player will put, on average, $175 into action per tournament, instead of $100. Player A will be earning $17.50 (10% of $175) per tournament, on average, if he rebuys the $100 chip in every tournament and Player B does not.

You should note here that Player A's rebuy does not alter his 10% win rate, but simply forces more action from Player B. By causing the tournament to last longer, Player A is getting a bigger dollar return with his 10% win rate. And, in this case, poor Player B cannot negate Player A's advantage by rebuying himself. If Player B also purchases the rebuy chip, he will cause the tournament to last even longer, further increasing Player A's dollar return on his 10% win rate.

So far, all of this indicates that it is wise for a skillful tournament player to rebuy, because his extra chips will force unskilled players to give him more action. It indicates that if you are a skillful player in a multiple rebuy tournament, it is not only to your advantage to rebuy multiple times as needed to maintain your chip stack, but it is also to your advantage when unskilled players rebuy multiple times!

In fact, the more rebuys you add to a tournament where one player is a skilled coin-caller and the other is not, the more money the skilled player will ultimately win per tournament. There is, in fact, as a general rule, no maximum number of rebuys that the skilled player should restrict himself to in order to maximize his winnings. In a simple tournament like this, as long as he has a percentage advantage over his competitor, he is making a mistake if he sets a loss limit on the number of rebuys he is willing to make.

The only time a skilled player should stop making rebuys in this coin-flip tournament where he has an advantage over his competitor is when he runs out of funds to continue. In this case, he probably should not have entered the tournament in the first place because he was under-bankrolled for the normal fluctuations. (In real poker tournaments, a skilled player may be facing a mixture of both skilled and unskilled opponents at his table, in addition to an escalating blind structure. These factors can create conditions where rebuying would cease to be the optimal strategy, even for a skilled player.)

The best strategy for the unskilled player, on the other hand—other than not entering the tournament at all—is to cut his losses by never making a rebuy. When unskilled players rebuy—kicking up the prize pool—the ones who profit are the skilled.

Strategic Power of More Chips

The above examples show how chips can be used to gain a mathematical advantage in a simple coin-flip tournament, but that is not the whole value of chips in a poker tournament. In a game like no-limit hold'em, chips also provide psychological and strategic power beyond what can be illustrated with simple coin-flip examples.

For example, in a no-limit hold'em tournament, if the blinds are at $50-$100 and the short-stacked player under-the-gun pushes all-in with his last $300 in chips, it would be highly unusual for him to get away with stealing the blinds. Most players at the table would figure that a player this desperate for chips when he's about to be entering the blinds could be taking a shot with just about any hand. In most cases, this player will find numerous callers to his all-in bet.

But, what if the under-the-gun player has $3,000 in chips sitting in front of him and he enters the pot with a standard raise to $300? Same position, same size bet, all the same players at the table, but in this case only a player with a pretty strong hand would call this bet. Nobody wants to tangle with an under-the-gun raiser who has a big chip stack. The big stack has the power to do further damage later in the hand. He has *implied* power. It would not be unusual at all for this player to end up getting no action and just taking the blinds. It's a simple fact in no-limit tournaments that it's easier to steal when you have a big chip stack than when you're desperate. And by this point in this book, you should realize that there is a lot of value to winning pots without confrontation.

The advantage from this implied power can't be mathematically quantified as easily as you can quantify the value of purchasing rebuy chips at half-price. The important thing to remember is that chips have this additional strategic value, and it's not insignificant. Again, chips are one of the major weapons in a no-limit hold'em tournament. For a skillful player to decide to play a rebuy tournament without rebuying would be like a Samurai warrior deciding to enter a swordfight with a pocket knife. He may be good, but he's not too smart.

So, assuming you are a skillful player, your approach to rebuys in any no-limit hold'em tournament should be to always have the maximum number of chips available to you sitting in front of you and ready to use.

GENERAL RULE

Always buy the extra chips, as many as you can, as soon as you can.

There are exceptions to this rule, and I'll discuss these exceptions below, but the idea is that, all other things being equal, you should maximize the power of your chips as a weapon. Now, let's look more closely at strategies for specific types of rebuys.

"DEALERS' BONUS" CHIPS

Not all tournaments offer dealers' bonus chips. These are chips available only at the time of your initial buy-in, and that can usually be purchased for a nominal amount of money compared to the buy-in price. For example, with a tournament buy-in of $40 for $400 in chips, you may have an option to purchase an extra $100 in chips for only $5 more. Poker rooms sell dealers' bonus chips in order to compensate the dealers who are assigned to the tournament tables. Tips to dealers in small buy-in tournaments are uncommon, and poker dealers generally survive on their tips. The dealers' bonus chip sales ensure the tournament dealers of a fair hourly wage.

The funds collected from players who purchase the bonus chips do not go into the prize pool. For this reason, there are always a few players who decline to purchase the chips. I've heard some of these players complain that, because the funds collected for these chips do not go into the prize pool, the chips are a "bad investment," or explain that they "don't believe in tipping dealers."

Is this a good decision?

Right off the bat, you have an example of a fairly common type of voluntary chip purchase not covered by the prior coin-flip examples. In this case, there are two opposing forces. On the upside, you get more chips and that's good. On the downside, if you purchase the bonus chips and others don't, you are essentially paying a higher commission to play in the tournament. This is money you will never get back, even if you win.

If you analyze the purchase of dealers' bonus chips in a coin-flip tournament where neither player has any skill advantage, it becomes clear that the value of this purchase will depend on the discount. For example, if Player A purchased an extra $100 chip for the full $100 price, and the funds from that purchase did not enter the prize pool, and Player B decided not to make the purchase, both players would be screwed. With his two chips versus one, Player A would again win twice as often as Player B, as in the earlier example, but the prize pool will contain no profit for him when he wins. That is, he'd be paying $200 to enter and rebuy, while the total money in the prize pool is only $200, or the total of his and Player B's initial $100 buy-ins. In the meantime, when Player A loses, he will be out $200. So, for every three tournaments, Player A would be out $200. Player B will be bad off as well, though not quite as bad off. When he wins, again, once out of every three tournaments, he makes a profit of $100. But he loses $100 on two out of every three tournaments. So, for every three tournaments he plays, he loses $100. Where do all of the profits go? To the dealer! The dealer makes out like a bandit, earning $100 per tournament.

But this doesn't mean that dealers' bonus chips are always a bad investment. What if the dealers' bonus chips are discounted, as they almost always are in a poker tournament, so that Player A can purchase the extra $100 chip for only $1? And again, let's specify that this $1 will not go into the prize pool, and again, let's have Player B refuse to make this purchase. In this case, Player A will again win twice as many tournaments as Player B, though Player A will earn a profit of only $99 when he wins, while Player B will win a full $100 when he wins because he didn't spend the $1 on the bonus chip. In this case, Player A comes out way ahead. On two of every three tournaments he'll win $99, while on one of three he'll lose $101. That would give him a $97 profit for every three tournaments he played (or a 32% win rate), and Player A's profit comes directly from Player B.

Since Player A will win this tournament two out of three times when he has two chips versus Player B's one chip, you can pretty quickly figure out that Player A will make a profit on his bonus chip purchase, assuming Player B does not make the purchase, as long as Player A is paying less than one-third the value of the chip. If he pays $33 for the $100 bonus chip, he'll break even in the long run. If he can purchase the chip for any amount less than this, he'll profit from the purchase.

And if Player A has a skill advantage over Player B, then purchasing a discounted bonus chip when Player B does not will again increase the dollar return on his advantage, as he will not only be reducing his average cost per chip, but forcing Player B to give him more action in each tournament.

What if neither Player A nor Player B has any skill advantage, and the $100 bonus chip is sold for $1, and both Player A and Player B make the purchase? In this case, this tournament will go back to being a 50/50 proposition for both players. Each player will lose exactly the cost of the bonus chip per tournament ($1 each), and the only winner will be the dealer, who will profit the exact amount of the bonus chip purchases ($2).

For Player B, however, it would be a very wise investment to purchase this bonus chip if he knows that Player A has made the purchase, as it will lower his average loss per tournament from $33 to $1. Moreover, if Player A has a 10% skill advantage over Player B, but Player B purchases the $1 bonus chip while Player A does not, Player A's 10% skill advantage would be insufficient to overcome the 32% advantage Player B obtains from paying substantially less per chip than Player A.

This means that the purchase of dealers' bonus chips are a good defensive play for any player—even if the chips themselves provide no advantage—if you are playing in a tournament where all or most of your competitors will make the purchase.

In real-world tournaments, I've never seen a dealers' bonus chips offer that would double a player's starting chip stack. Dealers bonus chips will usually increase your initial chip stack by somewhere between 20% and 50%. And, again, in every case I've encountered, dealers' bonus chips have been offered at a significant discount.

For example, Orleans has a tournament with a $40 buy-in for $300 in starting chips, with a dealers' bonus chip option of $75 in extra chips at a cost of $5. In this case, you are purchasing the bonus chips for exactly half the price per chip of the initial buy-in chips, and increasing your starting chip stack by 25%. Binion's has a $60 tournament that provides $1,000 in starting chips. The dealers' bonus chip offer is $10 for $500 more. In this case, the bonus chips are available at one-third the price per chip of the initial buy-in chips, and you are increasing your starting chips by 50%. The Plaza has a $50 tournament that provides $1,500 in starting chips. For $10 more, you can get $500 in dealers bonus chips. That is a 40% discount, and you are increasing your starting chip stack by 33%. Other Las Vegas poker rooms have similar offers.

Would I make these real world bonus chip purchases? In every case, yes—in a heartbeat. I am a winning player, so the chips have both mathematical and psychological value. Deciding not to purchase dealers bonus chips because you don't like dealers is like deciding not to eat because you dislike the food industry.

There could in theory be a dealers' bonus chip offer that would not be worth a purchase, if, for instance, the bonus chips were not discounted and most other players were not buying them. But all of the dealers' bonus chip offers I've seen in real poker tournaments have been good deals. In my opinion, this is a no brainer. Buy the chips.

REBUY FORMATS

There are two common rebuy formats in fast tournaments— the single rebuy format and the multiple rebuy format. The multiple rebuy format also usually includes an **add-on**, which is a final purchase of rebuy chips allowed to all players at the end of the rebuy period. Single rebuy tournaments also sometimes allow an add-on. Unlike the funds collected for the dealers' bonus chips, the funds the poker room collects for rebuys and add-ons do go into the prize pool. Because of this, the prize pools in rebuy tournaments, especially in the multiple rebuy tournaments, are often quite large relative to the initial buy-in costs.

Let's look at these different formats, how they work, and how you should approach them.

The Single Rebuy Format

This format allows any player to make a single rebuy at any time during a specified rebuy period. A rebuy period in a fast tournament typically lasts for two to four blind levels—most commonly for the first hour of play. The single rebuy format also typically allows this purchase of rebuy chips at any time during the rebuy period, regardless of the number of chips a player has when he chooses to make the rebuy.

In some single rebuy tournaments, the number of chips available as a rebuy is the same as the number purchased with the initial buy-in, with the cost of these chips the same as the initial buy-in cost (minus the house fee). In other single rebuy tournaments, the rebuy chips are discounted significantly—for example, with a $40 buy-in for $300 in chips, you may be allowed a rebuy of $300 more in chips for only $20. It is also not uncommon for rebuy chips to provide a greater quantity of chips than purchased with the initial buy-in. For example, you get $300 in chips for your initial buy-in, but $500 in chips for your rebuy. And, in some tournaments the rebuy chips are both discounted and of a greater quantity than the initial buy-in chips—say, $400 in chips for an initial $60 buy-in, with an additional $800 in chips for a $40 rebuy.

Some players will pay $60 to enter such a tournament with absolutely no intention of making the $40 rebuy, but they're making a mistake. A tournament with this format should be viewed as a $100 tournament in which players get $1,200 in chips. The majority of players in these types of tournaments, however, do recognize the value of the discounted rebuy chips, and 90+% will make the rebuy.

When the rebuy chips are not discounted, however, it is more common for players to pass on making the rebuy. In most cases, this is a mistake as well. I will discuss the reason below, in the section titled "Rebuy Misconceptions," but for now, just know that you should never enter a single rebuy tournament unless you plan to make the rebuy, especially if the rebuy chips are discounted. Remember the general rule:

♠ **Always buy the extra chips, as many as you can, as soon as you can.**

The Multiple Rebuy Format

Multiple rebuy tournaments are usually structured so that players may make a rebuy during the rebuy period only if their current chip stack is at or below the starting chip amount obtained with the initial buy-in. For example, if you started with $400 in chips, and you currently have $405 in chips, you may not rebuy. Multiple rebuy tournaments also sometimes allow players to make a double rebuy if they lose all of their chips on an all-in bet.

In a multiple-rebuy tournament that prohibits rebuys unless a player is at or below his starting chip allotment, players are usually allowed to make their first rebuy before the first hand is dealt. It is always in your best interest to do so. Otherwise, you may win an early small pot and find yourself unable to rebuy, facing other players at your table who made the allowed rebuy, and who now have you vastly out-chipped. I will say this one more time, to emphasize the point:

♠ **Always buy the extra chips, as many as you can, as soon as you can.**

The Add-On

Most multiple rebuy tournaments, and some single-rebuy tournaments, also allow players to make a single "add-on" at the end of the rebuy period. The add-on cost is usually the same as the regular rebuy cost, and the number of chips received is also the same number as for a rebuy in that tournament. The main difference here is that the add-on can only be made once, at the end of the rebuy period, and any player can make the add-on regardless of how many chips he currently has. By now, you should know the general rule for whether or not you should purchase the add-on chips.

But there will occasionally be exceptions to the rule. If, for example, you have already lost most of your starting chips, and the add-on would simply provide you with a short stack to continue, then you might decide to forego the add-on. If you would not initially buy into a tournament with such a serious chip handicap compared to your opponents—even at a discounted price—then the add-on is a bad investment. Go home. There will be better tournament opportunities in which to invest your money. But unless you are down to the felt, and the add-on is full price, you should probably take the add-on. When the add-on is discounted, you are usually getting the right price to take a shot with a short stack.

There is a common but mistaken belief among players in fast tournaments that you should forego the add-on if you make some massive amount of chips during the rebuy period, and the add-on amount is small relative to your current chip stack. For example, if a player has $3,000 in chips at the end of the rebuy period, with a big chip lead on the other players at his table, who have an average of $1,000 in chips, many players would advise the big stack to forego the $300 add-on. To think like this is to ignore the speed with which any player's chip stack can be decimated in a fast tournament.

I once had $3,200 in chips at the end of a rebuy period when most of the players at my table had in the neighborhood of $1,000 in chips. I made the $300 add-on. One player commented that I was crazy to buy more chips with the stack I had. Within about ten minutes, however, I called a preflop all-in bet from a player who had $1,800 in chips. I had pocket aces. He cracked them, and my chip stack immediately dropped to $1,700. I was truly glad I'd purchased the extra $300 in chips, as he would have brought me down to $1,400.

Chip positions change very rapidly in fast tournaments. You will rarely have a big stack that remains a big stack from the first hour of play until the end. It just doesn't happen.

REBUY MISCONCEPTIONS

I have heard many arguments against my general rule to always buy as many chips as you can get, as soon as you can get them, but I've never heard a convincing argument. The arguments I've heard against my do-it-now rebuy rule are most often voiced in the single rebuy tournaments where all players have the option to rebuy at any time during the first hour, and the amount of chips available for rebuy doesn't change as the blind levels progress. Here are the arguments I hear from the players in these events:

1. "I never make a rebuy. If I can't win with my initial buy-in, then the cards just aren't going my way. Rebuying is like chasing your losses."

2. "I only make a rebuy if I lose my starting chips. If I get lucky and make enough money with my initial buy-in, then I won't have to rebuy."

3. "I like to play loose at the beginning when the blinds are small. I like to see a lot of flops and try to catch something. But it's dangerous to have a lot of chips if you're playing loose because you can lose them all on marginal hands. If I think someone's bluffing with an all-in bet, and I think my hand is better than his, I want to be able to call him down cheaply without risking busting out."

4. "I like to allow myself a mistake or two in the early stages of a tournament. If I get all-in with the second best hand, it's not that big of an error if I lose fewer chips."

There are a dozen variations on the above arguments, all of which boil down to two main points:

- ♠ I want to win by getting lucky
- ♠ I want to win despite playing poorly

Neither of these strategies is a wise approach to a no-limit hold'em tournament. Players who wait to make a rebuy until they "need" it play hands they would never play, in ways they would never play them, if all their chips were on the table. Any time I sit down at a table in a single rebuy tournament, the first thing I do is look to see which players have made their rebuys off the top, as these will usually be the smarter, more dangerous, players. Those who are waiting to make the rebuy are more often weak players who will get involved in too many pots with mediocre cards.

Here's a true story of a hand I watched at one of the Orleans Friday night tournaments. The $65 buy-in (which includes $5 for dealers' bonus chips), gets you a total of $500 in chips, and the one $40 rebuy allowed during the first hour gets you $800 more, for a total of $1,300 in available starting chips. (Chip allotments in this tournament have since changed.)

Near the end of the first hour, with the blinds at $20 and $40, a player who had not made his rebuy yet—and whose starting chips had dwindled to $175—limped in from the button after the rest of the table had folded. The small blind called and the big blind checked. The flop came down J-J-9, with two clubs. All three players checked.

The turn card was a 7 of clubs, putting three clubs on the table in addition to the straight possibility. The small blind pushed all-in. The big blind pushed all-in. And the player on the button pushed in his remaining $135 in chips. The small blind turned up two rag clubs for a flush. The big blind showed down an 8 and a 10 for the straight. The button player held pocket 7s for a full house.

The side pot between the blinds—both of whom had made their rebuys—was much bigger than the main pot. The small blind, with his flush, was the big winner. The button player managed to win only $350 for his full house, and now had a total of $525 in chips. As the hands were exposed, he said happily, "Yes! I knew if I just waited for a hand I wouldn't have to rebuy!"

Now, think about this comment. If the button player had made his $40 rebuy for the $800 in rebuy chips, he would have tripled up on $975 instead of $175, and would now have had a total of $2,925 in chips instead of $525. And he's celebrating his brilliant decision not to rebuy!

The next blind level was $30-$60, so he was already short-stacked despite his triple-up. So, did this player save $40 by avoiding the rebuy, or did he waste $65 by entering the tournament in the first place?

REBUYING NEAR THE END OF THE REBUY PERIOD

As with add-ons, it is not always wise to make a rebuy at the end of a rebuy period. With fast blind levels, if you lose all of your chips near the end of a rebuy period, or you are desperately short-stacked, it may be best to call it a day and go home. It is not wise to be starting over in a tournament with a smaller stack than most of the players at your table when the blinds are already double or triple their first level. Again, if you would not enter a tournament with such a structure in the first place, then rebuying into it is a bad investment. This is especially true if the rebuy chips are not discounted, and you can only obtain the same amount as you got with your initial buy-in.

If rebuys or an add-on provide substantially more chips than the initial starting allotment, however, then it may be fine to rebuy at this point. Before the purchase, ask yourself what the next blind level is, how many big blinds the rebuys and add-on chips will give you for that level, how far behind in chips you'll be from the average player at your table, and how high you rate your opponents on skill. In other words, how well will you be able to compete at that point with the actual players and chip stacks at your table?

MULTIPLE REBUY STRATEGY

Multiple rebuy tournament structures often make small buy-in tournaments extremely loose and aggressive during the rebuy period. This is especially true if the rebuy chips are sold at a discount from the initial buy-in chips, and even more true if players get more chips with a rebuy than they got for the initial buy-in. These types of multiple rebuy structures are common for small buy-in tournaments.

Wild betting during a rebuy period is also encouraged in some tournaments by policies that allow players who lose all of their chips during the rebuy period to make double rebuys. The crazy betting and all-ins that result add an immense luck factor to everyone's results during the rebuy period.

Essentially, this type of tournament starts out as a lottery, with players buying chances at lucky hands. With enough players willing to both make and call all-in bets on draws or modest hands like top pair, there are simply going to be an inordinate number of big wins with mediocre cards and suck-outs. At the end of the rebuy period, after an hour of these constant all-in confrontations, there will be a few lucky players sitting there with massive chip stacks.

When rebuys are unlimited and rebuy chips are discounted, it is a mistake to play solid conservative poker during the rebuy period. Got that? *A mistake*. You've got to get in there and mix it up or you will inevitably find yourself on a short stack when the rebuy period ends. To be competitive after the rebuy period in this type of event, you should try to at least double the maximum number of chips you can buy at any one time. You cannot expect to do this with conservative play because you can't expect to be dealt enough premium hands.

Keep in mind that many of these fast format tournaments have blind levels that last only 15 minutes. This means that at the end of the rebuy period, you will be entering the fifth blind level. You must take a shot at making some money during that first hour of wild play to give yourself a meaningful chance of survival when the "real" tournament begins.

At the 2004 World Series of Poker, tournament pro Daniel Negreanu raised a lot of eyebrows in the $1,000 rebuy event by making 27 rebuys. He later defended his loose rebuy strategy by saying that he didn't mind buying a lot of chips for the players at his table, because he felt he could outplay them and get the chips back. Some players felt that Negreanu erred in investing so much money in rebuys. Whether or not Negreanu played too loosely during the rebuy portion of the tournament might be debatable, but as the coin-flip tournament examples showed, a skilled player's willingness to rebuy as many times as necessary to remain in the tournament is not disadvantageous in itself. Negreanu did finish second in that tournament, a finish that paid $100,000, profiting $72,000 despite the high rebuy costs.

REBUY STRUCTURE DECISIONS

You will sometimes have to make weird decisions based on rebuy structure. I once called three all-in bets after the flop with second pair (9s) when my kicker was a lowly eight and there was a jack on the board. It was the last hand of a rebuy period, and I felt certain that at least one of the players in this pot had a jack. My 8 and 9 were suited clubs, but only one of the cards on the flop was a club, so although I did have backdoor straight and flush possibilities, both of these possibilities were remote.

But my decision to call this all-in bet was not based on standard poker logic. It was based on the fact that, if I folded, the only way I could add chips to my stack was with a $300 add-on. I had just $10 over the initial $300 buy-in amount—too few chips to give me a competitive stack, but too many chips to qualify for both a rebuy and an add-on. Meanwhile, the average player at my table had made two rebuys by this point, and had about $900 in chips, which would soon be $1,200 for those who made the add-on. Folding would condemn me to having a very short stack of $610, when the blinds were about to go to $30-$60. A stack this short would give me only a poor chance of surviving in the tournament.

If I busted out, on the other hand, I would be allowed a double rebuy of $600 in chips, plus the add-on ($300 more in chips). In other words, if I folded, the biggest stack I could have would be about $600. If I busted out, on the other hand, I could have $900, and the rebuy/add-on chips were being sold at a 50% discount!

I called and won the pot with a runner-runner 10-7 to make a straight. The player who was holding pocket jacks, and who had flopped top set, was livid at my call. How could I call with second pair and no kicker? Was I a complete idiot?

What the question comes down to is was it worth a high risk of losing $310 and incurring the cost of the rebuys to have 50% more in chips than the $600 I would be limited to if I folded? My answer was yes. The implied value of the bigger chip stack was based on the fact that I felt there were many weak players at my table whose chips I could win by taking shots at them when they tightened up their post-rebuy play. I already had an hour invested in assessing my competition at this table. It goes right back to the principle that having more chips increases your advantage if you're playing with an edge, even if there is a cost to those chips.

In addition, I had believed I had more outs than I turned out to have—when we all turned up our cards, I was surprised to see I was up against trip jacks. With no straight or flush possibilities on the board, I had believed that one or more of my all-in opponents probably had a single jack in hand, and that I might win this giant pot if one of my 8s or another 9 came down. It was definitely a loose call, but I figured I probably had five outs with two cards to come to make two pair or a set, and the pot was so big—I would have more than quadrupled up—that I felt it was worth the shot in combination with the rebuy allowance if I busted out.

To give you a better idea of how loose these rebuy periods are, the other two all-in calls were made by players who each had an ace with no pair and bad kickers. They were both calling an all-in bet on the basis of having a single ace overcard in hand! So, here's another question for you: were these players wrong in calling with a single overcard?

As a matter of fact, one of these players with a bad ace was definitely wrong in calling this all-in bet, but the other player was probably not. One player had so many chips that, even after losing this bet, he was still not eligible for a rebuy. So, there he was, in an excellent chip position prior to this hand, making a loose call that decimated his stack. That's a terrible way to play. The other bad ace player had a chip stack similar to mine, and was just taking one last shot at getting lucky. Like me, he had no chip stack to protect. When he busted out, however, he exited the tournament. He had, incidentally, already made numerous double rebuys. I was sorry to see him go, but I guess he decided he'd spent enough on chips already. He was probably right.

The player who made the biggest mistake on this hand, however, was the player with the pocket jacks. He didn't raise before the flop! I might very well have thrown away my 9-high starting hand with a standard raise and two calls in front of me, and just resigned myself to making an add-on. But instead of raising, he just limped in, prompting the two bad aces to limp in behind him, and giving me the odds to call with my suited 9-8 to see if I could get lucky. I ended up getting really lucky.

So, multiple rebuy structures can sometimes make busting out a good strategy for increasing your chip stack. Whether or not you should do this is a judgment call based on many factors: how much it would improve your chip position, how this chip position will compare to the chip positions of your opponents, your feeling for the skill levels of the other players at your table, the probability of your all-in call actually making you the best hand, the amount this pot would mean to your chip position if you win it, and the actual rebuy chip cost. But don't make a crazy all-in call to improve your chip stack with rebuy/add-on chips unless those chips will provide you with better than ten times the size of the big blind at the next level. No matter how much more skilled you are than your opponents, you have to have sufficient chips to be able to use that skill.

When You Must Lose Starting Chips in Order to Rebuy

The Mirage rebuy tournaments require players to be below their starting chip allotment before making a rebuy. You cannot make a rebuy right at the start of the tournament when you still have all your chips. You must first lose some chips. The best strategy in these tournaments is to limp in on the first hand with any cards from any position in order to get rid of the minimum amount of chips that will make you eligible for a rebuy. This is not an uncommon strategy with this type of rebuy restriction, but neither is it the norm among the players who show up for fast tournaments.

Because chips are one of the major weapons in a no-limit hold'em tournament, and you want this weapon to be as powerful and dangerous to your competitors as you can make it, it's a mistake in a tournament with this format to chance winning a small pot early, before you have made a rebuy. If this happens, you cannot make a rebuy unless or until you lose chips you have won.

In one Mirage tournament, with starting cards of 8-4 offsuit, I limped into a pot to see the flop come down K-8-4. I went on to win a small pot from a player who had paired his king, but I also negated my ability to rebuy. Because the chips I had won were far below the amount I would have been allowed to rebuy, I made a mistake when I didn't just fold my two pair to his bet on the flop. Instead, when he bet, I raised and he folded, showing me his K-2 and saying, "I'm sure your kicker is better than mine."

You will also occasionally face these types of must-lose-to-rebuy decisions after the start of a tournament. In a multiple rebuy tournament, for example, if at any point in the rebuy period I lose enough chips to sink back down to close to my starting stack, I will often throw in a cheap call on a hand I have no intention of playing just to get into a chip position where I am allowed to substantially increase my chip stack with a rebuy.

How Pot Odds Change During the Rebuy Period

The normal math you use to figure out pot odds in order to justify calls with drawing hands does not apply during a rebuy period, if, in fact, you intend to rebuy if you lose your chips. The types of situations discussed above—where I could actually have more chips if I busted out than if I folded—occur frequently with drawing hands. Normally, I wouldn't get involved in a pot with a nut flush draw, for example, if I was getting only 3 to 1 odds, because I need better than 4 to 1 to mathematically justify the call. But if the drawing situation occurs when I can do a double rebuy at a 50% discount if I bust out on the draw, in which case I'll have the same number of chips (or more) if I bust out, while I'll have a triple up if my flush card hits, then this is a call I would be incorrect not to make.

These types of calls that are correct because the rebuy structure allows you to retain or improve chip position even if you lose the pot, but increase your chip position substantially if you win the pot, are not exactly free rolls, because you have to pay the cost of the rebuys. But if those rebuy chips are discounted substantially from the initial buy-in cost of the chips, then the pot odds you're getting on the underlying money represented by those chips are increased by the reduced cost of the rebuy replacement chips.

Here's a simple rule of thumb for estimating the altered pot odds when you must make a decision on calling a bet that would put you all-in when you are in this type of a multiple-rebuy tournament:

If the rebuy chips are discounted 40%, then I would lower the pot odds I need to call by 20%. For a two-way straight draw, for example, which normally requires pot odds of 5 to 1, I'd call with pot odds of 4 to 1. If the rebuy chips are discounted 50%, then knock 25% off the pot odds normally needed to call. For example, for a flush draw that requires pot odds of roughly 4 to 1, I'd call if getting better than 3 to 1. If rebuy chips are sold at the same price as the initial buy-in chips—no discount—then you always need full pot odds to call with your drawing hands.

This altered pot odds concept only applies when the rebuy and add-on chips you can purchase if you lose the hand would either maintain or improve the chip position you'd have if you folded. If you can replace chips for which you paid $100 with an equivalent amount of chips that cost you only $50, then the value of the chips you must put into the pot to draw is no longer $100. Their precise value not only depends on the discount percentage, but also the percentage of your original chips that you can replace at the discounted price. The lower the percentage of your original chips that you can replace, the more expensive your chips are overall, and the closer to full pot odds you need to call.

If you try to do the exact math on this at the table, you'll go nuts. As a rule of thumb, use regular pot odds unless you can replace 50% or more of your chips at a discount. If you can only replace 75% of your chips at a discount, you need higher pot odds than if you can replace your full chip stack at a discount. And if you can get more chips at a discount than you have in your current stack, you can reduce the pot odds requirements even more. So the simple rule is this: if you're short on chips and you can replace your stack or most of it with discounted rebuys, make the call.

MAXIMIZING YOUR EXPECTATION IN MULTIPLE REBUY TOURNAMENTS

There are two adjustments you must make to normal fast tournament strategy to maximize your expectation in multiple rebuy formats. One is that you must enter the tournament with the intention of making every rebuy you are able to make in the course of practicing sound strategy, and that you have the money with you to do that. If you must put a limit on the dollar cost of a multiple-rebuy tournament, make it something sufficient to cover at least three or four rebuys.

In fact, if you are an unskilled player just learning to play tournaments, then putting a limit on your rebuys is smart. Remember, in the real world you cannot turn a negative expectation game into a positive expectation game just by throwing more money into it. Until you have the ability to beat these tournaments, you will essentially be buying chips for the skilled players at your table when you rebuy. There is no way to learn to beat tournaments other than by playing in them, but don't overextend yourself financially.

And if you are a skilled player, but you really can't afford at least three or four rebuys, then these are probably not the tournaments that you should be playing. The cost of three or four rebuys is part of the real buy-in cost, and if you're not prepared to pay that, you're short-chipping yourself for the tournament. That is not a bright idea in any no-limit game.

The second adjustment you must make is to play loose as hell. Limp into the pot with as many hands as you can. Go ahead and play that K-10 offsuit, and your pocket 3s, and 9-7 suited, and lots of other marginal hands that would generally do nothing more than get you into worlds of trouble in no-limit games.

If your starting cards are real junk, go ahead and throw them away from any early or middle position. But if you're in late position and the pot is unraised, throw in your call no matter what you have. Take a shot. If the flop doesn't hit you at all and the betting is aggressive, get out of the way. Don't just throw your money away. But if you've got any decent shot at having the best hand, keep your hand alive. If you've got any good draw, you're usually correct to go for it, and when rebuy chips are discounted, keep the altered pot odds in mind.

The Orleans has regular Monday and Tuesday night multiple-rebuy tournaments. The initial buy-in is $40 and the rebuys are $20, and the rebuys provide the same quantity of chips as you get with your initial buy-in. The average player in one of these tournaments rebuys 3.5 times (or, 2.5 rebuys plus the add-on). That means the average player pays $110 to play this tournament. Because the rebuys go straight into the prize pool, and the house takes no percentage of the rebuy dollars as commission, these rebuys have real value to the players—the same value as if the buy-in cost was simply $110 per entry.

Again, to enter a tournament like this with the attitude that you will pay $40 to get in, and never make a rebuy, is a huge mistake. Your competitors are essentially entering this tournament with a lot more chips than you if you intend to forego rebuys or even limit yourself to a single rebuy. Since the rebuy chips are cheaper to purchase than the initial buy-in chips, rebuying multiple times also lowers the cost you are paying per chip for your ammo.

Unless you are at a very solid and conservative table during the rebuy period—and such tables do occur occasionally—forget about making position plays or attempting to steal pots with bluffs. Much of what I have advised regarding these types of strategies in fast tournaments does not apply during wild rebuy periods. Players do not fold to position plays, nor are they afraid of the guys with the big chip stacks. Neither should you be. In fact, the best players to get involved with are the players with big chip stacks because they will often be playing looser than the other players, and they are the players who can double you up.

What you really want to do in these multiple rebuy tournaments is play loose, but slightly tighter than your opponents. So, there isn't any generic starting hand advice based on your position that I can provide. It really depends on the character of your table. But you should think of this rebuy period as the time to increase your chip stack significantly, because those chips will be very valuable when the rebuy period ends and the real tournament starts.

SINGLE REBUY STRATEGY

In a single rebuy event, you should always make your rebuy right at the start of the rebuy period—before you've even played a hand, if that is allowed. Because you are playing on a limited number of chips, however, it is not correct to play as loosely during the rebuy period as you would in a multiple-rebuy event. In fact, if you are at a table where many players have not made their rebuy, you will usually make money from their tendency to play too loosely—often making very poor decisions, *as if they could make unlimited rebuys.*.

Players who have not yet made their rebuy are often not good choices to bluff at, or to make position shots at, because they will not have the fear of busting out that these types of plays require for success. In addition, they will very often call raises—and even all-ins—on draws, or with second pair, or just overcards, so if you have a legitimate hand, make them pay for their wimpy decision to rely on the rebuy as a form of insurance.

When you have a premium hand, play it aggressively, and don't hesitate to push all-in with it on any player who has not made his rebuy. You will make more money than you lose when you give them a chance to play bad poker at you.

REBUY MANIACS

A rebuy maniac often announces to the table before the first hand of the tournament is even dealt that he will be going all-in in the dark. He then proceeds to do just that on every hand. And he soon gets a number of willing callers who realize that any above-average hand is the favorite to beat his random two cards. They're right about this, and, what the heck, rebuys are cheap. Yet, rebuy maniacs almost always make money during the rebuy period. It's always surprising to see how often two random cards beat better than average hands like A-J or K-Q or medium pocket pairs.

The players who participate in the all-in/rebuy madness, however, will generally come out ahead as well, and will often be very well set up in chips compared to players at tables where this nonsense did not occur. Since this type of maniac play is not a violation of any tournament rules, the advantage play when you have a rebuy maniac at your table is to join in.

To make money from a rebuy maniac at your table, call him down with any hand better than Q-7. Specifically, call any all-in in-the-dark bet with any ace, any king, any queen with a kicker of 8 or higher, any J-10 or J-9, any suited connectors down to 8-7, and any pair.

I never instigate rebuy mania myself, as it is an expensive strategy and I don't think there is sufficient value to going all-in in the dark. Rebuy maniacs buy a lot of chips for the table, and if you call them down with better than average hands, you'll get your share. That's why it's nice to have these maniacs at your table. But though they often acquire better than average chip stacks themselves during the rebuy period, they pay too much for their chips. The section of this chapter on coin-flip tournaments showed that a player with an advantage can afford to make unlimited multiple rebuys, because he'll only force less-skilled opponent to give him more action, and increase the skilled player's win in dollars. But a rebuy maniac who pushes all-in in the dark is pitting his random hands against nine other players' selective (better-than-average) hands. That means he is playing at a strong negative expectation. This is the opposite of an intelligent strategy. There is one qualifier. If he is such a skillful player that he can overcome his immense disadvantage during the rebuy period with his even greater advantage once the rebuy period ends, then he can afford to buy chips for all of his competitors. By the way, new players who have not seen rebuy maniacs before will often get irritated by this move, when in fact this is the best chance an unskilled player may have to play with an advantage.

The rebuy maniac strategy is common, but it's not the norm. If a tournament starts out with 20 tables, it's unlikely that there will be a rebuy maniac at more than two or three tables.

REBUY DUMPING

If you play in multiple-rebuy tournaments, then you should also see the section on "rebuy dumping" in Chapter 26, which is titled "Cheating and Semi-Cheating." You will surely bump into rebuy dumpers occasionally, so you should know how to deal with them. Rebuy dumping is not technically cheating, but in my opinion it is unethical. Therefore, I describe the ploy, and how you can profit from rebuy dumpers, in the cheating chapter.

WHEN THE REBUY PERIOD IS OVER

Rebuys increase the variance on your overall tournament results. When you get lucky during the rebuy period, the extra chips will set you up in a very strong position for the remainder of the tournament. But when you are on the negative side of this fluctuation during the rebuy period, you will often have to face one or more opponents at your table who have small mountains of chips they have acquired through good luck. These giant stacks may make your fast-play and position strategies less effective against these players when the rebuy period is over.

The single rebuy format does not cause nearly as much early variance as the multiple rebuy format, but it too will increase your fluctuations. In the chapter on bankrolling your play, be sure to note that if you are playing in a rebuy tournament, you should add 10% to the minimum bankroll requirements shown in the chart.

PART THREE:
THE FINE POINTS

11

KNOW YOUR CARDS

Just as online players tend to neglect to total the number of chips in the pot when they first start playing in live games, they also often do not remember their cards after they peek at them, because in online games their cards are face up in front of them throughout any hand they are involved in. Rank amateurs, of course, share both of these weaknesses. What's more surprising is that the majority of players in fast tournaments forget their cards—even many of the better players. If you have this problem, you have to realize that you're giving information to your competitors that they can use against you. You must learn to remember your cards. It is simply a fundamental skill of poker.

Most players do tend to remember their cards in certain circumstances. If their cards are suited, they remember them because they are watching for that suit. No player with a K-J of hearts is going to have to look at his cards if two or three hearts come down on the flop. He's hoping to see those hearts, so his own hearts are easy to remember. And if a player has a pair, and both cards are the same color, say, two black eights, he will also usually remember this fact.

But if an amateur or online player is sitting there with an offsuit A-K, one red and one black, and the flop comes down with three cards to any suit, he will have no idea what the suits of his cards are. Does he have a nut flush draw, or perhaps a king high flush draw? Or are neither of his two hole cards in the suit on board? He has to peek at his cards again to find out!

But this repeeking of hole cards when the third card to a suit hits the board, whether on the flop or turn, tells you more than that the player doesn't remember the cards he looked at moments earlier. It also tells you that he absolutely, positively does not currently have a flush.

Thanks for the information, bud! Excuse me while I push all-in here with my trash hand. I can't tell you the number of pots I've stolen by representing a flush to players whose repeek of their hole cards told me they didn't have one—at least not yet.

If, on the other hand, you are up against a strong player who repeeks when the third card to a suit falls, be very careful. Strong players sometimes use this move when they do have a flush in an attempt to extract chips from a player who knows just enough to get himself in trouble. In fact, you can use this move yourself if you flop a flush, and you'll find it works very well at convincing your opponents that you do not have a flush, or are on a flush draw.

A variation on this move, for the truly brave or simply desperate soul, is to peek at your hole card after the fourth card to a flush hits the board, then push all-in. I've only attempted this move when absolutely desperate for chips, and after my opponent checked. It does tend to convince your opponent that you have a flush. The mathematical odds are about 2 to 1 against a single opponent's having a card in the needed suit, and if he checked when that fourth card to the suit hit the board, the odds are quite a bit higher against his having a high card in that suit. And even if he has a flush, he won't necessarily call an all-in bet.

I once made this move against a player who had a set of 6s, with one of the 6s in his hand giving him the flush, but when I pushed all-in on him, he folded, showing me his hand and saying, "I have a feeling you have a higher spade than mine." In fact, I had no spade at all, and I had no idea I was playing against a set, as he had played the hand so passively, slowplaying, I guess, with a plan to check-raise me at some point.

If you have difficulty remembering the suits of your cards, there are a lot of memory tricks that blackjack players use for this purpose. In some types of advantage play at blackjack, it's necessary for players to remember half a dozen two or three card sequences by both the suit and the value of each card, and then to recall each card and each sequence ten minutes later in the next shoe.

How do they do it?

One of the easiest memory tricks is to assign a character to each card. For example, the king of hearts is Elvis; the queen of hearts is Marilyn Monroe; the queen of diamonds is Madonna, etc. The face cards are easy. The system for assigning characters to the numbered cards can be any method that works for you. I know sports buffs who have named cards based on players' jersey numbers. You can name cards for friends and relatives, rock stars, politicians, historical figures, porno actresses, sitcom characters, school teachers, people you hate—whatever works. You'll have to practice with a deck of cards for a week or so, turning them over one at a time until you get a character assigned to every card in the deck, but once you have your system down, you won't even have to think about it again. When you peek at your hole cards and see Elvis and Napoleon staring back at you, instead of the king of hearts and five of clubs, you won't forget what suits your cards are when a third heart comes down on the turn.

If you don't need a system like this to remember your hole cards, fine. Don't waste your time with it. But if you're one of those chronic suit re-checkers, then do what you have to do to avoid giving players like me so much information about your hand. Suits matter in poker.

12

BOUNTIES

The Bay 101 Casino in Northern California hosts an annual WPT tournament called "Shooting Stars." In this tournament, which has a $10,000 buy-in, various poker "stars"—generally the big name players we've watched on TV—compete with hundreds of amateurs for the prize money. This tournament has a gimmick that adds to the fun for all participants. Each of the stars has a $5,000 "bounty" on his head. What that means is that any time a player knocks one of the stars out of the tournament, that player gets a $5,000 bounty—paid on the spot in cash—in addition to the bragging rights.

Some small buy-in tournaments also have bounty formats. Occasionally a single player will be chosen—often the player who knocks out the first player in the tournament—as the player with the bounty on his head. This is usually a small bounty, $5 to $10 or so. In a more popular bounty format, every player in the tournament has a bounty of $5 to $10 on his head from the start of the tournament to the finish.

HOW DO BIG BOUNTIES AFFECT YOUR STRATEGY?

In a major tournament like Shooting Stars, where many amateurs are likely to have entered through satellites, such players should definitely look for chances to take all-in shots at the bountied stars, assuming that the amateur has more chips than the star. In fact, any time a star was very short stacked, it would be wise to make an all-in bet or even call his all-in bet with any decent hand. That $5,000 bounty has such a big dollar value that it is probably any amateur's best shot at making some money in this tournament against experienced pros.

HOW DO SMALL BOUNTIES AFFECT YOUR STRATEGY?

In the small buy-in/small bounty tournaments, the prospect of earning the bounty should not affect your strategy at all. With the aggressive fast play described in this book, you will usually pick up more than your share of bounties if you make it to the final table, just as a natural byproduct of your play. In fast tournaments, you will often have to make or call all-in bets when you have a premium hand.

Most of the bounties you will earn on the way to the final table will not result from your being all-in. Instead, they will come from calling all-in bets from desperate players when you have a legitimate hand and they simply don't have sufficient chips to scare you out of the pot. Having a big chip stack will contribute to your bounty profits because you can call desperate all-in shots with pretty mediocre hands, knowing that if you lose, it won't dent your chip position significantly.

But again, I would not advise making loose calls simply for a chance at winning the bounty. In small bounty tournaments, the big money is in the tournament prize pool, not the bounties.

USING BOUNTY CHIPS AS TELLS

Many players like to stack their bounties like trophies next to or on top of their tournament chips. Most tournament regulations disallow players from having "foreign" (non-tournament) chips on the table. In bounty tournaments, however, an exception is usually made for bounty chips, often cashable $5 casino chips, that players have collected in that tournament. Players who display their bounty chips like this do so in an attempt to intimidate opponents. From my perspective, this display of bounty chips is not so much an intimidating factor as it is a tell that provides pretty reliable information on a player's overall tightness or looseness.

If I am desperate for chips and I find myself in a position where I must take a shot without a strong hand, I will avoid pushing in on a player who has a tall stack of bounty chips. That chip stack represents a loose aggressive player, one who will probably not back down from an all-in confrontation with a short-stacked player if he has any kind of playable hand himself. In this circumstance, you might conclude that those bounty chips are, in fact, working to intimidate me out of taking a shot.

If I do have a strong hand, however, this loose player is precisely the player I want to push in on, hoping for a loose call. It's still true that this player could bust me out of the tournament, but when I'm desperate and I really need to double up, this is the player against whom I have the best chance of accomplishing this goal. So, that big stack of bounties is a lure in this circumstance.

If it is late in a tournament, on the other hand, and a player has only two or three bounty chips displayed, I'll assume he is a tighter player, and I won't hesitate to take a desperation shot at him. Likewise, if he enters a pot with a raise, I'll be more hesitant to get involved without a premium hand.

I have always pocketed my bounty chips, or used them to toke dealers, rather than displaying them. Since I have found bounty display tells pretty reliable, I assume that other players also use them as a tell, and I don't like giving opponents information on how I play. If it's late in a tournament, I assume that any players who are not displaying bounties have either been pocketing them or flipping them to the dealers, as it's not easy to get deep into a tournament without picking up at least a few bounties.

A single bounty chip, incidentally, if used as a card protector, is not a tell. It does not necessarily mean a player has won only one bounty. Many players will use a bounty chip to cover their cards.

Some types of players rarely display bounties. Cagey codgers and other poker room regulars, whether or not they know much about tournament strategies, often pocket their bounties. It's the younger players who tend to display them. Cagey codgers are always aware of how they look in a poker room and generally have their poker face down to an art form, which is why they can slow play the nuts so effectively. Online players and beginners, by contrast, seem to miss many of the really simple visual tells they give off, and they also seem oblivious to these types of tells when other players exhibit them.

Because the bounty display is such a reliable indicator of a player's looseness, I always start watching how players handle their bounties right from the start of a tournament. But the information gets more reliable once you're past the halfway point and the loose players have had time to start piling up a display. This is especially useful information when you are moved to a new table in the late stages of a tournament, and you find yourself facing a group of players you have not yet encountered. A quick look at the bounty displays on the table will often give you a pretty good idea of some players' approaches to the game.

How reliable is this tell? In my experience, *very*. If there are two players at the final table with similar chip stacks, but one player has three bounty chips on top of his chip stack, while the other has ten or twelve bounties stacked up beside his chips, you should play your cards with the assumption that the player with the big bounty stack is the looser player. You will not often go wrong if you make this assumption.

Loose aggressive players do make more bounties, but many of the players who regularly go for a lot of bounties tend to bust out early because they play too loose.

Bounties do lower the variance of a tournament by spreading out the prize pool, but again, their real value is in the information that can be obtained from players' bounty displays.

13

BLUFFING

To make money in the fast tournaments, you must bluff players out of pots. Fortunately, bluffing is very effective in these tournaments because many of the entrants come from the casinos' low-limit games where bluffing is not common because it so rarely works.

Most of the position plays and chip shot strategies discussed in this book are essentially bluff plays, so this topic has been addressed pretty thoroughly already. But let's look at a few additional bluff possibilities you might want to add to your basic repertoire.

Typically, bluffing works best if you have recently shown down a powerful hand. It is also best done from late position, after you see how any opponents in the hand have entered the pot. When you are short-stacked, however, or at an aggressive table where the pot is often raised preflop, an early position bluff may work better.

EARLY AND MIDDLE POSITION BLUFFS

One thing to keep in mind is that early and middle position bluffs are generally taken more seriously than late position bluffs. A big preflop raise under the gun is scary to any player, including one who might have been willing to call a more standard raise. So, if stealing the blinds and antes is your only goal, this play can be an effective way to go. Early position bluffs are especially good plays to make when you are too short-stacked for effective postflop play, but have enough chips to scare away loose players before the flop. Late in a tournament, when the antes really add to the preflop pot, this steal has even more value. If one or two players have limped into the pot in front of you as well, the preflop pot may be substantial enough to nearly double you up.

It's true that there are real dangers to this move, since you have

THE POKER TOURNAMENT FORMULA

no information on any of your opponents and there may be a player sitting there with a high pocket pair, who inevitably will call. But the odds are against an opponent having a hand strong enough to call a preflop all-in bet, and this move will usually get you the pot.

LATE POSITION BLUFFS

One common late position bluff is to make a very big raise from the button against any number of limpers. This is a classic move practiced by most ball-cap kids. You'll often see this move from them early in a tournament, when most other players are thinking "survival." With the blinds at $10 and $20, and most players still pretty close to their $600 in starting chips, four players limp in for $20 and the kid on the button makes the bet $200. Classic. You see it all the time.

Bluffing a group of players like this is more dangerous than bluffing a single player, for obvious reasons. The ball-cap kids seem to have a pretty good grasp on this, and they are generally good at sizing their overbet to the situation. With only two $20 limpers in front of him, for example, the button player will probably take that pot with a bet of only $100.

I have a lot of admiration for these aggressive kids I see making final tables again and again. Their aggression makes it very difficult to put them on a hand and the best ones really do have bluffing down to an art. I've learned a lot from the ball-cap kids, and you can learn from them too, but there's only one way to do it: call them down with a legitimate hand when the board is truly dangerous and you really think they're just taking a shot. More often than not, they don't have it. What they have is guts and probably a pretty good read that you have top pair or some other far-from-the-nuts hand. If you call them down just once, and show down any marginal hand that takes the pot, they'll start to leave you alone. There are easier fish to catch.

THE MINI-RAISE

The **mini-raise** is a preflop, late position bluff that you'll find many opportunities to use if you gather a big chip stack.

211

This is a bluff that you can make when you get to the point in the tournament when there are many short stacks compared to the costs of the blinds and antes. This is the point when the average size chip stack in the tournament is short.

In fast tournaments, this usually occurs sometime just after the halfway point. For example, two and a half hours into the Orleans Monday night tournament, the blinds hit $150 and $300. This is a multiple-rebuy/add-on tournament, where the average player makes 3.5 rebuys, giving the average player about $1,350 in total starting chips. This tournament generally has about 200 entrants, and at this point about two-and-a-half hours in, about half of the players have been eliminated. This means the average chip stack for the remaining 100 players is about $2,700.

Since it costs $150 + $300 = $450 to go around the table once, the "average" player will be desperate, with only six times the cost of going through the blinds. But in fact, there will be very few players with average sized stacks at this time. There will be a few players with chips stacks well over $10,000, a few more with stacks of $5,000 to $10,000, and many who are hanging on by a thread. It is not unusual to see six to eight players at a single table with fewer than the average number of chips. This is when the mini-raise is a beautiful move.

Again, you can only make this bluff when you yourself are very well stacked with a stack of chips relative to the blind costs and the other stacks on your table. It's a bluff that's designed to cripple the short stacks, but you can often pick up the pot with it as well. The other conditions you need to make this move are:

1. You must be in late position, preferably on the button or in the cutoff seat.

2. Three or more players must have limped into the pot.

3. Two or more of the limpers must be short-stacked; the more short stacks in the pot the better.

You most often find these opportunities right after the blind level has increased, which further worries the short stacks. This is also the point in the tournament where you see how many truly poor players there are left in the field. It will not be uncommon at this point in the tournament to see a player with only $2,000 in chips limp into pot after pot, only to fold when an aggressive player makes a big raise. These players have no clue whatsoever about tournament speed factors, and they especially do not realize that with such short stacks, their only preflop bet should be all-in, unless they have aces or kings and are trying to get another player to make a move on them. Remember, when you are this short on chips, you should either be all-in, or stay out of the way.

In any case, here's how the mini-raise works: let's say the blinds are $150 and $300, and five players have limped in. Three of the limpers have only $1,500 to $2,000 or so. You are the chip leader at the table, and you have about $10,000 in chips. When the action gets to you, you simply raise the minimum amount. You make the bet $600. Your cards are immaterial.

This move will drive any of the "good" tournament players at your table bonkers. Even experienced aggressive players whom you know to be dangerous and whom you frequently see at final tables will be scratching their heads at your mini-raise. What the hell kind of raise is that? You can't even make this move without chuckling to yourself. But every player in that pot who just wanted to see a flop will hate you, and they'll have no idea how to read the meaning of that wimpy raise.

Essentially, what you're doing with the mini-raise is forcing already desperate players into greater desperation. You are single-handedly redistributing the wealth at your table. Because of your chip stack and position, you'll often take this pot postflop because that mini-raise is just confusing as hell. Do you have aces? Big slick? Queens? Nothing but a sense of humor?

Even if you don't ultimately take the pot, that mini-raise is good for you because it hurts so many other players. Most players will be compelled to call your mini-raise simply because the pot has grown so much since they put in their first $300. Often, a player who may have limped with a quality hand will go over the top of your mini-raise now that he's got a real pot to take a shot at, giving those short stacks a very tough decision, and an even tougher decision if they have already called your mini-raise before that other reraise. Obviously, if you don't have a playable hand, you fold to any reraise yourself.

If no player reraises your mini-raise, then you have position after the flop and a whole table full of players who entered with non-premium hands and who view you—the big chip stack—as the preflop aggressor. If no player takes a shot at this pot postflop, any normal bet of about half the size of the pot will usually deliver it to you. If there is a postflop bet, you'll have to abandon your hand unless the flop actually hit you. But you did your dirty work and you should be pleased with the result.

The mini-raise punishes limpers for treating a no-limit tournament like a limit ring game. One player will win a nice pot, but a lot of others will lose more chips than they intended to risk, and any short stacks will lose a lot more chips than they could afford to give up. The whole essence of a tournament is the redistribution of wealth, with the rich getting richer and the poor getting poorer. When you count yourself among the rich, anything you can do to make the poor poorer at a reasonable cost to yourself is a favorable result. You're accelerating your opponents' demise and getting yourself closer to the money. And, since you have position on this hand, you would at least have called all of those $300 limpers from the button anyway. There was just too much money in the pot for you to throw away any hand. So, that mini-raise only cost you an extra $300. If you count the strategic value of this bluff, which will give you the pot a good percentage of the time, it has little or no cost. I should point out that if you have a real hand here—say any high pocket pair or big slick, A-Q suited—you should not make a mini-raise. In that case, you should make a bet that at least matches the size of the pot. And that's no bluff.

SHOULD THE SMALL BLIND TAKE A SHOT AT THE BIG BLIND?

Many players feel that if they are in the small blind, and the whole table folds around to them, they have essentially had the button relinquished to them, so they should take a shot at the big blind. This is not true. The small blind is never the button.

The button is a great stealing position because if either or both of the blinds call the raise, the button has position after the flop. By contrast, the small blind is out of position to the big blind both before and after the flop. If you know the big blind is a wimp, then go ahead and take a shot at him. But you're in trouble if he calls.

If I am in the big blind and the small blind takes a shot at me, I will call his raise with a much more marginal hand than I would a raise from the button. Once the button and all other players to his right have folded, the big blind becomes the button.

Unless you know that the player in the big blind is a timid player who will only call a raise with a premium hand, don't take shots from the small blind. It takes a stronger hand to raise the big blind from the small blind than it does to raise both blinds from the button.

In fact, one of the most successful bluffs you can make is to raise the small blind from the big blind if the small blind limps in, and reraise him if he comes in with a raise.

THE STEAL-BACK (THE MOST SUCCESSFUL BLIND POSITION BLUFF)

If you're in one of the blinds and you get a raise from the button or cut-off seat, call. It's probably a meaningless position raise. When the flop comes down, bet.

That's it. Your cards don't matter.

To pull this off, you must have the right player raising preflop—generally a decent player who knows there's good money in blind-theft from the late position seats. He just does it as a matter of course (as you will so often do!). You can't do this on every one of his steal attempts. You have to give up a couple of blinds to him first when you don't have a hand to play back at him with. Not that you need a hand when you actually make the move, but your opponent must be convinced that you are not just a blind defender. In fact, the reason that you call instead of reraise, and then take the pot with a bet after the flop, is that it makes the move look better.

Don't worry that his raise might be based on a real hand. If he doesn't hit top pair or better on that flop, or actually have an overpair to the flop, he will go away. He may, in fact, have raised with queens, but if an ace or king comes down, and you bet after having called his preflop raise, this pot is yours.

The nicest feature of this bluff is that you can negate a number of his successful steals with a single steal-back. That's because he's only getting your blind on his steals, but you're getting his raised bet (substantially more chips!) when you steal back from him. For the most profitable play, make your move after the blinds have increased from his last steal. That way you'll be getting a raised bet based on a bigger blind level.

You can make this move from either the small or big blind, though it's safer from the big blind after the small blind has already folded.

DESPERATION FLUSH BLUFFS

These are bluffs you make when you are short-stacked and the board is truly dangerous, specifically when there are four to a flush on the board. These bluffs work best when the river card delivers the fourth card to the flush and you feel pretty sure that your opponent was not in the hand on a draw. Make this bluff against a single opponent only. The fact is, with only one flush card needed in his hand, your opponent may have made that flush on the river, even if he was betting on a legitimate hand before he made the "accidental" flush. But you can't worry about that. This is a desperation move that you make when your chip stack will not be competitive if you do not win this pot, while winning the pot would actually bring you up to a decent chip position. You've got to weigh the risk versus the reward.

This bluff is another that's most successful when you have position on your opponent, and he checks to you when the river card comes down. Very few players will bluff a flush when four to a suit are on board, though many will check if they make the nut flush, hoping to be able to check-raise. So, by checking on the river, your opponent will not feel that he is necessarily revealing to you that he does not have that flush. This would be a classic time for him to slowplay. If he does not have the flush, he will feel that if he checks and you check, then he probably has you beat with his quality hand. And if he bets and you call, then he is in trouble. You could never call his bet without having made the flush yourself. The last thing he would expect is for him to check and you to bluff that flush. Few players live that dangerously.

You do live that dangerously, assuming you still have enough chips to hurt your opponent. If there is $3,000 in the pot, and you have only a few hundred in chips remaining, you will probably be called down by any legitimate hand. But if you can bet anywhere near half the size of the pot, your opponent will fold if he does not have the flush. If your opponent is a weak player, you may take this shot even with fewer chips. He will fold to just about any bet because he could not imagine that you would push all in on the river with four to a flush showing unless you had the flush. This move is so bold it will often fold sets and straights.

It is much more difficult to make this move successfully if four to a straight are on the board. So, I consider it a flush bluff only. It's dangerous, but when you're desperate, and you've got a one-shot chance to pull your chip stack back into the competition, you've got to take the risk. This move will succeed more often than it will fail.

SHOWING YOUR CARDS AFTER A SUCCESSFUL BLUFF

It is just about always a mistake to show your cards after a successful bluff in a fast tournament. In a tournament with a slower blind structure, there may occasionally be some value to showing a successful bluff. That's because in a slow tournament you have both the time and the chips to see flops and wait for a really powerful hand for the next pot you get involved in. When you get such a hand following a displayed bluff, you're hoping for loose calls from players who don't respect your bets. But powerful hands are usually few and far between, and in a fast tournament, you don't have the chips to wait for them. You continually have to get in there and mix it up, often bluffing or semi-bluffing, using your position and aggressive betting more than your cards to take down pots. Successful bluffs are built on respect, and showing a bluff in a fast tournament can cripple you.

Some players believe that showing a successful bluff will put the bluffed player on tilt. That's often true, and again, this may be an effective tool in a slow tournament, where you have a lot of time after the bluff to set a trap for a player who's steaming. If you show a bluff in a fast tournament, however, you're only trapping yourself.

14

SHOWING YOUR CARDS

In the previous chapter on bluffing, I advised against showing your cards after a successful bluff in a fast tournament. But what about showing your cards when you didn't bluff? Unless you are called at the river, or are involved in an all-in situation, most of the time you will not have to show your cards to the table. Is it ever correct to show a hand when it's not required?

Rarely. And if you simply have a policy of never showing a hand unless required to do so, you will not make many errors.

SHOWING A WINNER

If you pick up a pot with a hand that's not really all that strong, do not show your cards. Even if you think you probably had the best hand, do not show your cards. In a fast tournament, you never want to show that you will bet in marginal situations. If your bet folded a stronger hand, you do not want to give this player the idea that he should make looser calls when you are betting.

Most of the information you acquire on your opponents will come from the showdowns when you get to see the cards they were playing. And whenever you show your own cards, you are giving your opponents information about how you play. Players will remember this information not only later in the same tournament, but from tournament to tournament as well. You will see the same players again and again in the fast tournaments you play. Believe me, I never forget the players who slowplayed a set of kings on me.

In poker, information is money. The attitude you should take about showing any winning hand, whether the nuts or a stone cold bluff, is: "If you want to see my cards, you must pay for the privilege. If you fold, tough luck. I win, and that's all that's important."

Players will often ask you what your cards were. You should

never respond truthfully. Say "five of a kind," or "two-three offsuit," or anything else that lets them know you're not about to provide them with any real information.

SHOWING A LOSER

The basic rule on showing a losing hand when not required to do so, is the same: Don't do it. Why give information to your opponents when you don't have to?

Weak players often show strong losing cards because they want their opponents to know they're smart. They want the table to see that their call on the river was justified—that they're not just calling stations, or reading the board wrong. If, for instance, there is an 8-9-10-J on the board, and a player holding pocket queens calls a raise by a player who shows down a K-Q, a weak player will find it very difficult to just muck his queens. He wants everyone to know that he's not an idiot who called that bet with pocket kings. He couldn't get away from his hand and he wants everyone to know he was playing intelligently.

Poor decision. Muck the damn queens and say, "Nice hand." If your opponents at the table believe you make mistakes that you don't actually make, that will eventually work in your favor. Do you really want them to see how you played those queens preflop and on every street?

The losing hands weak players tend to show most are the sets with which they called the bets of players who made straights or flushes. You will get so much information from these players when you see the set. Did they flop it? Hit it on the turn or river? Slowplay it? Were they checking? Calling? Raising?

Once you start realizing how much valuable information these players are giving to you for free, you will realize how dumb it is for you to give free information to them. The more of an enigma you are to your opponents, the less accuracy they will have in putting you on a hand, and the less profit they will be able to extract from you.

SHOWING ONE CARD

Occasionally, a player will show a single card to an opponent who folds to his bet. If, for example, an ace and two rags come down on the flop, and one player bets and the other folds, the player who bets will often turn over just the ace, not the kicker, to show he had it. This is a courtesy show. Players who do this generally feel that it is good to show a strong hand so that opponents will get out of their way later when they bet. By not showing the kicker, they're not giving full information on what hand they raised with, just enough information to tell their opponent they were betting with the best hand.

Or, let's say you are in the big blind with 7-2 offsuit. The aggressive player on the button raises, and you reraise him. He calls. The flop comes down with an A-2-2, giving you trip deuces. You check your trips, he puts in a pot-sized bet, and you go over the top of him all-in. He folds.

Do not show your deuce. There is too much fancy play here. You reraised out of position with a trash hand. Let him fold thinking you must have had a strong ace, maybe even pocket aces or AK. Leave him in the dark. There is a huge temptation to show your cards here because of the amusement value for the table, but you are making a big mistake if you do this.

Showing the "Wrong" Card

Some players like to show one card to an opponent to make him think that his play was a mistake. For example, let's say a player holds an A-10, and at the turn the board is 7-8-9-J, giving him a straight to the jack. An opponent bets, he raises, and the opponent folds. It will often drive a player nuts if just the ace is shown. In all likelihood, the original bet indicated that the opponent had at least a pair of jacks, and he may even have had an overpair, two pair, or a set, but he folded because of the straight danger, and he will be kicking himself for not calling.

Or, say he has pocket nines and the flop comes down A-K-9, giving him bottom set. His opponent bets and he pushes all in. The opponent folds. It will drive the folded player nuts if he is shown a single 9, as if the player pushed all in on bottom pair.

I personally love watching these types of plays, but in fast tournaments, moves like these can backfire. The player showing the wrong card may later find it difficult to get an opponent out of a pot. This is similar to showing a successful bluff. No matter how big the temptation, don't do it.

What you really want to remember is that other players will do these things to you. If a player shows a single ace after you've folded top pair because you thought he had the straight, don't believe it. Don't let it affect your game, or your future reads on that player. Any player who shows one card in that type of situation is toying with you. He is more likely a dangerous player and your fold was most likely correct.

15

TABLE IMAGE

You might think that fast play and the position and chip shots of the rock-paper-scissors strategies will make you appear to be a loose player, entering many more pots than players who look primarily for premium cards. But this is not true. My table image is pretty tight. Not the tightest, by any means, but most of my opponents put me on being a solid conservative player because I do not get involved in all that many pots.

The importance I place on position, and on being the first player into a pot, and on avoiding multi-way pots, has me throwing away many hands that my opponents would play. The players in these small buy-in tournaments are very loose by my standards. Many will call raises with suited aces and even suited kings. Many will limp into pots from any position with hands like K-J or Q-10, hands I would throw away in an instant unless I was making a position or chip play. The fact that I might throw away my A-J offsuit in the face of a raise and reraise, then raise with a 9-2 offsuit on the very next hand because I had position, would strike many fast tournament players as incomprehensible.

But position shots pay off much more frequently than hands played with marginally good cards. Position raises don't usually get called, and when they do, you can usually pick up the pot with a bet on the next round. Good cards played out of position, by contrast, often run into dangerous boards and scary aggression and must be abandoned.

The tight image you acquire by following the rock-paper-scissors strategy pays dividends in that your raises are so often given respect. You appear to be very selective in the cards you play, when actually you're just selective about the pots you get involved in. You're not only viewed as a pretty solid player, but as an aggressive and tricky player.

I once made a final table without ever having shown down a hand. It's not that my cards were so miserable in that tournament that I only took position shots, but when I had a hand I couldn't coax any action out of anyone. Pocket aces, pocket queens, big slick—no callers. But somehow I managed to steal my way to the final table betting on air, and needless to say I was one of the shorter stacks when I got there.

On the very first hand at that final table, I was on the button. The whole table folded around to me and I looked down to see Q-3 offsuit. In this same situation one table earlier, I would have pushed all-in. I had a very tight image at that table, and unless the players in the blinds had strong hands, I knew they would have folded. But at this table, I had no image whatsoever with the players in the blinds—since I'd just arrived—and I knew nothing whatsoever about them except that the big blind was sitting behind a mountain of chips and might call my all-in bet with any playable hand at all.

I hated the thought of mucking my cards on the button, so I decided to take a chance on not getting raised preflop and I just limped in. To my delight, the small blind folded and the big blind knocked the table. The flop came down J-10-10, not exactly a prime flop for my hand. But what disturbed me more was that the big blind seemed to be spending a long time trying to figure out how to play his hand. Did he have a jack or ten? A straight draw? Had he flopped a full house or quads? Why was he taking so long to decide what to do?

He checked. With no hesitation, I pushed all-in.

Now he spent so long trying to decide whether or not to call that I knew he had something. I was hoping it was the low end of a straight draw, 8-9, so that at least my queen might hold up if he didn't hit one of his outs on the turn or river. But I really didn't want a call.

Naturally, he called. I tossed my Q-3 face up, and he showed me pocket 9s.

I said, "Good call," mentally adding, "you bastard."

Now I'm standing up, ready to exit in tenth place if one of my three outs, the queens, doesn't hit on the turn or river. The turn card was a 5, but the river brought an unexpected surprise—an out I hadn't considered, another jack! That put two pair on the board—jacks and tens—counterfeiting the two pair he'd held—tens and nines—and giving me the better kicker!

It was nice to win that hand since I really needed the chips, but so much for my tight image. I knew that on the next hand I played I'd better have something better than a position shot. The next pot I entered turned out to be the very next hand. For this hand, I was in the cut-off seat, and the table folded around to me. I looked down to see two jacks. I considered pushing all-in, but I wanted to get more than the blinds if possible, so I made a standard raise, about three times the size of the big blind, and got one caller, the player on the button.

The flop came down with three rags, something like 9-4-2. I pushed all-in.

Now the button player was taking so long to decide on whether or not to call me that I knew I wanted the call. If he had any pocket pair better than jacks, he'd have called in a heartbeat. I knew I had the best hand, and I was now guessing he had something like A-K or a small pair, and he was wondering if he had the best hand since he'd seen the crap I'd pushed all-in with on the previous hand.

He called. I turned over my jacks, and his face dropped as he showed me K-J offsuit.

Now that was a loose call, especially since he didn't have that many more chips than me. I felt great for about two seconds. Then the king came down on the turn, and there was no miracle river card for me. My unlikely suck-out and double-up on the previous hand was all for naught. I went out tenth, damning the poker gods for teasing me so mercilessly before my fall.

So, the way this table image thing works, you'll have a pretty tight image if you follow the rock-paper-scissors betting strategy, but you can blow it really fast if you get called down on a position play. Then you've got to be careful for a while. The thing is, the player turnover in these fast tournaments is also fast. So, even if you do blow your image, you'll either get moved to a new table or get some new faces fairly quickly, and then you should be able to start taking shots again.

That is, if you're still in the damn thing.

16

MISTAKES

When you first start playing tournaments, you will be oblivious to most of your mistakes. In fact, you will likely attribute your losses primarily to bad cards (*I just couldn't get any playable hands!*) and "bad beats" (*Everyone kept sucking out on me!*). To most players, a bad beat is any hand that is a favorite to win, that gets beaten by an inferior hand. If, for example, you raise before the flop with A-K, and the flop comes down Q-J-10, giving you the nut straight, most players would consider it a bad beat if they were beaten on the turn or river by a player making a flush or full house.

However, it's only a bad beat if you played the hand correctly. For example, if there were two cards to a flush on the table, and you slowplayed the straight, giving free cards to your opponents, it's hard to call it a bad beat if one of your opponents makes his flush. Likewise, it's not a bad beat if you place a bet so small that any player with a flush draw or set has the pot odds to call your bet to try to draw out on you. You are the player in this hand who made the mistake. Your opponents played correctly. It's not the cards that make a bad beat a bad beat; it's the way the players play their cards.

In addition to simple mathematical errors based on odds and outs, there are many other types of mistakes players make in the course of a tournament. They misread the cards on the board, misread their opponents, overbet or underbet the pot, fold when they should call, call when they should raise, raise when they should fold, and so on.

THE BIGGEST MISTAKE

But the single biggest mistake most amateurs make is obsessing about their bad beats. Good players never think twice about a bad beat. The fact is, if you're a 2 to 1 favorite in a hand, then you should expect your opponent to win in these situations one out of every three times they occur. That's what 2 to 1 means. If you get into half a dozen of these situations in a tournament, where you are always the 2 to 1 favorite, then you should expect your opponent to suck out on you twice, based simply on mathematical expectation. This is why it is so difficult to get into the money in long, slow tournaments. Even if you play every hand correctly, and you are dealt a lot of premium hands, there's nothing you can do to avoid the mathematics of suck-outs.

One of the first signs that you are advancing as a player, and that you may have what it takes to make money in tournaments, is when you start ignoring your bad beats and focusing on your actual mistakes instead. This is very difficult to do in the beginning, but after a few dozen tournaments, you will have experienced so many bad beats that you should realize they are just a normal part of the game. Incredibly, for reasons known only to their therapists, some players never give up their bad beat focus. I don't get it. I have met players who have been playing poker for years who still whine incessantly about bad beats. It's like people complaining about the sunshine in August.

Because this bad beat focus is so common among amateur poker players, I feel I must address this issue. If bad beats at the tables are causing you distress, then you've got to do something about it. Every time you enter a tournament, make a vow to yourself that you will not dwell on a single bad beat that occurs, no matter how bad it is. Instead, you will focus on the things over which you had control—hands you misplayed, hands where you would have won more or lost less if you had played them differently. This is the only way you will ever improve.

And never, ever, tell a bad beat story to another poker player. If the player is any good, he will immediately start sizing you up as a fish. He will know that you are either a rank beginner who hasn't seen enough hands to know that bad beats are part of the game, or one of those perpetual losers who—despite years of experience—will never advance beyond the fish level.

I have seen players telling bad beat stories to other players while standing in line to sign up for the tournament. And I have seen some very sharp players going out of their way to draw out the details from the story tellers. "How much did you raise?" "How much was in the pot?" "Did you have position on him?" "Did you put him on the flush draw?"

Hey, why don't you just tell this guy who may soon be sitting across the table from you everything you know and don't know about the game, because that's what he's asking you. He doesn't give a damn how bad your bad beat was; he just wants to know how bad of a player you are.

So, the first mistake you've got to stop making is the mistake of dwelling on your bad beats. Get the bad beats out of your head. In the first 50 tournaments you play, you will make dozens of mistakes in every tournament, though you will not know it. By the time you've played 100 tournaments or so, you will recognize the fact that you were making uncountable mistakes in your earlier tournaments. Now your job is to find the three or four mistakes you will make in the tournament you play *today*.

You will soon identify the types of hands and situations that give you the most problems, and you will also begin to stop yourself from making many errors.

And remember to pay attention to mistakes even when they don't cost you money. You will find yourself in many situations where you've misread either a player or the danger on the board, and in the course of facing an unexpected superior hand, *you suck out*. Pleasurable though this may be, chalk it up in your mind as another mistake you've made, and try to recognize similar situations in the future.

It's actually a good sign if you frequently get sucked out on. It means you got your money into the pot with the best hand. In fact, if you only rarely get sucked out on, you're probably playing against opponents who are too tough for you.

THE MOST COMMON TYPE OF MISTAKE

By far, the most common type of playing error you see in the fast tournaments will be the failure to play with sufficient aggression. If you are the first player into the pot preflop, you should almost always come in with a raise, regardless of your hand or position. If you do not feel comfortable raising with your hand, then throw the hand away. Do not limp into a pot unless there are other limpers in front of you and you feel that the table is passive enough that no player yet to act will come in with a raise behind you.

Never just call or "slowplay" high cards or any decent pair before the flop in a fast tournament. If you have aces, kings, queens or jacks, tens, nines, eights, sevens, A-K, A-Q, A-J—*raise* if the pot has not already been raised. And with A-K or any of the high or medium pocket pairs, you should reraise and seriously consider pushing all in on any player who raised in front of you.

With the medium pairs, the decision to reraise or go all-in is a judgment call based on your assessment of the player who raised the pot. If it was a canasta lady, you should probably throw your pocket 9s away. If it was an aggressive ball-cap kid, push in on him. Put him to the test. You will occasionally bump into hands strong enough to call you down, and hands that are better than yours. So be it.

There are several reasons why aggression pays in fast tournaments. First, when you have any premium hand, your raise makes others *pay* to try to beat you. Second, you will collect a lot more chips from players who are afraid to call you than you will lose to players who do.

It is possible to be aggressive to the point where it's a mistake, but even then aggression is less of a mistake than being a wimp. Players who are too aggressive make more final tables in these fast tournaments than players who are not aggressive enough.

If you want to make money in the fast tournaments that don't cost $10,000 to enter, leave your finesse at the door. Instead, come in with a killer instinct, and always go for the jugular.

MISTAKES WHEN AN OVERCARD HITS ON THE FLOP

One of the most common and costly mistakes players make is failing to bet when an overcard comes down on the flop, even after their opponents have shown weakness. Let's say you raise with pocket kings and you get one caller, the big blind. The flop comes down A-9-6, all hearts, and your opponent checks. You not only hate the ace overcard, but neither of your kings is a heart. What do you do?

Bet! He checked. You bet. He does not have an ace.

How much should you bet? Against a single opponent, at least the size of the pot.

If this guy was lucky enough to have flopped a flush, and he's slowplaying it, let him check-raise you. If he's got an ace, or pocket 9s, but he's afraid to bet because he doesn't have a flush, then he's a wimp and you get this pot. If he was afraid to bet when he saw the flop, believe me he'll be afraid to call your pot-sized bet. You very likely have the best hand, so take this pot while you still have the best hand. If he has a single heart in his hand, you cannot afford to give him any free cards.

DON'T GIVE UP THE LEAD

Now, how would you play this hand if you were out of position and had to bet first? Again, you make a pot-sized bet. Against a single opponent, you have to take a shot at this pot with a bet big enough to make it a mistake for him to call on a flush draw, and to seriously consider folding if he has an ace in hand but no hearts. If there are multiple players in the pot, all of whom called your preflop raise, you should still take a stab at the pot, but bet only half the size of the pot. You might steal this pot from any player with an ace who fears the flush, but any bet bigger than half the pot-size is dangerous. Some desperate player with A-K or A-Q may call you down, especially if one of his cards is a heart. If no heart falls on the turn, you might want to push in on a player who called your raise on the flop. He almost certainly doesn't have a flush, or he would have raised you on the flop. If you really have a feeling he might be slowplaying a flush, then you should just check and fold if he bets.

Any time you raise before the flop and one or more players call behind you, you are in a risky situation because you do not have position after the flop. Since the flop will miss your hand a lot more often than it will hit it, you will often be in a quandary as to how to play after the flop. Any time you raise with a pocket pair, even kings, queens or jacks, one or more overcards might come down. But in almost all cases, giving up the lead in betting is incorrect.

If you don't bet, you are usually relinquishing the pot. If your opponents are wimps, or are slowplaying the nuts, they may not bet when you check, but most decent players in position would challenge you with a bet in this situation, and you would pretty much have to fold.

For an extreme example, let's say you raise in early position with pocket 7s, get three callers, and the flop comes down, A-K-Q, about as bad as a flop can be for your hand. What should you do? Bet. At least half the size of the pot. Just do it! Believe me, if anyone goes over the top of that bet, they've got the goods and you can throw your 7s away. If you get one or more callers, now you're entering poker territory. From here on out, you're on your own. Who called your bet and what do you think they called with? Can you steal the pot with an all-in bet on the turn? Do you just have to check and fold from here on out? That flop is so dangerous, and missed your hand so completely, that your decision on keeping the lead on the turn must be based on factors no book can teach you.

But the standard rule is this: if you raised preflop, and you get one or more callers who have position on you, then you must bet on the flop no matter what comes down. Push out a bet of at least half the size of the pot, and don't even think about not betting. If you are called on the flop, bet again on the turn. If you are called on the turn, then you have a judgment call to make on the river. If you put this player on a draw, did he hit one of his outs on the turn or river? If not, does he have a hand so strong he won't go away? If you really think this player is hoping you don't make it any more expensive for him, then push all-in. Sometimes you will lose money on plays like these, but much more often you will take the pot.

You've got to start developing your instincts in these situations, and not just clinging to your fears.

OVERCARD PARANOIA

The general rule is that you should not be afraid of overcards if you are against a single opponent who is simply checking and calling. Nor should you try to see a free card that might improve your hand if you already have a made hand. If, for instance, you have pocket 8s, and the flop comes down K-J-6, and your opponent checks to you, bet! Don't check hoping another 8 might hit the table, giving you the miracle set. Your opponent may be a wimp with A-J, afraid of the king on board. If you check, he'll know you don't have the king, and when the turn card hits the table, he will bet his second pair (unless he's such a wimp that he never bets when an overcard is on the table).

I'm not saying that you should always bet when your opponent checks, just most of the time. If you are on a strong straight or flush draw and you want the free card—especially if you think your opponent may be slowplaying a strong hand—then go ahead and take the free card. But in the above situation, your 8s are a made hand that really may be the best hand, and it's a hand that's unlikely to improve. You have a scary board and a weak opponent. So bet. That pot is yours to take right now, but it may not be yours one card later.

GO EASY ON YOURSELF

Finally, regarding mistakes, you should realize that not every losing call you make is a mistake. For example, let's say you raise with A-K and you get one caller, the player on the button who happens to be very aggressive and whom you know bluffs a lot. The flop comes down A-K-9. You bet, and he raises all-in. You call. He shows down pocket 9s, and you are knocked out of the tournament.

Don't beat yourself up over this "mistake." There isn't one player in a thousand who could read that player for having flopped a set, and most of the players who would fold in this situation would be wimps. They are dead money from the get-go. If at some point in your tournament career you acquire the ability to read a set in an opponent's hand with unfailing accuracy, more power to you. But any time you exit a tournament because of your aggressive play, whether you are making the all-in bet or calling it, you should feel proud of yourself for playing with guts and determination.

On the other hand, any time you exit a tournament after having been slowly blinded off while you waited for a "playable" hand, you should try to think of every possible opportunity you had in that tournament to make money. Think of all the pots you saw taken by players who bet and didn't get called. Do you really believe every one of those players had a strong hand every time he took the pot? Why didn't you take some pots that way? Did you pass up any opportunities to steal chips with position play? Were you aggressive enough against the blinds? Are you basing too much of your play on your cards?

The prime cause of mistakes by smart players is making decisions too quickly—simply not taking the time to think through the situation. Always stop and look at your opponent. There is a huge difference between a minimum raise from a player who has a mountain of chips and a player who is so short-stacked that this minimum raise has him pot-committed. You will not be able to get the short-stacked player out of this pot, and his raise seems to be begging for a call or a reraise. The big stack could just be taking a shot. You've always got to consider your opponent, his chip position, your chip position, his table image, your table image. You cannot simply play your hands according to a chart.

There will be many tournaments where you simply do not get decent hands, and when the opportunities for making money are few and far between, even when you are doing all that you can to take advantage of your position when you have it. So it goes. There's another tournament tomorrow. But even in the most miserable of tournaments, where you never really had a shot at the money, you probably made some mistakes. Forget the bad cards and the bad beats. Look for the few hands you could have played better. Any time you don't make it into the money, at least get the value of the education. Every tournament will teach you something.

17

TAKING A STAND

To have any hope of success in these fast tournaments, you must have the guts to take a stand with your hand, even in the face of danger. You cannot fold top pair to a big raise every time there are three to a flush or three to a straight on the board. You will almost never have the nuts and you must be willing to call big bets—and even all-in bets that could bust you—if your heart tells you that the bettor is just trying to bully you out of the pot.

If you're wrong, and you get sent packing, so be it. Even the best players make mistakes. Playing with courage and aggression will get you into the money far more often than solid, conservative play will.

Once a bully sees that he can push you out of a pot, he'll do it again and again, and any other bullies at the table will join in the feeding frenzy on your chips. For you to sit there thinking, "Wait until I have a really big hand—then I'll show them!" is just a fantasy. By the time you get that big hand—if you get that big hand—you won't have enough chips left to show anybody anything. You'll just be the short stack that got lucky in time to double up, so the sharks can start taking bites out of you again.

The best thing you can do is take your stand early—show the bullies at your first opportunity to do so that you're not an easy target.

Example: You have K-Q of spades and you make a standard raise from the button as the first player into the pot. The blinds are $50-$100, so you raise to $300. The big blind—an aggressive player who often steals the blinds himself—calls your raise. The flop comes down K-9-7, all hearts. You have top pair and a decent kicker, but no hearts in your hand. The flop looks good to you until the big blind pushes all in. He has more chips than you. What do you do?

First of all, you don't make a quick decision. You stop and consider the possibilities. You only have top pair, and you don't even have the ace kicker. All he really needs to beat you is A-K. He doesn't need the flush, but because the flop is suited, he may already have a flush. Or, he may have called your preflop raise with pocket 7s or 9s, in which case he flopped a set. That would make his all-in move more logical, as he would not want you drawing to the flush if you had a heart. Alternatively, he may have neither a set nor a pair, but the ace of hearts, giving him a nut flush draw. With the ace overcard and the flush draw, he would have 12 outs to beat your kings with two cards to come. That means that even though you currently have him beat, you are only a slight favorite to win the hand by the river. You are still the favorite, but do you want to risk all of your chips right now on the possibility that he's only on a draw?

With the combination of all of these possible ways your top pair can be beaten, the decision seems simple—just fold. A fold will only cost you your initial preflop raise, so it may seem a wise decision to simply wait for a better opportunity to take a stand. But before you fold, consider the fact that this situation has all of the elements a bully is looking for in order to steal a pot. One, he is up against a single opponent, and if he views this opponent as a solid, conservative player, all the better. Two, the flop looks dangerous. Any player who does not have two hearts in his hand could already be drawing dead. And three, only a player with a flush, or at least a set or an ace of hearts in his hand, could really consider calling this bet, and all of these possible calling hands are long shots.

All-in bullies court danger continually. They never stop putting their opponents to the test by representing hands they don't have. Many of these bullies are poor players, except for this understanding of raw aggression, yet they often amass a lot of chips by pushing players out of pots. In most tournaments, these bullies meet their demise either by representing a hand that their opponent actually has, or by bumping into a superior player who can read their bluff for what it is. The truly talented bully is the one who knows when to take his shots and when not to based on his read of his opponent.

In the all-in situation described above, the bully knows that the odds against your having an ace of hearts in your hand are more than 20 to 1. The odds are even higher against your holding two hearts. (The actual odds against you would depend on whether or not the bully himself had a heart in hand. Obviously, if he had two hearts, he would not be bullying you so much as playing a strong hand very aggressively, just praying that you hold an A-K or some other hand you can't or won't lay down.) Because this is such a classic situation for a bully to take advantage of, however, ask yourself one question before you muck your cards, and answer it as honestly as you can: "Do I believe in my heart that this sonofabitch is just trying to steal this pot?"

If your answer to that question is yes, but you still muck your cards, you will never make it in no-limit tournaments. Hang it up. You are wasting your time and money. If you don't have the guts to follow your heart in these small buy-in tournaments, when serious money is not at stake, you will never advance as a player. I'm not suggesting that you become a calling station, refusing to fold any top pair you make. Nor am I suggesting that you never make a good laydown when you have a legitimate hand but feel your opponent has you beat. But you've always got to look at the exact situation. If you fold to every possible flush or straight you see on the board, you are nothing but prey.

I'm not trying to portray the above situation as an automatic call. It's not. I purposely set up a situation in which a call would be difficult to make. It's a call I would find difficult to make myself— and in most cases I would not make it. What I am trying to convey here is that you must learn to follow your heart in scary situations. No-limit tournaments present these situations time and time again. If you always fold under pressure, you will exit every tournament after watching your chips dwindle while you're waiting for that monster hand that never seems to arrive.

Later, as you think over what happened, you'll be saying to yourself, "I should have called that aggressive bastard who kept pushing in on me. I'll bet I had him beat. He couldn't have made all those great hands." But there you are, driving home, while he's at the final table with all of your chips.

Making tough calls is the only way to learn if your gut-level feelings are right. If you never make these scary calls, not only are you assured of losing, but you won't even find out if you are good. You may have better reads on your opponents than 99% of the top pros. But your reads are worthless if you don't back them up with your money. Following your heart on these tough calls will also teach you when your reads are wrong. When you follow your heart, you'll start to see patterns of play that indicate not only the bluffs, but the monster hands you shouldn't have called, so that you can start basing your decisions on factors you weren't even aware of previously.

You have to view these small buy-in tournaments as a chance to get a cheap poker education.

18

LAYDOWNS

A **laydown** is a fold of a strong hand when you believe your opponent's hand is stronger. You will almost never have the nuts—the best possible hand given all of the possibilities with the community cards. And you will frequently find yourself having to make a decision on a call that could end your tournament if your hand does not hold up. If you can fold your good hands when you know you are beaten, you will survive in many tournaments where you otherwise would have busted out.

In a fast tournament, you should be less prone to laying down a competitive hand than you might be in a long slow tournament. Many tournament players pride themselves on their good laydowns, but many of these players are also fooling themselves, laying down the best hands in the face of aggression, rather than taking a stand against a bully.

There are a number of factors that should contribute to your decision to laydown a good hand—the degree of danger presented by the community cards, your read on the player who is raising, and the effect of the laydown on the health of your chip stack. If, for example, you are in desperate need of a double up to have any chance of survival in a tournament, you should be far more reluctant to laydown a competitive hand—no matter how dangerous the community cards—than if the laydown would have little effect on your ability to continue.

Let's consider some specific laydown situations, starting with the best hands and working down to the more marginal hands.

WOULD YOU EVER LAY DOWN A...
Straight Flush?

Ha!

No. Never. Not even if it's the low end of the straight flush and you fear your opponent may have the high end. If you lay down this hand, you get the wimp of the year award. Don't lay it down. If you get beaten by the high end of the straight flush, live with it. You played it right, so take it up with the poker gods. They owe you one.

Quads?

No. Never. Not even if there are four cards to a straight flush on board, or if there are two pair on board and you have the "small" quads.

Full House?

Believe it or not, you will have rare opportunities to lay down a full house. You may find it impossible to do so, but there will be times when you will know it is the right decision. For example, you are in the big blind with a 6-3 offsuit. A player in early position limps into the pot, and no other players enter. The flop comes down A-3-3, giving you trip 3s. Hoping your opponent has an ace, you make a pot sized bet, and he raises. You reraise, and he calls your reraise. Because he entered the pot from an early position, you do not believe he has a 3, so you must assume he has an ace. Because he called your reraise, you are just hoping he did not limp in with pocket aces.

The turn card brings down another ace. Now you have a sick feeling. You have just made a full house, 3s full of aces, but if he has just a single ace, he has you beat with aces full of 3s. Your only hope in this hand is if he may have limped with a hand like K-3 suited, and actually has the same hand as you.

Would this player do that?

In any case, as I say, there are times when you will know you should lay down a full house, in all cases because you have the baby full, and the big full is such a distinct possibility. I would not advise laying down a full house unless there are two pair on board, you had the trip card to the small pair, and you have pretty good reason to believe your opponent has a trip card to the big pair because of the way the betting has gone.

Flush?

It's very difficult, and usually incorrect, to lay down a flush if there are only three cards to the flush on the table. But with four community cards to the flush, it's a pretty easy laydown if your flush card is small. Flushes are hands that aggressive players like to represent. But with four to a flush on board, it takes more guts than most bluffers have to represent the flush. With a pair on board, you also must be concerned that your opponent has a full house. Try to imagine the cards he would have to have in his hand in order to have one of the possible full houses with that board. Think about how the betting went, and make your decision. But you are usually wrong to lay it down.

Straight?

The low end of a straight is an easy laydown if there are four to the straight on board. With three to the straight, it's not so easy in a fast tournament, and it's usually incorrect to lay it down unless there are four to a flush on board. A straight is such a premium hand that in a fast tournament where hands this good are rare, you probably want to play it to the death. As with flushes, aggressive players will often crank up their aggression when three to a straight are on the table, but they will be more cautious when four to the straight are on board.

Trips?

It's very difficult, and usually wrong in a fast tournament, to lay down three of a kind. You will sometimes encounter situations where you have trips and there are either four to a flush or straight on the board, and you will be fairly certain your hand is beat. In this case, lay it down. With three to a flush or straight, you're usually wrong to lay it down. The big bet will more often represent a straight or flush draw—or just a bully taking a shot.

Two Pair?

There are lots of hands that beat two pair, but this is still a premium hand, especially if one of your pairs is the top pair. I would lay down two pair in a fast tournament only if there were very strong possibilities of straights or flushes on board, or if I sensed a cagey codger slowplaying me with a set to raise me all-in on the river. If you have two pair because you have an invisible pair in your hand, however, and there is another pair on board, that's a different situation entirely. How good is your pair? If it's an overpair to the board you should be much less willing to lay it down than if there is one or more cards on the table higher than your pair. With a small pair, if it doesn't improve to a set, just get rid of your hand with any betting at all. You're probably beat.

Overpair?

It's not easy, and usually incorrect in a fast tournament, to lay down a pair in your hand that is higher than any of the cards on the table. It depends on how dangerous those cards on the table are. In a fast tournament, you should generally play an overpair very aggressively after the flop, all-in if you are getting close to short-stacked, in order to keep other players from drawing out on you.

Do note that this hand, like many of the other hands I am saying it is usually incorrect to laydown, are incorrect to laydown because of the fast tournament structure, where good hands are rare, good flops are rarer, and aggressive players take a lot more shots with nothing. In a ring game or even a slower major tournament format, an overpair is still just a single pair, and that's nothing to write home about. With danger on the board, this should not be a difficult hand to lay down if you don't have many of your chips already invested in it. Throwing away a pair of aces is something that some players can never bring themselves to do.

Top Pair?

If you're desperate for chips, you may have to play top pair to the death, even with a lousy kicker. If you're not desperate, then you have to consider why your opponent is trying to raise you out of the pot. How dangerous is the board? How much of a bluffer is he? It shouldn't be that difficult to lay this hand down, but you don't want to lay it down at just any sign of aggression.

Second Pair, Third Pair, Bottom Pair, Overcards?

Against a single opponent, you don't automatically lay down these lesser pairs in the face of betting, and you're generally correct in a fast tournament to stay in the pot if you've paired one of the lesser board cards and the other card you have in the hole is an overcard to the board. In fact, it usually pays off to reraise a weak bet in this situation. But if your opponent is really aggressive, you're usually correct to relinquish a lesser pair unless you are very short-stacked.

The ability to make money on a hand like this, however, is something that sets the pros apart from the amateurs. Most amateurs will immediately throw away second pair in the face of any betting. Skilled players will take their time and think it through.

There's no magic formula for when you should lay down a hand like this, and when you should put more money in the pot to keep your hand alive, but here are two basic guidelines:

1. Don't be so quick to throw your hand away against a single opponent. In a multiway pot, however, muck your cards if there is a bet and a raise among your opponents.

2. If you are not desperate and you don't have much invested in the pot, don't invest much more in a hand like this. If you bet and get raised, get out.

19

THE ACCIDENTAL NUTS

Raising with trash hands sometimes puts you in position to take down a big pot with a hand no opponent expects. Players in the blinds sometimes make the accidental nuts, simply by getting into unraised pots. But most players are very careful when playing against the blinds in unraised pots, because they realize these players can be in the hand with virtually any two cards. By contrast, if you're not in one of the blinds, and especially if you enter a pot by raising or calling a raise, most players expect you to have high cards, a decent pair, or strong suited connectors. But if you play the basic position strategy correctly, your opponents will often be wrong in this assumption.

Let's say you're in the raising seat, two seats to the right of the big blind, with a 5-7 offsuit. And let's say your standard raise of three times the big blind gets two callers—the button and the big blind. Oh, what a joy to have the flop come down 4-6-8. I had this happen once and I tripled up on the hand. The big blind, with a short stack and an A-8, pushed all in on his top pair with ace kicker. Hoping to keep the button player in the pot, I simply called his all-in. Then the button, who had pocket kings, reraised over-the-top all-in, and needless to say, I called him too.

Oh, the pain and misery at that table when we all turned up our cards. The player on the button had, in fact, made an error not reraising before the flop, which may or may not have gotten rid of the short-stacked big blind, but definitely would have gotten rid of me.

You will be surprised at how often a trash raise turns into a real hand when the community cards hit the felt. It doesn't happen so often that you expect it, but you definitely remember it when it happens, and the chips you can win with these unusual hands are way in excess of what you can make with top pair and an ace kicker.

This is another reason why calling standard raises from late position has benefits. When you flop the accidental nuts, you will almost always make money on the hand. Even with a good flop that is not the nuts, you stand to make money. Having a 7-3 when the flop comes down A-7-3 is a huge profit opportunity. In a fast tournament, any A-K will likely call your all-in bet. Any decent ace—A-Q, A-J, A-10 suited—will call a big bet, and may push in on you if they are first to bet.

Most of the discussion in this book on position play has considered it from the standpoint of using your position to bully opponents when you have no cards to speak of. But a side-benefit of getting involved when you have position, and only position, is that you sometimes end up with a strong hand that your opponents could never suspect.

When you show down a hand like this, the players at your table will remember it. You will get looser calls, so you must be more careful for a while about preflop shots. But postflop, they'll never be able to have much of a handle on you. You'll get more top pairs to fold when the board presents any danger and you're betting with aggression.

20

THE WOLF PACK INSTINCT

Do you remember the scene at the beginning of Jack London's *Call of the Wild* where one dog in a pack started biting another dog, and as soon as the other dogs realized that the bitten dog was weakened, they all joined in and viciously tore it to shreds? The protagonist of the story, Buck—the friendly dog who had been brought into this world of snarling beasts from a family home where all he'd ever known was security and comfort—realized for the first time that the world he was now in was literally a dog-eat-dog world. As London put it, "So that was the way. No fair play. Once down, that was the end of you."

When you enter a poker tournament, take a tip from Buck, for this is how you should view the world you are entering. If you show weakness, expect no mercy. If you are injured, expect to be attacked. Likewise, when any opponent at your table takes a big hit to his chip stack, don't hesitate to join the feeding frenzy on his remaining chips.

Whenever a player is desperately short-stacked, a kind of implied collusion sets in among the other players at the table to "get that guy." If this player makes any move on the pot, every player with any decent amount of chips who could not be significantly hurt by the loss should be in that pot. No matter what hand the short-stacked player holds—and you can expect that he will be playing very loosely on his small stack, looking for any two cards that might take the pot if he's called—his cards are a lot less likely to hold up against a group of players than against any one player.

If this player makes his all-in move, and you happen to be holding A-K suited, this is not the time to raise other players out of the pot. You do not want to limit the field for your own hand at a time like this. Just call. You want as many players as possible in this pot to put the short-stacked player out of his misery once and for all. He might have pocket 7s. You don't want your raise to fold an opponent who's holding Q-J offsuit. If you push other contenders out of the pot, a queen or jack might hit the board, and the short stack's 7s might double up on your A-K. You've got to make that short stack beat every hand, not just yours. This is a matter of life and death to the short stack, and his death is a good enough turn of events for your chances in this tournament that it should supersede your worries about some player besides you taking the pot. And unless you make a truly monster hand with the cards on the board, do not make any move that might drive other players out of the pot. You're all in this together, a pack of ravenous dogs circling a bloodied, defenseless victim. *Kill.*

There will be times when you'll see a desperation all-in move by a short stack, and another player at the table who has a lot of chips will push all-in behind him, saying, "I'll give you some protection." By that, he means—literally—that the short-stack will probably not have to beat a lot of other players at the table, just him. All of the players with more marginal hands will fold to the big stack's all-in move, whereas they may have called the all-in bet of the short-stacked player. Let me just say that the player who "gives protection" in this way had better be holding pocket aces or he is a fool. He truly is giving protection to the short stack, and that is not the way to go in for the kill. You want the minimum chance of doubling this guy up and the maximum chance of busting him out. That means teaming up against him.

You may be sitting there with some pretty sharp teeth—A-K, pocket jacks or queens—and that short stack may have so few chips he's liable to be pushing in with little more than a prayer. But don't raise. Just call. Let the pack in on this kill. You want to really give that short stack something to pray about.

You will generally find that the better players in the fast tournaments understand this strategic aspect of the game. In these baby tournaments, these types of situations are constant. In fact, one of the reasons you must avoid getting really short-stacked is that if you do, you will not get a chance to go up against a single opponent when you finally decide to make a stand. If you get too short, you'll most likely have to face a full pack of dogs that smell blood.

21

CHOPPING IT UP

Fast tournaments rarely get played out to the end. There will almost always be deals cut at the final table—mutual agreements among the remaining players to chop up the prize money. Most often, these agreements are reached when there are two to four players remaining, though I have been at final tables where there was a ten-player chop. Not a single hand was played at that final table.

The decision to cut a deal among the final players has to be agreed to by every player involved. If four out of five players want to chop it up, but one player wants to continue playing, then the tournament must continue. I have seen instances where players were pressured into agreements to chop up the prize money when they obviously wanted to continue playing—usually because they were among the chip leaders at the table and felt they would make more money if the tournament continued—but they let themselves be coerced by the group to accept a deal. No player should ever let himself be pressured into an agreement. The poker room management generally stays out of such agreements—as they ought to—so they will not step in if an agreement is reached, even if it looks like some player is getting a raw deal.

There is no standard way to chop up a prize pool. Generally, those players who have the most chips must agree to relinquish some of the first place prize to be distributed to the players in the lesser chip positions. If three or four players are all fairly equal in chips, then they might just decide on an even three or four-way split. For example, if three players are chopping up the prize money, and they are fairly close in chips, they might agree to chop the first, second, and third place prizes of $4,000, $2,000, and $1,000 by taking $2,333 each. This way all players get slightly better than second place prize money.

If one player in this example had substantially more chips than the others, then they might agree to this player taking $2,600, while each of the others take $2,200. Most players will usually agree to the actual chip leader taking a slightly larger share.

Some players feel that chopping up the prize money is a cop out, a sign of weakness. These poker purists believe that every tournament should be played to the bitter end, with each player taking the prize delivered by his actual finishing position. In a slow tournament, where there are a lot of chips on the final table, this may make sense. Short-handed play requires much greater skill, and as players are eliminated, players who have superior abilities at reading their opponents and representing hands will often beat players who are being dealt better hands. A final table at a major tournament can often go on for many hours. In a long, slow tournament, chopping up the prize money would be the right decision for any player who felt that he was less skillful than his opponents. It might also be correct for any player who was concerned with controlling fluctuations. Chopping up the prize money will lower the variance on any player's tournament results.

In a fast tournament, however, chopping up the prize money almost always makes sense. When you arrive at the final table of a fast tournament, the average chip stack will typically cover only three to six rounds of blinds and antes, if that. Most often, half of the players will arrive at the final table desperately short-stacked.

A few players will be in better chip condition, with the chip leader perhaps having sufficient chips to cover the cost of a dozen or more rounds of play. These players with the most chips will rarely be open to chopping agreements at this point, and I agree with this position. Within twenty to thirty minutes, a few of the shortest stacks will have been eliminated. Players usually start thinking about chopping it up when there are six or fewer players. By this point, the blinds will have gone up one or two levels, and every remaining player will be feeling their cost.

When even the chip leaders' stacks are down to the cost of only half a dozen rounds or so, most players realize that the tournament has reached a point where the lucky cards will win. Every ace is all in, regardless of kicker, as is every hand that has two high cards, such as K-J. Even the smallest pairs—deuces and trays—will take all-in shots and even call all-in shots. In fact, the only practical bet to make is all-in, because of the huge number of chips in the pot from the blinds and antes. At this point, players can do little more than take turns making all-in bets, and taking the preflop pot. Players get bumped out whenever two of them have the misfortune of having strong hands on the same round, such as A-Q meets pocket 10s. The next five cards then decide who gets the money and who gets the shaft.

Since there is no poker skill involved in the game at this point, the smartest move for the remaining players is to agree to chop up the prize pool. Continuing with the tournament at this point is just gambling, seeing who gets dealt the lucky cards, who hits a pair on the flop, who sucks out on the turn or river.

From the perspective of a professional gambler, it is foolish *not* to chop up the prize pool at this point in a fast tournament. Professional gamblers don't actually like to gamble. They only want to play when they have an edge. If I want to gamble, I'll go play craps or slots. That's not why I play poker tournaments.

So, here are some guidelines to follow when it comes time to chop it up:

1. If the chop is between five or fewer players, it's usually only the top place that has to give up any amount of prize money. With six or more players in on the chop, first place will give up the most and second place may have to give up a little.

2. If you are the chip leader when the choppers' chip stacks are all very close in quantity, always insist on getting slightly more than your fellow choppers. This gives you first place bragging rights. It doesn't have to be a big difference. If three of you are chopping up $6,000, then instead of agreeing to take $2,000 each, as chip leader you should demand $2,050, with $1,975 each for the other two choppers. They're unlikely to reject the deal, even if they think you're just nitpicking over a few bucks.

3. If there is a big disparity in chips, then make the chop reflect the reality of the situation. For example, if your chip stack as chip leader is anywhere near double that of your closest opponent, then insist on more of a piece for your cut of the prize. But don't try to short-change the other players too much. They will not agree to chop the prize pool unless they see some dollar advantage to it.

4. Never try to coerce another player into a chopping agreement. If someone really wants to play it out, then play it out. I don't know why this happens, but in almost every case where I've seen a player stand his ground and refuse to chop when all the others concerned wanted to cut up the cash and go home, the hold-out ended up regretting it. One player, who was second in chips and refused to chop when the table was down to five players, literally went out on the very next hand when he went all-in on the chip leader, got called, and lost. His pocket queens went down to big slick. That fifth place finish paid him $1,000 less than he would have been paid had he agreed to chop one hand earlier. In any case, those who refuse to chop are generally making a mistake, so let them make it.

5. Never chop if one or more players are in a truly desperate chip position. If some player can't even afford to go through the blinds and antes one more time, let the cards decide if he's going to be in on the chop.

6. A two-way chop gives you the best leverage when you are the chip leader. If you have substantially more chips than your opponent, say double or more his chip stack, he'll usually be agreeable to taking any amount more than the second place money. If he's closer in chips, just try to negotiate the best deal you can. You definitely want to get a bigger piece, even if it's only a small amount that gives you first place bragging rights.

Sample Chops

Let's say there are four players remaining at the final table with a total of $150,000 in chips on the table. Here are the remaining prizes to be awarded:

1st Place:	$3,500
2nd Place:	$1,800
3rd Place:	$1,200
4th Place:	$1,000

Here are the players' current chip stacks, and a chop I would consider fair:

	Chips	Chop
Player A:	$56,000	$1,950
Player B:	$34,000	$1,850
Player C:	$31,000	$1,850
Player D:	$29,000	$1,850

Note here that Player A, the chip leader, is giving up enough of the first prize to provide all three of his opponents with slightly better than second place prize money. This is a deal that all would probably go for.

Your immediate reaction to this chop may be that Player A should take a bigger portion of the prize pool, since he has 60+% more chips than his nearest competitor. That is not the way to think of it. All three of his opponents are so close to each other in chips that none would likely consider a chopped prize of less than second place prize money.

Player A's chip lead, in fact, is very precarious with three players so close in chips and all at better than 50% of his chip position. He should be happy getting better than second place finish money along with the first place bragging rights.

By contrast, if Player A and Player D were the only two remaining players in on the chop, Player A should go for a settlement more favorable to himself. If the two top prizes were

$3,500 and $1,800, Player D might be willing to accept a bump up to $2,300 for second place, leaving Player A with an even $3,000.

In the first example with four players chopping, Player A had three opponents to outlast rather than one, and all of them would likely feel decently positioned for the second place prize money. For them to agree to chop, first place has to give them enough to make it worth it.

Now look at this situation with four players again and the same prize pool, but with a different chip distribution:

	Chips	Chop
Player A:	$56,000	$2,000
Player B:	$51,000	$1,900
Player C:	$23,000	$1,800
Player D:	$20,000	$1,800

Again, if you're looking at those chip totals and thinking the chop should more closely reflect the chip distribution, you still don't get it. What you're looking for when you chop is a deal that all involved will agree on. Since tournament prize money is so heavily skewed toward first place, that is where the money for the chop has to come from. It just about always works out that the first place prize takes a big hit, while the other prizes get better, especially the lower prizes.

The easiest way to accomplish a chopping plan when no player has a huge chip lead is to start by taking the total remaining prize pool (or $7,500 in the above examples) and divide it by the number of players in on the chop (or four in the above examples). So: $7,500 / 4 = $1,875.

Now figure out a way to give slightly more than this amount to first place, while making the other players happy with a settlement that's bigger than what their current position would get them if that was where they finished.

This would not, however, be appropriate in a situation with a big chip discrepancy, such as:

	Chips	Chop
Player A:	$98,000	$3,000
Player B:	$19,000	$1,500
Player C:	$18,000	$1,500
Player D:	$15,000	$1,500

In this example, if Players B, C, and D really want to chop, Player A should not give up more than a few hundred dollars, possibly accepting $3,000 instead of the $3,500 first prize. That will leave $4,500 in the remaining pool, or $1,500 each for the three short stacks. This would be a payout between the second and third place prizes. They would probably not all accept such a deal, however, since one or more would likely feel like shooting for the $1,800 second place prize money.

In this case, Player A would be making a mistake to give up more of the first place prize money with such a big chip lead on all his opponents. Within a few rounds, one—if not two—of the shorter stacks would exit. And the fewer the number of players in on the chop, the better it will be for those who remain. This type of chip distribution will often lead to a two-way chop between Player A and one survivor, and that will be far more lucrative for both.

22

SATELLITES

Satellites are a form of fast tournament, but they have many differences from regular fast tournaments. The book *Win Your Way Into Big Money Hold'em Tournaments* (formerly titled, *Championship Satellite Strategy*) by Tom McEvoy and Brad Daugherty is good for discussion of specific satellite hand situations, with strategic advice based on your cards, position, chip stack, and opponents. In this chapter, I'm primarily going to provide comments on the differences between optimal satellite strategies and regular fast tournament strategy.

A satellite is a tournament that does not award money to the winners, but instead awards an entry to a tournament that has a bigger buy-in cost. A **single table satellite** will usually start with ten players, and will typically award one winner a seat in a tournament that has a buy-in of about ten times the cost of the satellite. A **super satellite** is a multi-table satellite that will award multiple seats into a major tournament, with the exact number dependent on the number of entrants in the satellite. Let's look at optimal strategies for both types of satellites.

SUPER SATELLITES

Let's say the Four Queens is having a super satellite with a $100 buy-in (plus the house fee of $10 or so) for the $1,000 no-limit hold'em event at the annual Four Queens Open. And let's say 200 players enter. This tournament will play out like any fast tournament, and the formula in this book can be used to determine the patience factor, as with any other fast tournament.

But although this tournament will play out like any other fast tournament for the number of hours that it is in progress, it will never reach a final table. In fact, it will come to an abrupt end right at the point where any normal tournament would start to get interesting. In this super satellite, twenty seats would be awarded to the last remaining twenty players. A super satellite ends when the number of remaining players equals the number of main event seats that will be awarded.

In a super satellite, there is no first place, second place, third place, etc. Regardless of the final twenty players' chip counts, these remaining players will all win the same prize—a seat in the $1,000 buy-in event. So, even though a super satellite of this type may have the same patience factor as a regular tournament, and even an identical blind structure and number of starting chips, the best strategy is not at all the same.

The prize pool in a regular tournament that plays out to the end is heavily weighted toward the top end payouts. In regular tournaments with 200 entrants, there may be twenty players finishing in the money, but those players who finish in 11th to 20th place will usually get only something of a courtesy prize—enough to cover the cost of the buy-in, with perhaps a few bucks extra. This $100 buy-in event might pay $120. Even 9th and 10th places at the final table would rarely pay much more than $200-$300. By contrast, first place in most tournaments pays 30% or more of the prize pool. In this example, first place would pay around $6,000.

This weighting of the top-end payouts in any regular tournament means you should always be shooting for the highest place finish you can get. There is such a big difference between $120 and $6,000 that it is a huge disappointment to get 11th place in a tournament like this. You were so close to a big payout you could taste it, but all you got was your buy-in cost returned!

In a super satellite, however, 20th place pays exactly the same as 1st place. This difference in the prize structure makes super satellites much more about survival than domination.

In a regular tournament, for example, if twenty-five players remained and my chip stack was below average, I would be blasting away with maximum aggression in an attempt to get myself not just into the money, but into the money with enough of a chip stack to give me a shot at the top prizes. This would be a mistake at the same point in a super satellite.

In a super satellite, with only twenty-five players remaining, I would be so close to the top available prize that a below average chip stack would not be reason enough for all-out aggression. Depending on how desperate other players are at this point, I might already be pretty close to assured of being in the money. There would surely be quite a few players well below average who would be much more in danger of elimination than I was.

Also, if I was in tenth place or better at this point, I'd be crazy to get involved in a hand at all. I'd throw away pocket aces. Why risk a suck-out when I am already assured of a win? I'd let the more desperate players—the players who know they're on the edge of extinction—grapple for position with each other. Don't bother me, I'm meditating.

The first thing to do when considering strategy for a super satellite is to figure out how many chips you'll need in order to win a seat. In the 200-player example described above, let's assume that each player starts with $1,000 in chips. That would make $200,000 worth of total chips in play, and the last twenty players would have an average of $10,000 in chips each.

In the actual tournament, some players in the final twenty will have considerably more than $10,000 in chips, and some will have considerably less. But that $10,000 average chip allotment among the winners is a very useful number to keep in mind along the way.

The Early Rounds

Many super satellite players understand the survival emphasis of this type of tournament, so they tighten up their play right from the start. This is a mistake. In the early rounds, the blinds are at their lowest in relation to the players' chip stacks, so you have sufficient chips at this point to see more flops and take some shots without seriously damaging your survival chances. And because so many of your opponents will be playing tighter than they would in a normal no-limit hold'em tournament, your aggression and position plays will be more successful.

Your initial goal in the first stages of a super satellite should be to build a decent stack as early as you can while the survivalists are waiting for the nuts. If you build any kind of a big stack early, you will find stealing pots to be easier than in any normal tournament.

If you play fast early, you can play more carefully later when others are forced into fast play because their stacks are so short. If you take some hits during this early fast play, don't slow down. Speed up. You cannot afford to lose ground in the early stages.

In the early rounds of a super satellite, you should use all of the fast play methods described throughout this book for fast tournaments. In these early rounds, there is little difference between a super satellite and any other fast format tournament.

The Middle Rounds

If you have not increased your chips substantially in the early rounds, you are in trouble. You should not be satisfied with keeping pace. You need more than an average chip stack by the middle rounds. Let's define "average." If 100 of the 200 original players have been eliminated in the above satellite, then each player will now have, on average, twice his $1,000 in starting chips, or $2,000. But you need substantially more chips than this, because the blinds will have gone up more than double their initial level.

So, if you are anywhere near the average number of chips or below it, you must start taking shots now. There is no time to wait. Satellites have one thing in common with all tournaments, which is that you will bust out more often than you will get paid. But if you play with aggression, and take some risks when you're in danger, you will win often enough to make money on your dollar investments in satellites. These middle rounds are your last chance to get a competitive chip stack, and if you don't play the chips you have now, instead of letting them get eaten up by the blinds, you'll never see the later rounds of this tournament, let alone get close to the money.

Assuming you have gained chips in the early rounds, now is the time to start thinking of that average stack that the winners will have at the finish—$10,000 in chips in the example given above. Think of this as a goal in the middle rounds. If you make some huge mountain of chips—say $15,000 or more—as a result of a few hands where you had premium payoffs, then slow down. You may already have sufficient chips to ride into the money. During these middle rounds you must constantly be aware of the number of opponents left, how short the short stacks are, and how close you are to success.

The Late Rounds

Keep the blind costs in mind. If you've got $10,000 in chips but the blinds are $500 and $1,000, that $10,000 average winner's chip stack is in jeopardy unless you are within a few desperate players of the final number of winners.

A general rule is that if you have acquired a chip stack that will equal the average chip stack of the winners, then you may be able to just slide into the money if at least 85% of the initial players have already been eliminated (assuming 10% of the players are getting the payday, as in the example above). So many players will be so short-stacked at this point, and your chips will be so well above the average amount, that you can probably just sit and watch the desperate players take shots at each other.

If you have a chip stack that is more in the range of the current average chip stack, but well below that $10,000 target, then you will probably have to make some chips if you're going to survive the blinds and antes. You should be looking for opportunities to increase your chip stack, but the kind of aggression that is effective in the early rounds won't cut it now. There are too many desperate players for you to expect opponents with legitimate hands to fold. If you're just not getting the cards, then look for strong position shots where you can be the first player into the pot with a big raise. You're going to have to make some moves, so make them with as much power as you can. Remember the rock-paper-scissors power relationships. No formula can guarantee you success, but the rock-paper-scissors power model will at least have you making your moves when you've got the upper hand.

SINGLE TABLE SATELLITES

Single table satellites, usually played with ten entrants, typically award one seat to a bigger tournament (though some award two). When only one seat is awarded, you must beat the whole table to win anything. There is no second place prize. Because of this, you can only rarely slow down your aggression, even if you build a big stack.

If you have watched a lot of the WPT and WSOP televised final tables, you may think that optimal strategy for a single table satellite is similar to the play you have seen at these tables. It's not. At the final table of any major event, there are a lot of chips on the table. Although one or more players may be short-stacked, there will also be players with mountains of chips and all the time in the world to be selective and make moves.

Single-table satellites are also different from the single-table sit'n'gos that are so popular online, although both sit'n'gos and single-table satellites share very fast blind structures. In the sit'n'gos, there is usually a prize structure that pays first, second, and third place. This makes the sit'n'go more of a survival event than a total domination event. In a sit'n'go, the best strategy is to get into one of those last three pay positions before you crank up your all-out aggression. Sit'n'gos do provide good practice for short-handed play.

In any satellite, you will sit out many hands with bad cards and poor position, letting your opponents take aim at each other. It helps you whenever the player with the bigger chip stack knocks out the player with the smaller chip stack. But you can't win if all you do is just watch your competitors play against each other. You need to be knocking out some of those players—and collecting their chips—yourself.

Two Seats Awarded

Single-table satellites that award two seats instead of one have twice the buy-in cost but reward skillful play more than the single-seat-awarded format. They lower variance as well, and so are a better investment for skilled players than the single-seat-awarded satellite. Most satellite blind structures are so fast that by the time they're down to two players, both must play just about any cards dealt to them on every hand. The lucky cards win. Awarding the top two finishers lowers the luck factor.

When two seats are awarded, the play gets most interesting when the table gets down to the last five players, who cautiously jockey for position until each of the next three players is eliminated. The final five players all know that they have a decent shot at winning one of the two seats if they can just survive. Nobody has to win it all. You can skate in on a short stack if the other guys knock each other out.

At the same time, the short stack is the one player who has to play because he will be the first to get blinded off. So, the satellite becomes an open season on the short stack, with all players trying to knock him out and collect his chips, before going on to the next shortest stack. The bigger your stack is at this point, the less you want to get involved, unless it's a wolf-pack play where all players get involved by calling some piddling all-in bet by the short stack. Most often, it's the next-shortest stack that takes on the short stack, because if he can beat him, or even just bully him out of pots with bets that threaten his survival, then he may not be the next-shortest stack for very long.

If you are the short stack, you must make a move to pick up some chips and get on more secure ground. If you are the second shortest stack, you too must make a move, although it's safest to make a move on the short stack if you have anything less than a premium hand. If you are in any of the top three chip positions, you've got to be careful about taking shots at the truly desperate. Let the children play with each other.

The Competition Defines Your Strategy

Optimal single-table satellite strategies can change radically depending on the players at your table. With timid players who are waiting for premium hands, you should play very aggressively. A really aggressive player can grind down an entire table of opponents if they are all afraid to get involved without premium cards. Many players new to satellites play more cautiously than they do in regular tournaments because they feel so close to the money right from the start. In a multi-table tournament that will go on for hours, most players feel like they're a long way from the money for the first few hours of play. In a satellite, these players feel as if they're already at the final table. They can see every player that must go down before them, and as each player is eliminated, the feeling that "I'm almost there" is strengthened. This makes weak players get more cautious the closer they get to the money.

If you are at a table with many weak players, then you should be careful when any of these players show aggression, unless they are so desperate that they might play any hand at all. Once three or four players have been eliminated, however, the really weak will run into trouble. Many weak players know little about short-handed play, and they don't realize how costly it is to sit there waiting for a hand while the cost of the blinds is not only rising but coming around to them more frequently. So, at a table full of weak players, turn your aggression up as you get deeper and deeper into the satellite.

Single-table satellites are really not for beginners, though they are filled with beginners who flock to the satellites trying to get a cheap seat into a bigger tournament where they really don't belong. All of the principles of fast play and position play apply to satellites, but because so much single-table satellite play is short-handed, they also require real skill at reading players and situations, since so much play is done with less than premium cards.

My general rule when you're not sure what to do in any single-table satellite when you're getting short on chips is this: *go all-in.*

23

LAST-LONGER BETS—EVERYONE INTO THE POOL!

Occasionally, players in a tournament will make side bets with each other to see who will last longer. Typically, a group of two to four friends will each put up a twenty-dollar bill, and the player who is last to bust out of the tournament gets all of the twenties. I have been at tables where as many as eight out of the ten players agreed to a last-longer bet. I've also seen last-longer bets in single-table satellites.

Players who get into last-longer side bets tend to play much more conservatively than they should. Rather than thinking in terms of winning the tournament, they become overly concerned with outlasting their last-longer opponents. Because of this, if you have last-longer players at your table, it tends to be easier to push them out of pots. And they rarely take shots themselves, so when they do bet, take it seriously.

If you have a situation where half or more of the players at the table are participating in a last-longer pool, it may be worth the $20 investment to get your money into the pool as well. Your joining the pool may encourage the few stragglers who have not yet joined to get into the pool, and give you a table full of tight and careful players. Another reason for joining the last-longer pool is that last-longer players often play even more conservatively against others in the pool, as they are particularly concerned about giving chips to a player who could beat them for their $20 side-bet as well as for the chips in the pot.

Just be sure, if you join the pool, that you do not allow the money in the pool to tighten up your play. Instead, you should loosen up and increase your aggression against your last-longer opponents.

24

BREAK OUT OF THE MOLD

This is something I learned from blackjack, and it is equally important in poker. Most blackjack players fall into one of two categories—those who have never read a decent book on the subject, and those who have, but never went beyond what they read. If you know much about blackjack, you can quickly categorize the players at your table into one of these two groups. The casino game protection personnel can do this just as easily, because the surveillance guys have all read the same books. So, if you want to become one of the few players getting rich playing casino blackjack, you have to come up with a way of playing beyond what all the books tell you to do.

In the no-limit hold'em tournaments, there is a similar situation, with most players falling into one of these same two groups. In the fast tournaments, roughly half of the players seem entirely clueless, with their poker education having come primarily from TV, while most of the rest of the players all seem to have read the same books.

With the clueless players, fancy poker will not be very effective. They do not understand position, and they can't read the board well enough to feel threatened if you represent a hand. So, there's no use taking shots at them. You pretty much have to wait and let them beat themselves. These really poor players rarely make it past the halfway point of a tournament. Play your premium hands against them when you have the cards, and watch as their chips slowly get divvied up among everyone else.

There's a lot more money to be made from the players who have all read the same books. Although these better players differ from each other in degrees of aggression and looseness, the difference for most of them is a matter of style, not substance. Essentially, they play the same. A raise from early position means a very strong hand—a high pocket pair or A-K. Limping into an unraised pot means a small pair or medium suited connectors. You don't have to be much of a reader of players to tell what they have. If an ace comes down on the flop and he bets, you know he has an ace. If the ace comes down and he doesn't bet, you know he doesn't have it, unless he's slowplaying a set of aces, or a set of anything, which you will figure out as soon as he check-raises.

One "truth" to which these players adhere, and which is spouted in book after book on the game, is that it takes a stronger hand to call a raise than it takes to make a raise. In limit hold'em games, this is generally true. Raisers, and especially raisers in early position, do tend to have strong hands, and you're unlikely to get rid of them with fancy play. In the fast no-limit hold'em tournaments, however, nothing could be further from the truth.

In the fast tournaments, the actual rule to remember if you want to get into the money is: "It takes a stronger *position* to call a raise." Remember, in a fast tournament, position is generally stronger than cards. If you are up against a solid poker player, one who has read all the books and generally plays legitimate hands accordingly, he will be very concerned if you call his preflop raise. He will automatically assume you must have a medium to high pair, or else A-K, or maybe A-Q suited, simply because he knows that "it takes a strong hand to call a raise." He does not understand that all you really need to call his normal raise is a seat to his left. Your seat is stronger than his hand. Now, if he raised with pocket aces, he may be giddy with excitement to get your call. But most of the time, it's not aces. If he raised with kings, he may be similarly excited, but that will be a short-lived excitement if an ace comes down on the flop.

Players who are used to limit games have no comprehension of the power of position or chips in no-limit tournaments. The rock-paper-scissors power relationship is not in their consciousness at all. To these players, paper is the most important factor in the game, and they evaluate every move you make based on what they think your cards are.

If you practice playing position in the dark as described in the chapter on position strategy, you will often find it hard to avoid cracking a smile. Here's what will happen: an early raiser whom you called from the button will check on the flop. You will then bet half the size of the pot. He will then spend a god-awful amount of time staring at you, trying to pick up information on what your hand is. But you don't even know what your hand is. Every time this happens, you will be struggling desperately to keep a straight face.

What you're really doing when you use the rock-paper-scissors betting model is finding reasons to bet that have nothing to do with your cards, reasons beyond the mental world of many players who have read all the books, or who are coming from a limit hold'em, non-tournament background.

You should never stop looking for ways to bet or play your hands in unconventional ways. Use the rock-paper-scissors model simply to determine who has the power, and be creative with your approaches.

Here's a simple example of how a postflop position play works:

A player in middle position makes a standard raise before the flop. On the button, with no other callers in the pot, you call. Your cards are trash. You have nothing except position. Both blinds fold. The flop comes down with a king and two rags. He bets half the size of the pot. You reraise the minimum allowed. He throws away his hand in disgust.

To an experienced player, a postflop bet of half the size of the pot is a meaningless bet. Sooner or later, many hold'em players learn that a player should not give up the lead if he was the preflop raiser. And it's true that this is smart play. If I am the preflop raiser, I bet after the flop. It's just standard. A player who keeps the lead in a case like this is betting that the king did not hit you, and that his queens, jacks, A-Q or whatever he has is still the best hand. This is generally a pretty good assumption, and most preflop callers who have hands like A-J, pocket 9s, or whatever, will immediately fold to that bet on that flop.

Your raise on the flop from the button, however, isn't based on your having a king. It's based on your bet that this player is simply keeping the lead in the hand, which is more likely than his having a king. He might have raised preflop with A-Q, J-10 suited, any big or medium pocket pair, or he may be just taking a shot with trash himself. Mathematically, the greatest likelihood is that he has no king, and his postflop bet is just a standard hold'em keep-the-lead bet. So, the mathematically correct play for you in this situation is to raise.

This is not to say that you should make this move every time an out-of-position player bets after the flop. I don't. I may fold, based on my feeling for the specific player and the specific flop. I may even call, hoping to get another keep-the-lead bet out of him on the turn before I raise. I don't know of any foolproof formula for always making the right move in this situation. It's just something you'll get better at the more you play.

Now, if this opponent reraises my raise, I'm generally out of there. But that is a hell of a gutsy move if he doesn't have at least a king in his hand or better. You'll soon learn from the chips you'll earn with these plays that few competitors in these fast tournaments can read players well enough to play back at you. These postflop steals are where a sizable amount of your final table chips will come from. You don't bet on your own luck, you bet against the other guy's luck. Ironically, in a fast no-limit tournament, nothing is less lucky than to be dealt good cards in a bad position.

Position steals are even stronger if you have both position and a big chip stack. In fact, the best way to make the most on a position steal is when the early raiser also has a big chip stack. You will be the one guy at the table he doesn't want to mess with. The best way to get the most out of this type of player is to call-call-call, then move in. You can take half of his chip stack on this play.

Preflop, you call his raise. On the flop, you call his bet. On the turn, you call again. On the river, if he checks, you push all-in. And if he makes a standard bet, say up to the size of the pot, you push all-in.

On the river, if he makes a bet that will pot-commit him (more than half his chips), or he pushes all-in on you, too bad. You just lost a lot of your chips. Either he has the nuts, and his small bets were simply designed to milk you, or he put you on some draw that he decided you didn't hit, or he read you like a book, didn't believe your calls, and decided to punish you. Of course, the worst punishment would be for him to let you go all-in, and then call your bluff.

But in these fast tournaments, you just don't bump into many players this sophisticated. When you do, you'll remember them, and you can file them under dangerous for future tournaments. The most talented and experienced tournament pros actually do get reads on their opponents, make their position steals only when the play will work, and recognize position steals when opponents are trying to pull one on them. In a long, slow tournament, you may need this ability to read to last through days of play in which you must multiply your chip stack fifty times or more to get to the final table.

HOW TO BREAK OUT OF THE MOLD

In order to break out of the mold, you must know what the mold is. Start by reading the major authors on limit hold'em strategies as played in ring games, not tournaments. Really study these books.

Then put in a couple hundred hours or so at the low-limit ring games, either online or in your favorite poker room. I did. If you're used to the excitement of tournament play, it's like watching paint dry. But if you go through the trouble of actually playing the limit strategies recommended by the experts, you'll start to recognize why many of the tournament players you find in the fast tournaments seem to be playing the same way.

Watch how they "define" their hands with their bets in the limit games. They do the same thing in tournaments. Watch how the better ones "keep the lead" if they come in as the preflop raiser. They do this in tournaments, too, but usually with bets so small that they're defining their hands again when they do it! Once you start to recognize the standard low-limit hold'em mold, you can use aggression to trounce the players who fit into that pattern.

Be creative and brave. You will sometimes lose a lot of chips on the postflop plays you invent to steal pots from players who play by the book, but far more often, you'll make a lot of chips with a trash hand. Again, in the fast tournaments, you must make a lot of chips with trash hands because the scarce premium hands just cannot be depended upon. You have nothing to fear but the nuts.

25

THE LUCK FACTOR

In any tournament, you have to multiply your chip stack many times in order to get to the final table. There is no way that any player can expect to be dealt enough premium hands to win the number of double-ups necessary. So, how do you make the chips you need when you know you can't possibly expect to be dealt enough lucky cards? I'll tell you how. By betting that nobody else can be that lucky either.

WHAT IT TAKES TO MAKE THE FINAL TABLE

Let's look at a typical fast tournament that takes about 4 1/2 hours to reach the final table. Let's assume $1,300 in starting chips and a field of 200 players. For simplicity, we'll assume there are no antes, but otherwise a standard blind structure, with blinds increasing every twenty minutes. This chart shows the costs of the blinds at each level in this tournament:

	Blinds	Cost
Level 1:	$10-$15	$25
Level 2:	$10-$20	$30
Level 3:	$15-$30	$45
Level 4:	$25-$50	$75
Level 5:	$50-$100	$150
Level 6:	$75-$150	$225
Level 7:	$100-$200	$300
Level 8:	$150-$300	$450
Level 9:	$200-$400	$600
Level 10:	$300-$600	$900
Level 11:	$400-$800	$1,200
Level 12:	$500-$1,000	$1,500
Level 13:	$750-$1,500	$2,250
Total cost of blinds:		**$7,760**

Note that if you earned five times your initial chip stack ($1,300), you'd have $6,500 in chips, enough to get you through Level 12, but not Level 13. You might also note that the final table in this tournament will have a total of $260,000 in chips on it ($1,300 x 200), which means the average player at the final table will have $26,000 in chips—twenty times his starting chips. Any player at the final table with $26,000 in chips, however, will have to have won even more than this over the course of the tournament, as he will have had to pay the $7,760 in blind costs in addition to whatever chips he currently holds. That means that to have just an average chip stack when you arrive at this final table, you will have to have multiplied your starting chip stack roughly twenty-six times in 4 1/2 hours.

It's true that it's not necessary to arrive at the final table with $26,000 in chips, and half or more of the players at the final table will have less than this amount. But if you arrive at the final table with a stack well below the average of your competition, you will arrive as an underdog. Depending on exactly how short-stacked you are, you may find it difficult to steal at all, and you'll be a target for the bigger chip stacks.

HOW WILL YOU EARN CHIPS FOR THE FINAL TABLE?

In any case, if you are attempting to multiply your initial chip stack of $1,300 a minimum of twenty-six times in the course of a few hours of play, during which time you can expect to be dealt only half a dozen or so premium starting hands, how do you accomplish this?

Here's my breakdown on where your chips will come from if you make the final table in a fast no-limit tournament:

Preflop shots at limpers, blinds, and antes:	20%
Actual strong hands (preflop and postflop):	40%
Postflop position steals:	40%

These numbers are approximate and are based on my estimations from personal experience in fast tournaments. In longer, slower tournaments, the percentage of chips won based on actual strong hands is probably greater, as more starting chips and slower blind structures allow players to both see more flops and be more patient and selective in the hands they play, especially in the early stages of the tournament.

But I want to emphasize that every one of these factors is important. That 20% you make from preflop steals keeps your chip stack competitive during card droughts. In a tournament that takes four to five hours to reach the final table, just about every player will go through card droughts where virtually no playable hands arrive for periods of time ranging from half an hour to a couple of hours or more. During such droughts, it is absolutely essential that you take shots at the blinds regularly to avoid getting dangerously short-stacked. Those blind costs keep accelerating, and you do not have the luxury of waiting for good cards to play.

On your way to the final table, only about 40% of the chips you acquire will come from strong hands that hold up. In fact, when you fail to make it into the money, in almost every case you will go out on a strong hand, where you get your money all-in as a strong favorite, but then get sucked out on. That's poker. I have thought many times that if I could simply throw away all of my good hands, and restrict my play to stealing pots with trash hands, I'd get a lot further a lot more often. Unfortunately, you cannot afford to give up 40% of your potential chip earnings just to keep out of trouble. You might, in fact, make it into the money more often, but you would always arrive as the short stack, and your only shot at any real money would be extremely lucky cards at the end. The pots you win with your good hands will be crucial in determining your chip position at the final table.

The other 40% of the chips you earn on your way to the final table will come from postflop position steals. I have made it to a number of final tables in fast tournaments without ever having had a legitimate postflop hand, and without ever having shown down my cards. In fact, if I make a final table, I will only rarely have shown down more than one or two hands in the prior hours of play.

In a long, slow tournament, this would be impossible. But in four to five hours of play, you can easily have four to five hours of bad cards. Again, the key to getting to final tables in fast tournaments, despite your lousy cards, is to realize that every other player's card luck is, on average, just as bad as yours.

LUCK, STRATEGY, AND THE FINAL TABLE

When many players first start playing tournaments, they think that if they can just get dealt a few really good hands, and hit a few monster flops, that they'd have a real shot at making it into the money. But this is not the way to think of the luck factor in a fast tournament. Can you imagine entering any non-tournament ring game with a total of $1,300, and a plan to turn it into $25,000 after four hours of play? How often do you really think you'll get cards good enough to achieve this result?

Here's how to think about the luck factor:

When a dealer deals both you and your opponent two cards face down, would you be more willing to bet before either of you have looked at your cards that you have a premium starting hand, or that your opponent does not have a premium starting hand? We all know which bet is going to win more often.

You might argue that this isn't the same thing as betting against the existence of a premium hand among nine other randomly dealt hands at your table, and I agree. So, let me give you a great starting hand, say pocket queens—a hand that appears only once every 221 hands—and then deal five community cards onto the table. What are the chances that after the five community cards are on the board, you will still feel so comfortable with your queens that you would put your entire tournament on the line with them? If there are three to a flush or straight on board, this would be a huge decision. A single ace or king on the table would have you folding your queens without any hesitation. Any pair on the board, say 8s, would look dangerous because your queens may be up against trips, or worse.

Every premium starting hand will more often than not shrink

in value by the time the river card comes down. That's just a fact. Rarely will any player hold the nuts. So, instead of waiting for the luck of good cards to bet, bet *against* your opponents' luck.

In a fast tournament, if you can make just one postflop position steal when there are a lot of chips in the pot—especially a couple of hours into the tournament when short-stacked players are dropping like flies—that one play can be worth a dozen or more blind steals. It's always good to try to get a read on an opponent before you make your move. It's especially helpful to look for tight players with weak, hesitant postflop bets. But you don't have to be any great reader of players. Just play the math. Bet on the river that your opponent doesn't have the nuts, or even close to the nuts, and that he won't jeopardize a decent chip stack this far into the tournament.

Instead of entering a tournament hoping that you'll get lucky cards, enter with the hope that your opponents will get lucky cards when you've got position on them. Lucky cards will get their money into the pot; your position will get the pot into your stack. That's how you get to the final table.

26

CHEATING AND "SEMI-CHEATING"

There are a thousand ways to cheat at poker, including all of the classic card-cheating moves—from daubing or bending cards, to slipping in a pre-arranged cold deck, to working in collusion with the dealer, to false shuffling, stacking the deck, and delivering losing hands to unsuspecting marks. Most of these classic techniques, however, are more easily pulled off in private games. And although many of these techniques have been used in major casino poker rooms, they are not highly effective in tournament play, where players have little control over which house dealer is assigned to their table, which decks of cards will be used, and which players will be seated where in the tournament. So, I'm not going to waste much ink on the classic poker cheating scams.

If you play in big money games, and especially if you play in private games, I'd advise you to invest in a 2-DVD set by Sal Piacente titled *Poker Cheats Exposed*. Sal's new DVDs show many of the classic techniques and include a lot of moves I haven't seen demonstrated before. Also highly recommended, many of the classic poker cheating moves are described in detail in a new book by Steve Forte, *Poker Protection: Cheating... and the World of Poker*.

What this chapter will cover are the specific types of cheating found in today's casino poker room tournaments, because many types of tournament cheating are different from the classic card manipulation moves.

COLLUSION WITH OTHER PLAYERS

One common type of cheating in poker tournaments is **collusion** between two or more players who share information about their hands via secret signals. Because poker is a game based on trickery and deception, some players apparently feel that any type of deception is fair. To them, it's all poker. So, let me point out that collusion is wrong. It is cheating. It is not poker, but a form of theft.

Most players who attempt collusion cannot beat poker with skill. Thankfully, they are often just as bad at crime as they are at poker.

How Does Collusion Work?

Two players working in collusion attempt to steal pots by raising and reraising each other to get opponents with legitimate but marginal hands to fold. Usually, one player will have a strong, or at least playable, hand, while the other will be in the pot simply to jack up the bets to the point where everyone else folds.

Once the competition is gone, the weak hand folds to a raise, and the strong hand picks up the pot. The strong hand, assuming it is strong enough to warrant the aggressive play, can also voluntarily show his cards at this point to make his play look good. If the strong hand is truly a monster, the weak hand can stay in the pot for the purpose of building the pot to keep other players in it. For example, he can throw in calls to give marginal hands the incentive to stay in the pot. And if other players are aggressively betting, or are obviously not going to go away because they have so much already committed to the pot, the weak hand can go into the raising/reraising routine with the monster hand to suck in even more bets. The only important thing the weak hand must do in order to pull off this scam is refrain from showing down the cards he was playing.

And there are other advantages to collusion. Just knowing two other cards that are not available to be dealt is an advantage. If I am dealt an A-J and my partner has a J-8, I know that the value of my jack is greatly diminished. If I've got pocket sevens, and my partner has a J-7, I'll throw my sevens away before the flop since my chance of flopping a set has been cut in half.

If both colluding players have strong hands, the weaker hand can fold if another player is aggressively contesting the pot. The colluders will not give a third party any chance to beat both of them. For example, if I'm holding A-K, and my partner has A-Q, and an ace comes down on the flop, the A-Q will fold fast. If my aces get beat because an opponent shows down a set, that opponent will get my money, but not my partner's. In an honest game, the A-Q might not fold, and the winner might get twice what he got from me.

Many of these types of collusion plays are more effective in low-limit ring games than they are in tournaments, and they are especially strong in short-handed play where two or three colluders can work together to take off a single mark. One problem tournament formats present to colluders is the fixed number of chips each player in a tournament has at his disposal—and this is especially true in a fast tournament where players do not start with large chip stacks. Following are ways that colluders adjust their scam for tournaments.

Chip Dumping

The most common method of player collusion I've seen in fast no-limit tournaments is **chip dumping**. Two or more players who have an agreement to share tournament wins and losses play against each other very aggressively, with the goal of having one player end up with all of their chips. Simply, Player A dumps his chips to Player B.

Chip dumping can occur at any point in a tournament. It can happen at the first table when the tournament begins, and it can happen at the final table. In tournaments where players who are colluding in this way are assigned to different tables, there is simply an agreement to pull off the move if and when they get to the same table. In many of the small buy-in tournaments, this is not a problem. Players are often allowed to choose their starting table and seat, so colluders can simply pick seats at the same table. Even if seats are assigned in the tournament, there is still a good chance that colluders will get together at some point in the tournament, as many of these small buy-in tournaments have very small fields— often ten or fewer tables.

Many players believe, erroneously, that players on the same team might cheat by soft-playing each other. Not true. Soft-playing is what husbands and wives, or good friends (amateurs), do with each other when they play at the same table—checking instead of betting, giving up a pot instead of playing back with a legitimate hand. You frequently see this type of play in small stakes limit games. But in a no-limit tournament, it usually wouldn't make sense for a cheater to soft-play a cohort. The value is in the opposite approach—playing much harder against your teammate for the purpose of getting all of your chips into one stack.

Some poker rooms make it too easy for colluders to cheat in this way in the small buy-in tournaments. Allowing players to pick their tables and seats is a poor policy. Even worse is a policy that allows players who go all-in against each other to not turn up their cards, even when there are no other hands in action on the table. When players must display their hands for all-in pots, when no further action is possible, a chip-dumping team will at least have to find dumping opportunities where both players' all-in actions appear to make sense. With no requirement to show hands, the dumping is harder to detect. After the river card is dealt, the player with the legitimate hand turns over his cards, but all the dumper has to do is quickly muck his hand.

Because many experienced players will ask the dealer to show the mucked cards, chip dumping teams will have the player with the trash cards make the all-in move, and the player with the legitimate strong hand call the all-in. This way, if the bad hand gets displayed, it will simply look like the all-in raiser was making a move on the pot, hoping to steal it without a call.

Can anything be done about chip dumping? I doubt it. It would help if all poker rooms required all-in hands to be displayed when the action was completed. It would help if players were randomly assigned their tables and seats upon sign-up. But many small buy-in tournaments are not taken very seriously by the tournament directors. They see the participants as amateur locals and tourists who like to sit with their buddies and girlfriends in a social setting. They're simply trying to attract a crowd, not turn away potential players who are mainly looking for fun.

And even with more careful policies, the most talented chip

dumpers would not be deterred. Rather than dumping all of their chips to a cohort on a single all-in play, they could simply dump them on a series of plays, without ever going all-in, to avoid tough questions. Even when you see it—and I've seen it a number of times—how can you prove it?

Final Table Dumping

Cheats can get the most value out of chip-dumping from dumping chips at a final table. If two teammates are, say, 8th and 9th in chips when they arrive at the final table, and dumping can get one of them into 3rd or 4th place in chips—and in serious contention for first place—that is an enormously profitable play, because tournament prize money is heavily skewed toward the top-end finishers.

At a final table, soft-playing by two teammates might make sense if both players are very well situated to win, or at least finish in two of the top four places. But even at a final table, chip-dumping is by far the more profitable cheating move for players who own a piece of each other's results, unless both players are inordinately well-stacked.

I don't think there will ever be a way to stop poker players from forming team banks. Nor do I think that team banks should be disallowed. With the huge buy-in costs of the major no-limit tournaments today, and the enormous playing fields that make it a long shot for even the best players to make it to a final table, many of the top players do have prize-sharing arrangements with other pros. It's the only way to survive. Players in small buy-in tournaments do the same thing. Most players who own percentages of each other, or who are playing on team bankrolls, are simply trying to ride out negative fluctuations, not dump chips or find partners for collusion schemes. Pro gamblers have been making these types of agreements forever. It's an intelligent response to a very risky business.

But if two players who own a percentage of each other should wind up at a final table together, might not the player with the short stack feel better if he lost his chips to his teammate, as opposed to some other player at the table? Even without a prearranged chip-dumping plan, won't his natural instincts as a gambler tell him that this would be the advantage play?

Chip Passing

Two cheaters who are not at the same table can practice a variation of chip dumping in which one player surreptitiously removes some of his high-denomination chips from the table and passes them to his cohort during a scheduled break. Players have been accused of this type of chip dumping even in the big money tournaments, and it is very difficult to stop. In the major tournaments that last many hours or even days, players need only wait to palm chips until their table is being broken, or they are being moved to a new table where their opponents do not know what their chip stack looked like just moments before. The removal of chips from one player's stack, the passing to his cohort, and the addition of the chips to the cohort's stack may be hours apart.

In the fast small buy-in tournaments, players don't have this luxury of time, and that is why they sometimes get caught. In a tournament that lasts only five hours, the value of chips removed two hours earlier will have been diminished too much by the rising blinds. So, in the small buy-in tournaments, some cheats don't even wait for scheduled breaks to make this move. One player simply exits his table for a restroom stop or smoke break, and his partner at a different table follows him. If there are sharp players at the table of the player who pocketed chips from his stack, they will quickly inform the dealer that the absent player's stack is missing chips, and the tournament director will be called over before the player even gets to the restroom. I have several times seen players caught red-handed, with tournament chips in their pockets, attempting this ploy.

Auto-Dumping

Finally, I know of one player who has been caught in more than one Las Vegas poker room dumping chips to himself! He was removing high-denomination chips from one tournament, then bringing them into play in a different tournament. In some cases, he was reportedly buying the chips in a rebuy tournament where the chips were sold at a discount, then bringing them into other tournaments where the cost of chips was higher, most frequently when he appeared to have a good shot at the money. He was first caught doing this at a casino poker room downtown. They called a few of the other Vegas poker rooms where he was also known to play in tournaments, and one of the alerted poker rooms then caught him doing the same thing in their tournaments!

To show you how lightly the poker rooms take misconduct at the small buy-in tournaments, the player's penalty for this scam—and he was caught red-handed—was temporary suspension from playing tournaments at the two casinos where he was caught. His penalty time is now up, and he is back in the tournaments at these same poker rooms after having had his hand slapped.

CARD SWITCHING

Some cheaters are so brazen that they will actually steal a card by mucking only one of their hole cards, then bring it back into play later when they need it—often much later in the tournament and at a different table! I have been at tables where two cards of the same denomination and suit have suddenly appeared on the table. And I have seen another table where a dealer who was counting down the cards just after a table was broken came up short one card, and of course, the missing card turned out to be an ace. All the players at that table had already been sent to new tables. I only knew about it because it occurred at the table next to mine and I heard the dealer reporting the missing card to the tournament director.

Another player at my table who saw this same interaction told me later that he'd asked the tournament director whether the players from that table shouldn't be searched to find the player who had stolen the card. The tournament director said something like, "I don't have the authority to do that. I can't get ten security guards in here to escort all of the players from that table off the floor where we can conduct full-body searches. I can't stop the tournament for a few hours while this is going on. The casino manager would have to call Gaming Control for authorization to hold and search these players, and Gaming would probably tell us that we can't search ten players because one of the ten might have stolen a card from a table. I'll ask surveillance to look at the videos from that table to see if we can see who stole it. Or maybe we'll see where that ace shows up later, and we can identify one of the players from that table. But there's a good chance that whoever stole that card will be too scared to play it at another table, and we'll never see it again. He'll have a souvenir, that's all."

Professional poker cheats who specialize in mucking cards in and out of games never try to muck a card out of one deck and into a different deck. What they do is steal a card on one hand, then sneak it back into the same game when they need it, while the same deck is in play. This way, there is never a problem with a missing card, unless the dealer decides to count down the cards while the cheat has the stolen card in his possession, in which case that card will quickly find its way onto the floor beneath the table. More importantly, there will never be a problem with two cards of the same suit and denomination showing up on a hand. But small buy-in tournaments attract a lot of amateurs, and the cheating in these tournaments is amateurish as well.

Technically, cheating at gambling is a felony in the state of Nevada and carries a one-year minimum sentence for anyone so convicted. Personally, I'd like to see the penalty imposed. If a player is caught stealing chips from a casino blackjack game, you can be sure he won't just be temporarily suspended from the casino games, then invited back. Likewise, if an ace disappears from a deck of cards at a blackjack table, this will be taken very seriously by the casino's game protection personnel. Stealing money from other players, however, especially in the low stakes tournaments, is simply not viewed with the same concern as stealing from the casino itself.

REBUY DUMPING, OR SEMI-CHEATING

In unlimited rebuy tournaments, one of the most common and blatant chip-dumping techniques is the maniac group play. Two or more players will continually go all-in against each other before the flop, even when neither of them has a legitimate starting hand, and sometimes even in the dark. The player or players who bust out simply buy more chips, and keep making the same move. In some cases, these players will even announce what they are doing.

This type of team rebuy dumping can be very profitable in small buy-in tournaments because rebuy chips are often sold at a discount, and may also provide more chips than the initial buy-in amount. These tournaments usually require a player to be below his initial buy-in amount in order to make the rebuy. By continually going all-in against each other, rebuyers are dumping chips to players who are not technically eligible to rebuy. Rebuy dumpers can amass monster chip stacks for one or more of their group very cheaply. The strategy works well because, no matter how bad the dumpers' hands are, they are simply buying cheap chips for each other whenever they are the only players in the pot.

I've never seen this topic covered in any other tournament book, but I have seen numerous irritated players complain to tournament directors about players who are doing this. "They just keep going all-in against each other. Every hand. They're not even looking at their cards!" Tournament directors generally shrug it off. "What can I do about it? They're not breaking any rules."

Since rebuy dumpers are open about what they are doing, and since poker room directors can see what's going on but make no move to stop the chip dumping—and I'm not sure how they could stop it even if they wanted to—rebuy dumping is not really cheating. I label it "semi-cheating" because, although it may not violate tournament regulations in many poker rooms, it violates the spirit of the game. Poker is not a team sport. There should not be agreements between players, whether open or secret, to play or bet in pre-determined ways.

In a perfect world, there would be enforceable rules against rebuy dumping—and every other type of chip dumping. But in a no-limit tournament where a big part of the legitimate strategy is taking shots on bluffs, and where players are allowed to play like maniacs, betting in the dark, going all-in on trash, how could you enforce such rules?

So, rebuy dumping is simply an aggressive advantage play, unethical in terms of normal poker ethics, but not illegal. Players in major tournaments never have to worry about this tactic because the big money tournaments rarely have rebuy periods, and if they do, the rebuy chips are usually not discounted as they are in the small buy-in tournaments. You don't really need discounted chips to make the strategy work if you are a skilled player, but paying multiple full buy-in costs will vastly decrease the value of the move.

One thing you can do if you have rebuy dumpers at your table is play against them exactly as you would against rebuy maniacs (who are discussed in Chapter 10 on rebuy strategies) by calling their all-ins yourself with your better-than-average hands. As mentioned in the rebuy chapter, these hands are: any ace, any king, any queen with a kicker of 8 or higher, any J-10 or J-9, any suited connectors down to 8-7, and any pair. If you call rebuy dumpers down with these hands, you'll usually make a good profit during this rebuy period. You will have to rebuy more often than you normally would during a rebuy period, but the chips are cheap. Rebuy dumping is so common in small buy-in tournaments, and so blatant, that many of the tournament regulars figure it out and quickly respond with this defense.

I once played in a $40 buy-in, unlimited-rebuy tournament at Orleans where all of the players at one table had agreed in advance to go all-in on every hand. By the end of the one-hour rebuy period, the table had made a total of 113 $20 rebuys. In fact, the tournament director announced that this table had set a record at Orleans for the number of rebuys made by a single table. That comes to an average of about 11 rebuys per player, leaving the average chip stack at that table more than three times the size of the average chip stack at any other table, since at the other tables the average number of rebuys was approximately 3.5 per player.

But, were the rebuy chips purchased by the players at this table worth the price? This table paid more than $2,600 in buy-in and rebuy costs for a $40 buy-in tournament.

I busted out early and didn't stick around. One of the players who had participated in the rebuy dumping at that table—but didn't make it to the final table—told me later that the players at that table had no agreement to share profits and losses. Their only agreement was to go all-in on every hand during the rebuy period.

He said that three of the players from that table did make it to the final table, but he didn't know where they finished in the money.

If these three players all finished in the bottom five positions, they would not have made $2,600 between them to even cover the actual cost of the chips, though they might individually have profited a small amount since they were not sharing their wins. With middle position finishes, they might have had a break even play. If one of them finished first or second, then their rebuy dumping strategy paid off. Second place paid somewhere around $3,000.

In any case, if you have rebuy dumpers at your table, be prepared to make a few extra rebuys yourself. It will be worth it. The dumpers should set you up pretty well in chips by the end of the rebuy period. And before you get irritated with the dumpers, think of it this way: if a few smarter players, who may not be among the world's top poker players but have more savvy than the tourists, realize there's a way to "buy" a seat at the final table with a legal rebuy strategy, then I say more power to them. We're all in this for the money, aren't we? Believe me, if you call the dumpers down with better-than-average hands as defined above, you will make money in the long run from rebuy dumpers, so don't let them irk you. Any players who use this strategy against them will profit. So, take advantage of the rebuy dumpers whenever they appear at your table. Let them buy you some chips.

CHEATING ONLINE

There are two types of cheating that online poker players most worry about. One is play by bots, or computer software programmed to play the hands. Bots were never a concern in live poker rooms because they were never a possibility, and there is some debate over whether bots really qualify as cheating online. The other is collusion between two or more players who share information about their hands via telephone or private online messages. Collusion has always been a problem in live poker games, where colluders use secret signals to transfer information, and it's the same problem in the online games. Everyone acknowledges that collusion is cheating, but how dangerous is it, and what can be done about it?

Bots

There are two types of bots that may be of concern to online players. The first is a program designed to play a human player's hands automatically, without the knowledge or involvement of the other players at the table or the online poker room. The second type is a program employed by the poker room itself, which gives the appearance that all players at the table are human. In this case, the bot would be playing with the house's money against whatever real players are at the table.

I haven't heard much discussion of bots being used in online tournaments except in the single-table sit'n'gos. Even so, I don't think most players who are skillful enough to make money themselves should be highly concerned about such bots. Most skilled players would find it hard to believe that a computer program could beat them. Furthermore, many professional online players would acknowledge that their own online play—when carried out on four or more simultaneous tables, sometimes using multiple computer monitors—is not a whole lot different from what a bot might be programmed to do. This type of assembly line play precludes much attention to individual players at the tables, other than the players' prior actions on the current hand. The pros who employ multi-table tactics simply make their decisions on their hands according to a formula based on their cards, their position, the prior action on the round, etc.

More on the Human Bots

The Internet has provided a way for many skillful poker players to go from hobby level to full-time pro, even on a relatively small starting bankroll. A $10/$20 limit player who is capable of earning $10,000 per year in the live casino poker rooms really can't afford to quit his job and play poker full-time. If this same $10/$20 player moves his game online, however, he'll often find that he can earn $12,000-$15,000 annually. He'll lose the part of his win rate that he was getting from his ability to read his opponents' body language, but this loss is more than made up for by the speed of the games online, the savings on tips to dealers, the lower house rake, and the easy home access to play at all hours. He's simply able to play more hours per week, at a faster clip, and with lower expenses.

As soon as this player discovers that he can play two tables simultaneously almost as easily as one, then four tables almost as easily as two, his day job is likely to start taking a back seat to his poker play. Without increasing his strategic skills one iota, he's seen his game go from a potential $10,000 per year income—that he couldn't afford to quit his job to realize—to a real $50,000-$60,000+ in earnings per year.

The only online tournament players I know who use this multi-table approach use it in the single-table sit'n'gos. These tournaments are fast to get into, and very similar to each other, and generally compatible with formulaic play based on cards, position, action on a round, and the number of remaining players.

Personally, I have no moral objection to any player creating a bot to play and using his bot in the public online poker rooms. I admire such players for their ingenuity. Unskilled players have to learn to play poker, and whether they are schooled in the fundamentals by a bot or a human who plays like a bot makes very little difference. The lessons cost the same.

There are popular commercially available poker simulation software programs that essentially are nothing but a collection of poker bots that you can play against on your home computer. There are dozens of different cyber-players, from which you can choose your opponents, all set to play with varying degrees of skill and with varying degrees of aggression or passivity, looseness or tightness in starting hand selection, and so on.

If you practice with one of these programs, it's soon easy to beat these players. You know which players are tight, loose, or passive, which players try to steal pots, and which ones will call you down. No matter how good they are, they're predictable. And, frankly, these bots aren't very good players.

I think the main worry over players using bots is that as artificial intelligence advances, the bots may be able to beat more and more players at ever-higher levels, and gambling conglomerates may start to maintain armies of bots to get rich in the online poker rooms.

Should this occur, online poker as we know it may disappear. These bots could be used cheaply to dominate tables even at low-stakes levels. So, despite the fact that I would not categorize a player using a bot in the current Internet environment as immoral, I know professional gamblers well enough to dislike this trend.

But I definitely have moral objections to any poker room's use of bots to beat its own customers. Poker strategies are largely based on deception. Every player at every table employs deception and expects deception from his opponents. That's the game.

But whether online or live, this battle of liars must take place on a level playing field. That means that the information available in the poker room itself—from the dealers, the cards, the rules and procedures, the shuffle, everything—must be equally available for all players. If an online poker room can rationalize representing its own bots as human players, then why not have the bots electronically peek at the players' cards?

The poker room itself is never supposed to be part of the deception of the game in any way. Everything the poker room does must be above board. Think of how easy it would be for a poker room to devise a bot to beat its own players, even if the bot didn't peek at players' cards. The poker room has the hand histories of every player at its tables. Any poker room that would use its own bots to play hands, unless it purposely designed stupid bots that would lose, is not a poker room but a sting operation.

Collusion Online

During the five weeks of the 2005 WSOP, which was held mostly at the Rio in Las Vegas, the Palms across the street ran excellent daily $230 tournaments at noon. I was sitting at one of their tournament tables waiting for the tournament to begin, and the subject of online play came up. One player said he would never play online for any serious amount of money because it's too easy for players to collude with each other.

Another player said he didn't worry about that because the online poker rooms all have software for detecting collusion between players at the same table. The first player said, well, he and his buddies never got caught when they did it!

Then, a third player piped in and said he'd done it as well with some of his friends, but they had never been able to make any money with it!

So, far be it from me to tell you there's no collusion happening online. If two players sitting at a live poker table would discuss it so cavalierly in front of strangers, I suspect it's been tried a lot.

But, let me point out once more that collusion is wrong. It is cheating. It is not poker, but an attempt at theft.

It is much easier for players to collude online than it is for them to collude in live games. In live games, they need finesse and subtle signals and timing and no small amount of nerve. Online, two players can be on the phone with each other telling each other exactly what their cards are every hand. That doesn't take a lot of finesse.

But the online games also make it easier for colluding players to be caught after the fact. In a live game, once those cards hit the muck, everything about a hand is lost, except for what any players may remember. Online, there is no muck. The poker room has a history of every hand, with every card every player was dealt and every action on every game.

If you suspect collusion between two players, you can contact the poker room management and ask to have the hand histories reviewed. And collusion is not difficult to detect if you can see all of the hands.

How Does Online Collusion Work?

Online collusion works exactly the same as collusion in live games, except that telephone communication or instant messaging online between the colluders makes the scam a lot easier to pull off. Most collusion online would occur in the ring games, not the tournaments, though some colluders might work in the single-table sit'n'gos.

Most of the scams that colluders pull in the live games, from sharing card information, to jacking up pots then pushing others out with aggressive bets, to chip dumping schemes, can be done online as well. The only types of scams colluders do in live games that cannot be done online are dealer-player collusion schemes and in tournaments, any type of chip passing that might occur off the table.

Multi-Accounting

One form of online collusion that has occurred, even in the biggest and most popular poker rooms, is what the poker rooms call "multi-accounting." This is a single player who opens multiple accounts under different names for the purpose of entering all of his identities in the same tournament. In a sense, he can then collude with himself if two or more of his identities get to the same table. Again, this type of cheating would be stronger in ring games or single-table satellites, but players have been caught doing this online in bigger multi-table tournaments.

Those who get caught tend to be the dumb ones who don't really know how to disguise themselves technologically. They play their identities through the same computer, or enter their different identities through the same IP address, or set up phony accounts in some way that can be traced and exposed. I doubt there is any way that the online poker rooms can protect themselves from the smarter cheats who know how to avoid these amateur mistakes other than by the same methods they use to identify colluders who have different identities.

So How Can the Online Poker Rooms Combat Collusion Schemes?

In addition to an online poker room's ability to look at complete hand histories for their games, another problem colluders face on the Internet is that the poker room can see if two players always show up together, or move together from table to table, should they ever be asked to investigate a charge of collusion.

Unfortunately, there is very little legal recourse for players who have been cheated in online collusion scams. The U.S. has no laws regulating online gambling operations, and even if they did, none of the online poker rooms are located in the U.S. I do know of one instance where a multi-account tournament player had his account frozen by the poker room, and his last tournament win—where he was exposed as having played multiple identities—was redistributed to the other players in the tournament. So, you shouldn't hesitate to report suspected collusion if you see unusual betting patterns among two or more players. But don't generally expect any result other than getting the colluders kicked out of the poker room.

27

TOURNAMENT SKILLS CHECK LIST

Blackjack card counters have it easy. There is a lot of inexpensive blackjack simulation software on the market that allows them to input any set of casino rules and conditions, then test their card counting skills while the computer tracks every mistake, and the exact cost of every mistake. It's all math. This does not necessarily mean that a card counter who can beat his computer games will be able to make money in a casino. There are other factors involved. But at least he can test whether his strategy and betting spread have a positive expectation. He can even know close to his precise advantage on the game if he can carry out what he has planned to do.

Poker, on the other hand, is a game of arguments and options. One pro might say that he would fold in a certain situation, while another might prefer to raise. A third might call on the flop and try to steal the pot on the turn. And, depending on which pros are talking, all of them can be right.

No book or poker simulation software program can provide you with the correct way to play every single hand you are dealt in a poker tournament. It's the mixture of math and psychology—and the unknown skill levels and strategies of all of the players you must compete against—that makes poker an impossible game for which to formulate a perfect strategy.

Furthermore, because of the high variance, until you have a few hundred tournaments under your belt, your win/loss results are not highly significant indicators of your skill. So, is there any way to know if you have an advantage and whether you are likely to win?

I've devised a check list to help you to evaluate your ability to beat fast no-limit hold'em tournaments. There are ten questions on the list, and you should be striving to answer "yes" to all ten questions. If you have any "no" answers, then these are the areas you should work on improving.

Skills Checklist

1. Do you raise more often than you call?
Strong players do. Weak players call more often than they raise.

2. Do you usually win pots without a showdown?
Weak players call too much and can't get away from a hand once they have money in a pot. They often have showdowns on their winning hands, even when their cards are very strong, because they play them weakly, without raising, allowing competitors to get free cards to the river. This is also one of the reasons why they get sucked out on so often.

3. When you take a shot at the pot without a legitimate hand, do you usually take it down?
Strong players know when to make a move, and they rarely get called when they do. Weak players rarely take shots until they are in desperate chip position, and often get called when they bluff into real danger.

4. When you do have a showdown, do you usually show a strong hand and win the pot?
Strong players rarely show down a hand, and when they do, it's a strong hand. Weak players show down too many poor hands.

5. Do you regularly steal the blinds and antes?
Strong players pick up the blinds like clockwork. Weak players almost never steal the blinds. They only raise if they have strong cards.

6. Do you love seeing the blinds increase?

Strong players welcome the rising blinds because it makes the pots bigger and the increased bet sizes scare the weak players. Weak players find themselves dreading the rising blinds because the cost of sitting and waiting for a strong hand has become more threatening to their chip stack.

7. Is your decision to enter a pot more often dictated by your table position and the size of your chip stack than by your cards?

Weak players are almost always playing their cards, and only their cards.

8. When you fail to get into the money, does your bust-out usually result from playing a strong hand—usually the best hand when the money went into the pot?

Weak players usually get slowly blinded off until they are desperate for chips, then bust out when forced by their chip position to play a marginal hand.

9. When you bust out, is it rarely the result of being in a desperate chip position?

Strong players start taking position shots long before they are desperate.

10. When you look back on the tournaments where you failed to get into the money, do you primarily see mistakes you made and hands that you could have played differently to win more or lose less?

Strong players mentally replay many critical hands, and focus on their mistakes. Weak players look back at lost tournaments and see nothing but bad luck.

---

* **SCORING:** Give yourself 10 points for each "yes" answer. A passing grade is 100 points. A score of 90 is a failure. Work on it.

PART FOUR:
THE MOST IMPORTANT CHAPTERS IN THIS BOOK IF YOU WANT TO MAKE MONEY

28

HOW MUCH MONEY DO YOU NEED?

As a professional gambler, the first thing I think of when I see a profitable gambling opportunity is this: How much of a bankroll do I need?

All gambling is a high-risk investment, and the risk is caused by what mathematicians call **variance**—which is essentially just a two-dollar word for luck. Even with a strong advantage, a player can go broke playing poker tournaments unless he has enough of a bankroll to ride out his inevitable negative swings.

How many times have you seen it on TV? The amateur—who's a 95% underdog on a hand—sucks out on the pro by catching the only card that can save him. That's poker. In the long run, the pro is going to make a lot of money in these situations. But he's only going to make that money if he still has a bankroll to keep playing.

You can't stop suck-outs, runs of bad cards, and bad beats. But, believe it or not, there are mathematical limits on luck, and a professional gambler can actually control his own destiny—ensuring himself of long run profits if he simply bets within the limits of his bankroll. Managing your money well will turn these miserable events into nothing but small downward blips on the ever-rising upward trend of your gambling career. Managing your money well will also maximize your return on investment.

Near the end of this chapter, you will find a convenient one-page chart that shows bankroll requirements for tournament players based on tournament buy-in costs and the number of players entered. If you don't care anything about the math or how this chart was devised, just use the chart. I am of the opinion, however, that professional gamblers should get a handle on the mathematics behind their gambling investments, so the appendix will provide information on how that chart came to be, and exactly what the numbers mean.

Coming as I do from a blackjack background, it strikes me as downright weird that charts like the one in the appendix in the back of this book do not exist in other books on poker tournaments. It's the rare blackjack book these days that doesn't provide at least some information on such topics as standard deviation, the Gambler's Ruin formula, risk-averse betting strategies, the Kelly criterion, and various related topics, in addition to simplified charts of data that card counters can use to estimate their bankroll requirements.

Most poker books, by contrast, stick to strategic advice exclusively. Blackjack players learn early how to manage their bankrolls; poker players learn early how to hit up their friends when they go broke.

With the current poker tournament boom, all serious tournament players should start thinking in terms of bankrolling their play. The fluctuations in poker tournaments are pretty hairy, and it's not all that difficult to put some numbers on these things.

One way to look at the bankroll requirement for entering any specific tournament is to simply say, "This tournament has a total buy-in and entry fee of $105, therefore the total bankroll requirement is $105. Since I cannot lose more than $105, that's all I need."

This overly simplistic view is fine if you only intend to play one tournament, and never play another. Or if you only intend to play one of these tournaments every once in a while as entertainment, then your total bankroll requirement is $105 "every once in a while." No brainer. But that's not how it is for many tournament players. They play lots of tournaments, sometimes 100 or more per year. Or, although they're entering only a handful of tournaments each year, the tournaments are expensive. They are spending an amount of money that is dear to them, and they are counting on a return on their investment.

At the 2005 WSOP, I talked with one player who had come to Vegas with $25,000 that he had spent the better part of a year saving, solely for the purpose of entering WSOP events. $10,000 was earmarked for the main event and the other $15,000 for the smaller tournaments. This was not a professional player, but a California working man who had been doing well in small buy-in tournaments in Southern California's poker rooms. He was married and had two kids. To his credit, he was entering satellites daily to try to get cheaper entries into some events, but he fully intended to spend every penny of the $25,000 he'd arrived in Vegas with, and he wished he had more. More than anything, he wanted a bracelet, but he also felt sure that his poker skills were sufficient to get him into the money in numerous events, even if he didn't win. Each day, as the lists of players who finished in the money were published, I scoured the lists for his name. I never saw it. This chapter is for him too, and for hundreds of players like him who scrimp and save to try their luck in the big money tournaments. This man had laboriously saved enough money to launch a serious poker tournament career. Instead, he blew his bankroll on what were essentially a few high-priced lottery tickets.

Any experienced tournament pro can tell you that bankroll fluctuations can be drastic. To illustrate this, I've charted the results of my first seventy-five small buy-in tournaments. The line is definitely a steady upward trend, but also pretty jagged.

Here's the chart:

In the chart, I'm showing fourteen finishes in the money out of these seventy-five tournaments. You can see the wins in the chart

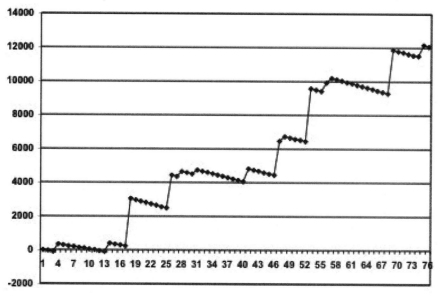

CARDOZA PUBLISHING • ARNOLD SNYDER

by every upward tick indicatng a winning session, and the losses by a downward tick. But the upward trend is driven primarily by only five substantial wins. Had it not been for those five wins, my overall result on the other seventy tournaments would have been a slow downward trend. I failed to make it into the money on fully sixty-one of these seventy-five tournaments. But my average win on the fourteen tournaments where I placed in the money was slightly more than $1,200, and my average loss on the sixty-one tournaments where I busted out with no payday was only about $70. (Note that I started out with cheap tournaments and so should you.) My overall win rate in these seventy-five tournaments was better than 230%. I was also fortunate during this early run of tournament play that my big wins, as well as my small wins, were fairly evenly distributed. This kept me from ever going into a real nosedive. That doesn't mean a nosedive is impossible. I've had them since.

As a professional gambler, I'm looking to play as many tournaments as I can play, knowing that I have an expectation of earning money in each of them, but also aware that I will lose my buy-ins and entry fees most of the time. With hundreds of tournaments under my belt at this point, I know from experience that in the fast tournaments I'll make the final table and finish in the money in about one tournament in five—on average—but these paydays are not always evenly distributed. I might place in the money on five out of seven consecutive tournaments, and then have a string of two dozen tournaments where I finish in the money only once. What interests me as a professional gambler is how bad the negative fluctuations could get.

Again, in the appendix, I provide an in-depth analysis of how to figure this out. But for now, we'll skip the math and show the results.

The chart that follows will give you a pretty good ballpark estimate of the minimum bankroll requirements for just about any tournament you're likely to encounter, assuming you are a skilled player. In using the chart, note that the cost includes not only the entry fee and buy-in, but any rebuys and add-ons you are prepared to make. You may also use the formulas provided in the appendix to analyze a tournament with a specific number of players and cost that is not included in the chart, or you may just interpolate the minimum bankroll requirement from the data that is provided in the chart.

Do not use this chart if you are playing primarily in multi-table tournaments with Skill Levels of 0 or 1, as these events are too luck-based to provide a skilled player with a strong enough advantage over his opponents. If you are playing and winning in Skill Level 2 or 3 tournaments, then double the bankroll requirements in the chart as the luck factor in these tournaments is also high. Use the chart as is for tournaments with Skill Levels of 4 or higher, assuming you have a sizeable advantage over your opponents. See the appendix for a more detailed discussion.

The chart is based on the bankroll you would need to play 100 tournaments at the prescribed buy-in levels and given the number of players. As you'll see, the greater the number of players in a tournament, the more of a bankroll you would need to ride out the expected fluctuations. It is easier to get into the money in a tournament with 50 players than one with 200, and that is why you would need more of a bankroll if you were playing, on average, bigger events.

One of the most practical uses of the chart is simply in determining if the fluctuations you are experiencing are within the realm of normal luck. If you experience a downswing greater than the chart entry for the type of tournaments you play in, then it may be time to begin questioning your strategy or skill. For instance, if you play $75 tournaments online, where the number of players averages about 200, and you are down more than $2,000 in 100 or fewer of these tournaments (the bankroll chart shows a minimum bankroll requirement of $2,121 for this situation), then I would seriously start to question your skill relative to the other players in this event. You may be a winning player on an unusually bad streak, but it's more likely that you're overestimating your skill level. I'm sure you have a hundred bad beat stories to go with all those losses, but I also suspect you are making some serious errors in your play.

MINIMUM* BANKROLL REQUIREMENT BASED ON 100 TOURNAMENTS

NUMBER OF PLAYERS

COST	40	60	80	100	150	200	250	300	500	750	1,000	2,000	5,000
$25	316	387	447	500	612	707	791	866	1,118	1,369	1,581	2,236	3,536
$50	632	775	894	1,000	1,225	1,414	1,581	1,732	2,236	2,739	3,162	4,472	7,071
$75	949	1,162	1,342	1,500	1,837	2,121	2,372	2,598	3,354	4,108	4,743	6,708	10,607
$100	1,265	1,549	1,789	2,000	2,449	2,828	3,162	3,464	4,472	5,477	6,325	8,944	14,142
$150	1,897	2,324	2,683	3,000	3,674	4,243	4,743	5,196	6,708	8,216	9,487	13,416	21,213
$200	2,530	3,098	3,578	4,000	4,899	5,657	6,325	6,928	8,944	10,954	12,649	17,889	28,284
$300	3,795	4,648	5,367	6,000	7,348	8,485	9,487	10,392	13,416	16,432	18,974	26,833	42,426
$400	5,060	6,197	7,15-5	8,000	9,798	11,314	12,649	13,856	17,8-89	21,909	25,298	35,777	56,569
$500	6,325	7,746	8,944	10,000	12,247	14,142	15,811	17,321	22,361	27,386	31,623	44,721	70,711
$1,000	12,649	15,492	17,889	20,000	24,495	28,284	31,623	34,641	44,721	54,772	63,246	89,443	141,421
$1,500	18,974	23,238	26,833	30,000	36,742	42,426	47,434	51,962	67,082	82,158	94,868	134,164	212,132
$2,000	25,298	30,984	35,777	40,000	48,990	56,569	63,246	69,282	89,443	109,545	126,491	178,885	282,843
$2,500	31,623	38,730	44,721	50,000	61,237	70,711	79,057	86,603	111,803	136,931	158,114	223,607	353,553
$3,000	37,947	46,476	53,6-66	60,000	73,485	84,853	94,868	103,923	134,164	164,317	189,737	268,328	424,264
$5,000	63,246	77,460	89,4-43	100,000	122,474	141,421	158,114	173,205	223,607	273,861	316,228	447,214	707,107
$10,000	126,491	154,919	178,885	200,000	244,949	282,843	316,228	346,410	447,214	547,723	632,456	894,427	1,414,214
$25,000	316,228	38,7298	447,214	500,000	612,372	707,107	790,569	866,025	1,118,034	1,369,306	1,581,139	2,236,068	3,535,534

*Add 10% more for rebuy tournaments

302

On the other hand, if you are playing in $75 buy-in tournaments with only forty players, I would advise you to start questioning your skills long before you hit $2,000 in losses. The bankroll chart entry for this situation is only $949, so if you have losses anywhere in the neighborhood of $1,000, it's time to start questioning your approach. Again, I'm not saying that such negative fluctuations can only result from a lack of skill. It is possible that your poor results really are caused by nothing but inordinate negative flux. That's poker—but if your results don't turn around soon, you need to start looking for softer games.

Again, this chapter is simply meant to provide you with a handle on the normal fluctuations in tournament play to keep you from getting in over your head. The message is that you should always play within the constraints of your bankroll. If you can get into the next WSOP main event on a $200 satellite, or even a $1,000 satellite, more power to you. But I would not advise any player to scrimp and save in order to enter these big money affairs with massive fields of players. The odds are too much against you even if you are among the top players in the world. If you're determined to play in major events, against the top competition, you stand a much better chance of hitting the money in the smaller WPT events, or WSOP circuit events, or many other $5,000 and $10,000 buy-in events available these days in poker rooms all over the world, where the field sizes are generally in the hundreds of players rather than the thousands.

At the 2005 WSOP, the best values in my opinion were the tournaments other than no-limit hold'em, as these events generally had only a few hundred participants each. But then, it's no-limit hold'em that everyone wants to play. The best no-limit hold'em values were the two $5,000 events, the second of which was the short-handed (six players maximum per table) tournament. These two events had 466 and 301 entrants respectively and—incidentally—were won by T.J. Cloutier and Doyle Brunson, respectively.

29

HOW FIELD SIZE AFFECTS TOURNAMENT SPEED

Just as the number of players in a tournament affects the bankroll requirements, it also affects a tournament's speed, which means it affects both optimal strategy and the role of luck. Chapter Three showed how to quantify a tournament's speed by using the blind structure to develop a patience factor. This chapter will show how a greater number of players cause the speed of a tournament to escalate as the tournament progresses toward the final table, particularly in tournaments with fast to medium blind structures. This speed increase takes many players by surprise and alters optimal strategy near the end of the tournament. These strategy adjustments as the tournament winds down to the final table are among the most important strategy adjustments you can make in a tournament—the ones that will get you into the big money. This chapter will also show why this is not as big a factor in most of the major events that have long, slow blind structures.

If you are playing in fast and medium-speed tournaments, it's a good idea to know in advance if a tournament will be speeding out of control in the later stages. If so, you want to do everything you can to set yourself up in advance with sufficient chips to survive the high-risk confrontations that will be inevitable once the average chip stack is approaching desperation.

ALL TOURNAMENTS SPEED UP AS THEY PROGRESS

To understand why players must be concerned not only with a tournament's speed but with the rate of the speed increase, you must understand that tournaments are structured to force players into confrontations that will result in players being eliminated. Since blinds and antes must be paid, and since these costs keep rising, players who do not win chips will be eliminated by default. When I say that every tournament's speed increases, I mean that the cost of paying the blinds and antes goes up faster than the average chip stack.

Here is a simple example of what happens in a fast tournament. The Rio Casino offered a daily noon tournament with 20-minute blind levels. These were the first four blind levels:

Level 1:	$25-50
Level 2:	$50-100
Level 3:	$75-150
Level 4:	$100-$200

So, after one hour of play, the blind level went to $100-200, which is to say that the cost of going through the blinds increased 400% from Level 1. During this first hour of play, some players were always eliminated, which meant that the average chip stack of the remaining players was bigger too. But the average chip stack would not have increased 400% during this time. For the average chip stack to increase this much in the first hour of play, 75% of the players would have to be eliminated, and this did not occur. Usually, in the first hour of a fast multi-table tournament, including this one, only about 10%-20% of the players are eliminated.

Hour after hour, as the Rio tournament progressed, the cost of the blinds continued to escalate at a much faster rate than players were eliminated, until the final table was reached, at which point virtually all remaining players were short-stacked in relation to the cost of the blinds. What happens in such fast-accelerating tournaments is that more and more players are forced into do-or-die confrontations as the blind costs go up, and they must get into these confrontations with hands of lesser and lesser value. This same thing occurs in tournaments with slow blind structures, but at a much slower rate. In a slow tournament, many players stay well ahead of the blind costs from start to finish.

In addition, the more players there are in the field, the longer a tournament lasts. When a fast tournament gets longer because of additional players, it gets to blind levels it would never have reached with fewer players. The need to make money for these additional blind levels pushes players into even more confrontations. If the number of starting players was really excessive for the tournament's fast blind structure, even the chip leader will be short-stacked in relation to the blinds by the time the final table is reached, and the luck of the cards—not skillful play—will decide who wins. As soon as you make cards the primary deciding factor in who wins the pot, you may as well be flipping a coin to determine the winner.

In a slower tournament format, by contrast, although some players may arrive short-stacked at the final table, the average chip stack will be well ahead of the blinds, and the chip leaders will be able to continue playing real poker.

There are both an upside and a downside to having more players in a fast tournament, the big upside being the increased prize pool. The first tournament where I ever finished in the money was a 40-player event at Sam's Town. When it got down to three players at the final table, we did an even three-way chop of the prize money, which came to about $500 each. A few weeks later, when I did an even three-way chop on the top three prizes in a 200-player Orleans tournament, my share came to $2,000. That's certainly a big difference, considering that both tournaments required similar dollar investments (about $60 each) and the Orleans tournament only added about ninety minutes to the playing time.

The downside to having more players in a fast tournament is that the tournament may cease to be a skill event before you get to the money, drastically reducing the value of those extra players. There are many big Internet tournaments, for example, that have thousands of entrants, but that have little value to skilled players because they degenerate into luck fests so very long before any players are in the money. This does not mean that these tournaments have no value whatsoever for skillful players, only that the skill factor diminishes as the tournament progresses and is usually a minor factor in the final finishing positions. In other words, players who play with skill early will have a great shot at getting to the later stages, but skill will have little to do with how they finish once they've gotten past the opening.

One way to judge how long a tournament will remain vulnerable to skilled fast-play techniques is to look at what the average chip stack will be when the players reach the final table. Will the average chip stack still be ahead of the blinds and antes enough to continue using fast-play techniques profitably, or will the blind costs be so high that no player will be able to go more than a few hands without trying to win a pot, and every confrontation will inevitably be all-in?

There are two simple methods for estimating the length of time that a tournament will take to get down to the final table, depending on what information is available to you in advance.

THE EASIEST METHOD

If your local poker room has a regularly scheduled tournament that you've played before, you should have a pretty good idea of how long it lasts. If not, ask the tournament director for a ballpark estimate of what time it ends. Subtract the starting time from the approximate ending time and you will know how many hours the whole thing lasts. Now subtract from this time the number of minutes for whatever breaks are scheduled, and subtract another half-hour to account for the final table play (I'm assuming this is a small buy-in tournament with a fast blind structure), and you'll have a pretty good estimate of the tournament's running time to get to the final table.

Based on how long each blind level lasts, you can now figure out what level the blinds will be at when you get to the final table. Just assume that with 15-minute blinds, you'll go through four levels per hour. With 20-minute blinds, you'll go through three levels per hour, and so on. If you figure the tournament will take 3.5 hours to get to the final table, and the blinds have 15-minute levels, then you simply multiply four blind levels per hour times 3.5 hours to calculate that players will have gone through 14 blind levels before the final table. In this case, the final table will start at the 15th blind level. The poker room should have a printed blind schedule that you can pick up, or at least a copy of one posted on the poker room wall. Find level 15 and see what the blinds and antes will be when the players in the tournament get to the final table.

Now, to figure out how many chips will be on the final table, multiply the number of starting chips each players gets by the total number of players. For instance, with $1,000 in starting chips and a tournament that typically gets around eighty players, there will be $80,000 in chips on the final table. Once you know the total number of chips on the final table, divide this number by ten (assuming ten players at the final table), and you will know the average number of chips each player will have. In this example, each player would have an average of $8,000 in chips.

Now compare the average number of chips on the final table with the blind costs at the 15th (or whatever) level, in order to see how desperate for chips the players will be at the final table.

If the tournament you're interested in is a multiple rebuy tournament, you may be stumped at this point unless the tournament director can tell you the approximate number of rebuys each player makes. I'll provide a few other accurate methods for determining the number of rebuys per player later in this chapter.

What do you do with this information? That's coming up shortly. First, let's discuss how to estimate how long it will take to get to the final table in a tournament where no advance information is available from the tournament director or other players familiar with the event.

THE FINAL TABLE ESTIMATED TIME OF ARRIVAL (ETA)

You need to know two numbers to calculate the time it will take for a tournament to reach the final table. The first is the number of players competing in the event. I call this the **field factor**. The second is related to the speed with which the blinds go up. I call this the **speed factor**.

Once you have these factors, simply add the field factor to the speed factor to get the length of time in hours that it will take for the tournament to reach the final table. You do not need to understand the math to use the formula.

Calculating the Field Factor

To obtain the field factor simply take the square root of the number of starting tables in the tournament. For example, let's assume that a tournament has 100 players.

Step One: 100 players equals 10 tables.
Step Two: The square root of $10 = 3.16$, and that's the field factor.

For convenience, there's a chart on the next page for quick estimates. This chart assumes that there are 10 players per table.

The field factor essentially gives you a base number of hours that any tournament will take to get to the final table—as a function of the number of entrants—if the tournament's speed factor is 0, which will never be the case. (The calculation of the speed factor, which must be added to the field factor, is described below.) Again, in calculating the number of tables, just divide the actual number of players by ten. If a tournament has 55 players, use 5.5 for the number of tables.

If the tournament is played with nine-spot tables, you should still use ten as your divisor. Although nine-spot tables would increase the number of tables by 10%, which would have the effect of increasing the field factor, having fewer players per table would also increase the rate at which players would go through the blinds by 10%—which would require an adjustment to the formula that would decrease the field factor. This would be true for a short-handed tournament as well but I would advise against using this formula for tournaments that are so different strategically from full-table tournaments. Use this formula (or the chart) for calculating the field factor for all tournaments that start with eight to eleven players per table.

FIELD FACTORS

# Players	Field Factor	# Players	Field Factor	# Players	Field Factor
40	2.00	220	4.69	750	8.66
45	2.12	240	4.90	800	8.94
50	2.24	260	5.10	850	9.22
55	2.35	280	5.29	900	9.49
60	2.45	300	5.48	950	9.75
65	2.55	320	5.66	1,000	10.00
70	2.65	340	5.83	1,100	10.49
75	2.74	360	6.00	1,200	10.95
80	2.83	380	6.16	1,300	11.40
85	2.92	400	6.32	1,400	11.83
90	3.00	420	6.48	1,500	12.25
95	3.08	440	6.63	1,750	13.23
100	3.16	460	6.78	2,000	14.14
110	3.32	480	6.93	2,250	15.00
120	3.46	500	7.07	2,500	15.81
130	3.61	525	7.25	2,750	16.58
140	3.74	550	7.42	3,000	17.32
150	3.87	575	7.58	3,500	18.71
160	4.00	600	7.75	4,000	20.00
170	4.12	625	7.91	4,500	21.21
180	4.24	650	8.06	5,000	22.36
190	4.36	675	8.22	5,500	23.45
200	4.47	700	8.37	6,000	24.49

The field factor is just the first step in estimating a tournament's estimated time of arrival (ETA) at the final table. Now you need to look at the number of chips each player starts with, and more importantly, how quickly the blinds are escalating relative to that number of chips.

Calculating the Speed Factor

To obtain the speed factor for a tournament, the formula is:

$$(P - 1) / 3$$

P is the tournament's patience factor.

That's all there is to it. For example, let's figure out the speed factor for the Orleans Monday night tournament, which has a patience factor of 5.50. (See Chapter 3.) Inserting this patience factor into the formula, I get:

$$(5.50 - 1) / 3 = 1.50$$

So, if I want to estimate the final table ETA for this tournament with 200 players:

First, get the Field Factor

Step One: 200 players equals 20 tables
Step Two: the square root of 20 = 4.47

Now, add the Speed Factor to the Field Factor.

$$4.47 + 1.50 = 5.97 \text{ hours}$$

Or, about six hours, which turns out to be pretty close to what actually happens in this event.

TESTING THE ETA FORMULA WITH WSOP EVENTS

Let's test the ETA Formula with some events from the 2005 WSOP. Here is the data:

Event	# Players	Field Factor	Speed Factor	Final Table ETA
$10,000 Event	5,619	23.70	24.75	48.45 hours
$5,000 Event	466	6.83	7.49	14.32 hours
$2,000 Event	1,403	11.84	5.45	17.29 hours
$1,500 Event	2,305	15.18	4.35	19.53 hours

I chose these tournaments because the blind structures are widely known and easily obtainable, so you can double-check my work if you want to. These tournaments had numbers of players that varied widely, from 466 to 5,619, and starting chips that varied widely as well, from $1,500 to $10,000. The $10,000 event had 100-minute blind levels. All of the others had one-hour blind levels. The $10,000 and $5,000 events had starting blinds of $25 and $50, versus starting blinds of $25 and $25 for the other two tournaments.

In the actual $10,000 main event, which started on July 7 at the Rio and hit the final table on July 16 at Binion's Horseshoe, the blinds were at level 30 ($50,000-$100,000 with a $10,000 ante) when the nine finalists arrived. With 100-minute blind levels up until this point, this meant that 2,900 minutes of actual tournament play had elapsed getting to the final table. 2,900 minutes is forty-eight hours and twenty minutes. The ETA estimate of 48.45 hours is right on the money.

In the actual $5,000 event, which started on June 14 and hit the final table the following day, the blinds were at the 14th level ($2,500-$5,000 with a $500 ante). Since this tournament has 60-minute blind levels, the formula's estimate of 14.32 hours as the final table ETA is also pretty darn close.

In the $2,000 event, which started on June 28 and hit the final table the next day, the players reached the final table at blind level 18 ($6,000-$12,000 with a $2,000 ante). The formula's estimate of 17.29 hours is also very close to how the actual event played out.

In the $1,500 event, which started on June 3 and hit the final table the next day, the players reached the final table at level 19

($8,000-$16,000 with a $2,000 ante), so the formula's 19.53 hour estimate is also surprisingly accurate.

Another WSOP no-limit hold'em tournament that I got data on was the other $2,000 event. (There were two $2,000 events and two $1,500 events in 2005.) This second $2,000 event had only 1,072 entrants, more than 300 fewer than the 1,403 in the event included in the chart. Since both tournaments had identical patience factors, the speed factor for both is also identical. The only change is in the field factor. With 1,403 players, the field factor is 11.84. With 1,072 players, the field factor comes to 10.35, or about an hour and thirty minutes less. In real life, the $2,000 event with 1,072 players arrived at the final table one blind level sooner—at level 17 instead of 18, more or less as the formula predicted.

Now let's look at the size of the average chip stacks upon arrival at these final tables, relative to the blinds/antes.

In the $10,000 event, the final table was played nine-handed, and the average chip stack was $6,243,000. So that $100,000 big blind wasn't much of a threat to most of these players. The average chip stack was about 62 times the size of the big blind.

In the $5,000 event, the final table was played ten-handed, and the average chip stack was $233,000. The chip leader had $630,000. So the $5,000 big blind was not much of a threat to most of these players yet either. The average chip stack at this table was about 46 times the size of the big blind.

In the $2,000 event (with 1,403 players), the final table was played nine-handed, and the average chip stack was $312,000. So the $12,000 big blind was definitely more of a factor here, and was definitely threatening to the average stack, which was just about 26 times the size of the big blind. Note that in the $2,000 event with fewer players (1,072), the average chip stack at the final table was about 30 times the big blind. That goes to show you the effect of field size.

In the $1,500 event, the final table was played nine-handed, and the average chip stack was $384,000. The chip leader had $728,000. So, that $16,000 big blind was not a big threat to the biggest chip stacks. But the average chip stack at that table was only about 24 times the size of the big blind. And the cost per player of going around the table once (9 hands) was $42,000, which meant that to have an average chip stack at that final table was to be very short-stacked. I should note, however, that in these WSOP events, blind levels last ninety minutes at the final table, contributing further to keeping the results skill-based, even with the huge fields these tournaments are now attracting.

The $2,000 and $1,500 events, with 1,403 and 2,305 players respectively, were a lot closer to being crapshoots at the end than the other two tournaments with their larger amounts of starting chips. If field sizes continue to grow, so that the $1,500 event might be played with 3,000 players (instead of 2,305), about two more hours would be required to hit the final table, and even with all those extra chips in play, the average chip stack would only be about twenty times the size of the big blind. If you do the math, you'll see that with 3,000 players, the average chip stack at the nine-spot final table will be $500,000, with the big blind at $24,000, the small blind at $12,000, and the antes at $4,000. The blinds and antes will cost each player at the table $72,000 in chips every nine hands, and with an average chip stack of only $500,000 each, that's fast.

USING THE ETA FORMULA
IN SMALL BUY-IN TOURNAMENTS

If you don't get the logic of the final table ETA math, don't sweat it. Just plug in the numbers for your local tournament, taking the approximate field factor from the chart above, and adding it to the speed factor, which is easy to figure out once you have the patience factor worked out. You'll see that it works fairly well.

The Orleans Saturday night tournament—one of the best small buy-in tournaments available in Las Vegas ($230 if you get the bonus chips and make the one allowed rebuy)—has a field factor of 2.65 with seventy players. This is a typical number of entries for this tournament. The speed factor is 1.96, which you calculate using the 6.89 patience factor listed in the chart in Chapter Three. So, after adding the field factor to the speed factor (2.65 + 1.96), you would expect to hit the final table at this tournament after 4.61 hours of play. Based on my experience, that's a good estimate, as the tournament starts at 7:00 p.m. and usually hits the final table around midnight, so that after subtracting the time for the scheduled breaks, the actual play time is generally just shy of five hours.

Because of the single rebuy structure and discounted rebuy chips, only a handful of players fail to purchase the rebuy—maybe five out of a hundred. So let's figure out the number of chips on the final table.

The total number of chips available to each player is $3,250, and sixty-five players purchase this full amount. Five players pass on the purchase of the $2,000 in rebuy chips, and have only $1,250 chips at the start. Taking 65 times $3,250, and adding 5 times $1,250, this puts the total number of chips in play at about $217,500. So, at the ten-player final table, each player will have an average of $21,750 in chips.

Next, you want to know what the blind levels are after 4.61 hours of play. In this tournament, the first three blind levels are twenty minutes each. All blind levels after that last twenty-five minutes. I picked this tournament blind structure to analyze precisely because it's a pain in the ass. With more normal 15- or 20-minute blind levels from start to finish, you can figure out the final table blind level simply by dividing the ETA hours by either 3 (for 20-minute blind levels) or 4 (for 15-minute blind levels). Or, even simpler, go ask the tournament director and he'll tell you the players usually get to the final table around midnight!

So, how do you figure out the final table blind level with this unusual blind structure?

Here's what I do. First, I convert 4.61 hours into minutes.

$$4.61 \times 60 = 277 \text{ minutes}$$

Next, I subtract 60 minutes for the first hour, since I know that with 20-minute blinds, this hour will use up exactly 3 blind levels.

$$277 - 60 = 217 \text{ minutes}$$

Now, how many blind levels will be used up by those remaining 217 minutes? Well, since the blind levels after the first hour last 25 minutes, all I have to do is divide 217 by 25. That gives us:

$$217 / 25 = 8.68$$

Finally, I add the three blind levels from the first hour to the nine blind levels I will go through after that, and I estimate that I will have gone through 11.68 blind levels, reaching the final table near the end of level 12, and as I am entering blind level 13.

Next, what are the blinds at level 13? I have to get this number from the tournament's blind structure printout, which tells me that the blinds are $1,500-$3,000 with a $700 ante. Since the average chip stack at this table is only $21,750, the average player at this final table will clearly be desperate. There will be a few players with chip stacks well above the average and these players will be able to wait a few rounds while the most desperate players take their shots at each other. But at this point, luck will rule. Note how much faster a fast tournament is than a slow tournament when you get to the final table. Final tables don't last long in fast events.

ESTIMATING THE TOTAL CHIPS IN MULTIPLE REBUY TOURNAMENTS

It's easy to estimate the total number of chips that will be in play on the final table of a non-rebuy event. You simply multiply the number of starting players by the number of chips each player begins with, and you have the answer.

With a single-rebuy tournament, as in the example above, it's again no problem as long as you have an estimate of how many players will purchase the rebuy chips and how many will not. This method isn't perfect, but it's close enough for our purposes.

But, how do you get this estimate for a multiple-rebuy tournament? When I started playing the Orleans Monday and Tuesday night tournaments a few years ago, I was stumped. On some nights, my starting table played conservatively through the rebuy period, with the average player making very few rebuys. On other nights, the players went wild with all-in bets, with some individual players making a dozen or more rebuys in the first hour.

So, how did I figure it out?

There are three ways.

The First Way

Some poker rooms use convenient computer displays that inform players about the tournament's progress. Typical information on this display will be the number of starting players, the current blind level, the number of players remaining, the prize structure and other information of this type that is updated as the tournament progresses. Some of these displays actually tell you the total number of chips in play, and some tell you the average number of chips each remaining player has. Even if you don't know the number of rebuys the average player made, that's all the information you need to know!

The Second Way

Many poker rooms either post or otherwise provide a printed list of the previous day's winners, along with the total number of entrants, the total prize pool, and the actual prizes awarded to each finishing position. As most poker rooms also print or post their **prize structures**—the percentage of the prize pool paid to each position and the percentage of the house commission—it is tedious but not impossible to figure out exactly how many rebuys were made. First, you figure out what the house commission was in dollars, based on their percentage, then you add the house commission back into the total prize pool, so that you know the total amount paid by players in buy-ins, fees and rebuys.

Since you know each player made the initial buy-in with entry fee, you multiply the number of players by the total buy-in and entry fee costs, then subtract this amount from the total amount paid by all players in buy-ins, entry fees and rebuys. The difference is the amount paid for rebuys. Now you simply divide this amount by the cost of a single rebuy and you have the total number of rebuys purchased. Divide this by the number of players, and you have the average number of rebuys purchased per player.

The Third Way

This is my favorite. Ask. One night after a tournament, as I sat at a vacant poker table trying to calculate average rebuys from the data I had gleaned from the prize allotments, I asked the tournament director if he had any idea how many rebuys the average player in this tournament made. Without hesitation, he said, "Just over three at the evening tournament, and just under three at the afternoon one." I asked him how much it varied from tournament to tournament. "Not much." I asked a couple of other questions about exactly how the house commission was figured—did it apply to the bonus chips, the rebuys, the add-ons—then finished figuring it out the long way. That night, the players made 3.1 rebuys each on average, just as he'd said they would.

So, the easy way to solve this problem is, ask someone who knows the answer.

IS THE ETA FORMULA ALWAYS ACCURATE?

I use the formula with confidence in no-limit hold'em tournaments that aren't short-handed, and that have patience factors of 3.0 and higher. It will usually get you within two blind levels of the final table arrival blind level. But I don't waste much time analyzing tournaments faster than that, so the accuracy may go down for lightning-fast structures. Also, you will occasionally run into situations where tournament directors decide to skip a blind level, or add an ante, or shorten the length of the blind levels in order to speed up the tournament—usually so they can go home earlier! Obviously, this kind of stuff will mess up your ETA predictions. In addition, some tournaments really do play out faster or slower on different nights due to unknown factors—perhaps the full moon or who knows what. But as a general guide, you will find it accurate in a wide variety of tournaments.

With regards to Internet tournaments, the ETA Formula must be adjusted for the actual hands-per-hour differences that exist from one online poker room to another. There is no simple way to adjust it for a generic online speed—you really have to time the speed at the place you're thinking of playing. Also, I've noticed that individual online tournaments tend to play out differently from each other even within the same online poker room.

If the online tournament you are interested in is a regular daily or weekly event, then I would suggest just watching the tournament to find out the chip positions of the players upon arrival at the final table.

Online tournaments play amazingly fast in hours relative to live tournaments, but they are real tournaments, where the players have sufficient chips and time to engage in skillful play.

WHY DO YOU NEED TO KNOW HOW FAST A TOURNAMENT IS?

Very few players know that the tournament structures have any effect on optimal strategy, and most play the same way in every event they enter. I had to invent the term "patience factor" for this book—which is the poker tournament equivalent to "deck penetration" at blackjack—because I couldn't find the concept discussed anywhere in the literature.

I suspect that some players who have years of tournament experience have a gut-level feeling for the speed of a tournament based on their starting chips and the blind structure, and automatically adjust to changes in speed as players' chip stacks change and the blind levels increase. The professionals must do this, because I don't believe any player can succeed in tournaments without adjusting his play for the speed of the tournament.

Why Do You Need To Know How Fast A Tournament Is?

Because the tournament's speed—not your cards—determines how you should play and bet. If you do not anticipate the effects of crucial tournament speed factors, you will not make it into the money often enough to pay your buy-in and entry fees, let alone make a profit.

CRUNCH TIME: THE REAL FINAL TABLE BEFORE THE NOMINAL FINAL TABLE

Every fast tournament, and many medium-speed tournaments, if they have large fields, has a critical time period that occurs before the final table is reached. This critical period is the last opportunity for players to earn chips by using position plays and chip shots, and I call it "crunch time." It generally lasts for about half an hour and you must take advantage of this period to earn chips with skillful play if you want to make money from tournament play in the long run. Once crunch time is over, it's too late to advance your chip position with anything other than lucky cards.

Again, your goal in fast tournaments should be not only to make it into the money, but to hit that final table with as many chips as possible. During crunch time, you must play with maximum aggression when you have a premium hand, but you cannot wait for a premium hand to play. There are many desperate players at this time, so the really short stacks will be taking shots left and right. Watch out for them. The players with medium-sized stacks—which, in almost all cases are really short stacks relative to the blinds, though these players don't know it—slow down at this point because they are so close to finishing in the money they can almost taste it.

These medium stacks are the players that you will feed on during crunch time. They are terrified of going out when they feel they've almost arrived. In fact, most of these players are doomed. With fast play you will eat them alive. Their chips will become your chips. You will play a high-risk game, but I guarantee you it will pay off.

It is absolutely imperative that you do not think like one of these doomed players. You do not want to finish in a bottom-rung money position. Finishing in a bottom money position is not much better than busting out in the first hour. You can't make money on these poor finishes, and if you've played this many hours you want more than just some meager courtesy win for making it this far. You make your money by finishing at the top. That's your whole reason for being here.

If you arrive at the final table with one of the monster chip stacks, you will almost positively be in on the final chop. Crunch time is when you put that monster stack together. Most players in fast tournaments do not realize that for all practical purposes, the tournament ends when crunch time ends. This isn't the case in the final tables they watch on TV. None of their books on tournament play tell them that the tournament ends before they get to the final table. In fact, most books on tournament play devote a whole chapter to final table playing strategies. (You may have noticed that this book's chapter on fast tournament final table "play" is little more than a discussion of how to chop up the prize pool.)

Once you grasp that crunch time is when you set yourself up for your finishing position, there are just two things you must do to prepare for it in any tournament. You must know when crunch time will start, so you don't let it pass you by, and you must know how to play when you're in the middle of it.

Predicting Crunch Time

How do you know when crunch time starts? If you have figured out what the average chip stack will be at the final table, that is a good indicator. Here's a basic guide:

♠ If the average chip stack at the final table will be less than the cost of five big blinds, crunch time begins three blind levels earlier. It will start when that blind level kicks in and will last throughout that blind level and the next. Crunch over.

♠ If the average chip stack at the final table will be more than the cost of five big blinds, but less than the cost of ten big blinds, crunch time begins two blind levels earlier. Once again it will start when that blind level kicks in, but in this case it will usually last through that blind level only. Crunch over.

♠ If the average chip stack at the final table will be more than the cost of ten big blinds, but less than the cost of twenty big blinds, crunch time begins one blind level earlier. Once again it will start when that blind level kicks in and will last through that blind level only. Crunch over.

♠ If the average chip stack at the final table will be more than the cost of twenty big blinds, crunch time begins at the final table. In a fast tournament, it will last for only one blind level. When the blinds go up, crunch time ends and luck takes over.

♠ Finally, in fast tournaments the predicted crunch time will never be exact. Use the prediction as a guide to know when to start watching for it. The remaining tables often get quiet as the desperation levels increase with the blinds, and you'll notice players busting out more frequently. It's hard to gauge the average chip stacks at your table because the discrepancies from player to player are huge, but you'll notice that most of the players have very short and desperate stacks.

How Should You Play During Crunch Time?

Generally, you should avoid confrontations with both the really short and really big stacks unless you have a premium hand. You should concentrate on the players in medium chip positions relative to the average chip stack at your table. These players will usually be short-stacked relative to the blinds, but their chief concern will be trying to stay alive until the desperate players have busted out. Because they are afraid of getting involved in pots at this time, they will be your main chip suppliers.

The pots at crunch time will be big because the antes will have kicked in. These medium-stacked players cannot afford to sit and wait for a premium hand, considering the cost of the antes and blinds, but they don't know it. If a player has $20,000 in chips and the blinds are $500 and $1,000, he will often feel that he is in fine chip position with a stack that's twenty times the size of the big blind. But at this level, there is typically a $200 ante, so the cost of going through a ten-hand round is actually $3,500. If he goes through these ten hands just one time, depleting his stack to

$16,500, the new blind level will be $700-$1,500 with a $300 ante, which means the next ten hands will cost him $5,500. Most players in fast tournaments just don't see this coming. To have a stack equal to twenty big blinds feels like safety to them, and when they're close to the money, they want to preserve their chips and take no chances.

If you have enough chips to knock one of these players out, you can almost always take the pot with an all-in bet. It is worth the risk of getting knocked out yourself to try to take these players' chips with more aggression than they want to deal with. I repeat: You do not want a bottom-rung money finish, and this is your last chance to build a stack that will accomplish your goal of finishing at the top. It is better to bust out trying to get the chips you need than it is to sit on your chips like the wimps and make it to the final table on the bottom rungs.

The Crunch Strategies

When you are chip rich compared to the other players at your table:

1. Avoid confrontations with other chip-rich players except as follows: push all-in against these players preflop with any pocket pair from 8-8 up, as well as with A-K and A-Q. Call a preflop all-in bet from a chip-rich player with pocket pairs from J-J up and A-K. Otherwise, get out of their way.

2. Avoid confrontations with desperate chip stacks unless you have a pocket pair from 8-8 up, A-K, A-Q, A-J, A-10s, A-9s, K-Qs, K-Js, or Q-Js, in which case you either push all-in or call an all-in from a desperate player. If a desperate player is so short-stacked that his all-in bet is less than three times the size of the big blind, call him with any two cards if you have better than 25 times the big blind.

3. Push all-in with any two cards on any medium-stack player, which usually means a player with fifteen to twenty times the big blind at this point, who either limps in or makes a standard raise (three to four times the big blind). But avoid multiway raised pots unless you have position. If you do involve yourself in a multiway pot, push all-in on your medium-stacked opponents if they check on the flop.

4. And, as always in poker tournaments, take into account your reads on the players that you are going up against. If you know a player with a medium chip-stack is a tight player who rarely plays a hand, don't reraise him all-in if he makes a standard raise. Only go over the top of him with a premium hand yourself: 10-10 to A-A or A-K. You must be brave during crunch time, but trust your reads on players and get out of the way of real danger.

When you are medium or short-stacked yourself compared to the other players at your table:

If you have fewer than 20 big blinds, then you are in desperate chip condition if the antes have kicked in. You must revert to the standard desperation strategies provided in the chapter on Chip Strategy.

30

CONCLUSION:
WHAT I CAN'T TEACH YOU

For twenty-nine chapters, I've been trying to teach you everything I can about how to win money in fast poker tournaments. In this chapter, I'm going to try to impart to you everything I *can't* teach you about this endeavor.

I can provide you with lists of hands to play and the best shots to take, but I can't teach you when it's best to depart from these strategies. And, unfortunately, if you're hoping for a career in the top-level poker tournaments, you will have to make these departures. Poker tournaments, especially at the higher levels, constantly deliver fresh puzzles to be solved—new types of players who must be read and new types of plays you have never seen before. If you play poker strictly according to the instructions in this book, you will make money in the tournaments with lower skill levels—and with the plenitude of online tournaments at low skill levels, you may be able to make a lot of money—but you won't make it very far up the tournament ladder from there.

Every professional gambler I know is addicted to solving puzzles. They do crossword puzzles, get hooked on computer games like Tetris and solitaire and minesweeper, get involved with fantasy sports teams, practice card tricks, or enter Scrabble competitions. Poker great Howard Lederer got hooked on the popular television game show *Who Wants to Be a Millionaire?* and figured out the best strategy for it. Blackjack legend Ken Uston was a Pac Man addict. He spent the better part of a year figuring out how to play this arcade game all day long on a single quarter. I once asked him why he'd bothered. "Geez, Arnie," he said. "I like getting the free games."

The big attraction to gambling for professionals, in fact, is never the money. It's always the game. As Poker Hall of Famer Johnny Moss put it years ago, "Money's just paper to gamble with."

Most books on poker will tell you to start out by playing very conservatively, and only add higher risk plays to your repertoire slowly as you gain experience at the tables. But that is not the approach puzzle-addicted professional gamblers would tend to take. Professional gamblers feel compelled to experiment, to push the limits for greater success, and this is how they advance as players. The fact is, higher-risk trial and error, and even sheer inspiration, will often take you in directions you could never have arrived at by logic, or even by way of years of experience with conservative play. You have to be willing to try something new to learn something new.

My advice to you, if you have ambitions to compete with the best, is to start out playing a very high-risk game, and only slowly incorporate more conservative play as you gain the table experience to tell the difference between real danger and just fear. In my opinion, our society tends to teach us to be far too cautious. People tend to go for the sure thing instead of betting on themselves and their natural ingenuity. In other words, society is always teaching you that, when you're not sure what to do, you should fold. I'm telling you that, when you're not sure what to do, you should not fold.

It's the hands where you're not sure what to do that are the best opportunities for learning. If you fold, you learn nothing. The next time that situation arises—and believe me, it will arise again and again—you will once again not know what to do. By contrast, when you don't fold, you learn right then and there if folding would have been the better play. And you may have to play through dozens of variations on this same situation before you start to see the subtle differences between them that tell you what to do. Don't worry— you'll get better. If you aren't making a lot of mistakes when you start, you're not doing enough for your own education.

So again, in violation of the common poker wisdom, my advice to you is that the less experience and skill you have, the looser and more aggressively you should play in poker tournaments. And you don't even have to worry that this experimental play will cost you more money. If you ask any pro whether he'd rather be at a table with a tight "solid" player or a loose aggressive player, he'll pick the tight player as an opponent any day of the week. Conservative players are easy to read and easy to beat. Loose aggressive players, on the other hand—even if they're not very skillful—are difficult to read and always dangerous. Since, as a beginner, you can't be good, at least opt for being dangerous.

This is as far as I can take you with a book. From here on out, it's up to you. So, go be dangerous, and see how much more you can learn.

APPENDIX

Figuring out bankroll requirements for tournaments is very different from figuring out bankroll requirements for a casino game like blackjack, or even for poker as played in a non-tournament format. A blackjack player will generally play about 100 hands per hour, so 10,000 hands would represent about 100 hours of play. If I expect to play 1,000 hours of blackjack this year, I might estimate my variance on 100,000 hands to see the range of probabilities for where my years' results can end up.

When I enter a poker tournament, however, I am making one bet, and that bet is my total cost of playing that tournament. If I enter a $100 buy-in tournament, then I am placing a single $100 bet. This is a very important point when it comes to estimating my bankroll requirements. There would be no point in estimating what my variance might be on 10,000 tournaments, let alone 100,000, because I will not play this many tournaments in my lifetime. If I am playing a lot of fast tournaments, however, I might well play 100 to 200 tournaments in a year's time, so I want to know how bad the negative fluctuations can be on that number of bets.

Statisticians use the "standard deviation" formula to estimate such fluctuations, and that's what we'll use. It's not that difficult to apply the formula to poker tournaments if you use a specific tournament's payout structure and make some assumptions about your expected results. But first, let's define what the term standard deviation means to a statistician. For simplicity, let's again use a simple coin-flip example.

COIN-FLIP EXAMPLE

If I flip a coin 1,000 times, and I bet $1 on each flip, winning a dollar each time the coin comes up heads but losing the dollar each time the coin comes up tails, I would expect to break even, assuming the coin and the flipper are honest. If you try flipping a coin 1,000 times and recording the actual results, however, you'd be highly unlikely to come up with exactly 500 wins and 500 losses.

Statisticians use the term **standard deviation** to explain such normal variations from an expected result. For instance, if you flip an honest coin ten times, betting $1 per flip, your expected result is to break even with five heads and five tails. If, however, you came up with seven tails and three heads, so that you lost $4 on these coin-flips, this would not be an indication that something was wrong. In ten coin flips, having seven tails come up would be considered a normal fluctuation. If, on the other hand, you flipped a coin 10,000 times, and it came up 7,000 tails and only 3,000 heads, giving you a $4,000 loss, any mathematician would call it a very abnormal fluctuation, and advise you that something was fishy with either the flipper or the coin. Even though the ratio of heads to tails has remained 7 to 3, the large number of flips makes such a highly skewed result suspect.

When you are considering even-money bets (bet $1 to either win $1 or lose $1), on a coin flip, you can figure out the standard deviation on your win/loss result for any number of flips simply by taking the square root of the number of flips. It is not difficult to figure this out on any pocket calculator that has a square root key. The square root of 100 is 10, so the standard deviation on our win/loss results in 100 coin flips betting $1 a flip is $10. The square root of 1,000 is approximately 31.62, so the standard deviation on the results of 1,000 $1 coin-flips is $31.62.

Once you understand what the square root of a number means to a statistician, you will understand why it can be perfectly normal for you to lose $4 with $1 bets on ten flips of an honest coin, but nearly impossible for you to lose $4,000 with $1 bets on 10,000 flips of that same coin.

The standard deviation on ten $1 bets equals the square root of 10 equals $3.16.

The standard deviation on 10,000 $1 bets equals the square root of 10,000 equals $100.

So, to have a loss of $4 in ten flips of the coin is to be just over one standard deviation ($3.16) away from our break-even expectation.

But to lose $4,000 in 10,000 flips of the coin, where one standard deviation (SD) is $100, is to be forty standard deviations away from our expectation. This is in the realm of the mathematically impossible.

How impossible is it?

Statistically, you expect to be within one standard deviation of your expectation 68% of the time. You will be within two standard deviations of your expectation 95% of the time. You will be within three standard deviations 99.7% of the time.

Let's put these numbers into a chart so you can get a clear picture of how the number of coin flips affects the extent of normal fluctuations:

COIN-FLIP FLUCTUATIONS ON $1 BETS			
# flips	1 SD (68%)	2 SD (95%)	3 SD (99.7%)
10	$3.16	$6.32	$9.49
100	$10.00	$20.00	$30.00
500	$22.36	$44.72	$67.08
2,500	$50.00	$100.00	$150.00
10,000	$100.00	$200.00	$300.00

One way I could use this chart would be to estimate my bankroll requirements if I was planning to wager on 100 coin-flip contests. I can see that 95% of the time (2 SDs) I would finish within $20 of my break-even expectation, and 99.7% of the time, I'd finish within $30 of my break-even expectation. So, if I've got $30 to play with, I can be pretty sure I'll last through the 100 coin flips without going broke.

And, suffice it to say that if you get a coin flip result that is forty standard deviations from your expectation, as in the 10,000-flip example mentioned above, either the coin or the flipper is crooked. You have a much better chance of winning your state lottery than you do of flipping 7,000 heads in 10,000 trials with an honest coin.

Now, the results on a poker tournament buy-in involve many complexities that are not involved in a simple $1 bet on a coin flip. First of all, not all of the money you pay to enter a tournament will go to the prize pool. Second, most tournament bets are not a 50/50 proposition. Unless a tournament is heads-up between two players of equal skill, a player will make it into the money far less often than he will bust out, and when he does make it into the money, his payout will depend on his finishing position. And, it's impossible to know in advance exactly what percentage of the time a player will finish in any given position. How do you account for all of these factors if you want to estimate your bankroll requirements for entering tournaments?

The actual formula for standard deviation is based on figuring out the fluctuations for all of the possible results, then figuring out the overall fluctuation on these combined results. I'm going to show you how to do this for poker tournaments, but first, I'm going to show you the math for dealing with standard deviation on a coin flip contest structured as a tournament, in order to prepare you for the more complicated math of actual poker tournaments.

In this example, each flip of the coin is one tournament. I want to be able to figure out the fluctuations I might expect if I entered, say, 100 tournaments.

Coin-flip Tournament Buy-in: $1
Possible Finish Results: First place pays $2; Second place pays $0.
Frequency of Finish Results: First place: 0.50; Second place: 0.50 (or 50% each)

Note here that we're calling a win (heads) first place, and it pays $2, while a loss (tails) is second place and pays $0. That $2 pay for first place is simply the usual $1 win, but here it is expressed as a tournament prize, or as the total delivered to the winner. Now we have the data you need to estimate the standard deviation on your win/loss results in a tournament. Let's put this coin-flip tournament data into a chart, in which the last column is going to be a formula for estimating the fluctuations on the individual first or second place results. At the bottom of that last column, you will find the total of the individual results.

Result	Buy-in (B)	Payout (P)	Frequency (f)	$f \times (P/B - 1)^2$
1st	$1	$2	0.50	.50
2nd	$1	0	0.50	.50
			Total:	$1.00

Standard Deviation per Tournament =
Buy-in ($1) x square root of total ($1) = $1.00

That chart may look like nothing more than a complicated way to come up with the number $1.00, but it will be useful later. And what exactly do we mean by the bottom line: "standard deviation per tournament?" Well, this is a very convenient number to have because if you want to know the standard deviation on your win/loss result for any number of tournaments, you simply multiply this number by the square root of the number of tournaments you intend to play.

So, if I'm going to play 100 of these coin-flip tournaments, all I have to do is multiply my SD per tournament ($1) by the square root of 100, which is 10, to find out that one standard deviation on 100 tournaments is $10—exactly what we got for 100 coin-flips before we put them into this more complicated tournament structure. But what we can do with this chart that we couldn't do before is use it to figure out much more complicated fluctuations on tournaments that have more complex payout structures.

Let's start with a simple poker tournament example. Let's assume that you are playing in a $109 buy-in tournament with 100 players, that the tournament will play down to the last ten players, and that each of the last ten players will receive the same $1,000 prize. This is not all that different from a typical super satellite format, except that the satellite will typically award a seat in a $1,000 tournament instead of $1,000 cash. The house commission on this tournament is $9, and that entry fee does not go into the prize pool.

In addition, let's assume that based on your current skills, you're playing a break-even game, so that you expect to break even with your competitors after 100 of these tournaments, winning ten times and losing ninety times. Because of the $9 entry fees, after 100 of these tournaments you expect to be down $900. But what is the standard deviation on your expected result (-$900) after 100 of these tournaments?

There are three things you must know to figure this out for any tournament. What is your buy-in cost? What are the payouts? And how frequently do you get each payout? Here's the data:

> **Buy-in:** $109
> **Payout for 1st-10th place:** $1,000
> **Payout for 11th-100th place:** $0
> **Frequency of win:** 0.10 (10%)
> **Frequency of loss:** 0.90 (90%)

Here's our chart:

Result	Buy-in (B)	Payout (P)	Frequency (f)	$f \times (P/B - 1)^2$
1st-10th	$109	$1,000	0.10	6.68
11th-100th	$109	0	0.90	0.90
			Total:	7.58

SD per Tournament =
Buy-in ($109) x square root of total (2.753) = $300

If you take out a pocket calculator and simply insert the proper variables for P, B and f into the formula that heads the last column, you should come out with numbers that match those in the chart. If you total the numbers in that fifth column, you should get 7.58, and the square root of 7.58 is 2.753.

Finally, as in the coin-flip tournament example, you multiply the buy-in ($109) times the square root of the last column total (2.753), to get $300. That is the standard deviation per tournament that you enter. And, yes, I know you're only paying $109 to enter each tournament. Read on.

As a statistical measure, standard deviation is pretty meaningless when you talk about one tournament, especially for any wager—or tournament buy-in—that does not have an even money payout. Obviously, if you only play one of these tournaments, you cannot lose more than $109. So, it would be impossible to have a negative fluctuation of one standard deviation on a single tournament. The reason the SD is so high per tournament is that it is averaging our positive and negative fluctuations, based on their frequency of occurrence, and those $1,000 wins you expect 10% of the time pull up the average. You don't have any use for standard deviation, however, if you only intend to play one tournament. You already know that you will either win $1,000 or lose $109, and that's all you need to know.

Standard deviation becomes a more useful measure when you intend to keep playing this tournament a couple of nights per week for a year. What will the standard deviation on your results be after 100 such tournaments? This is very easy to figure out once you know the SD per tournament. You simply multiply the SD per tournament times the square root of the total number of tournaments you expect to play, or 100. And since the square root of 100 = 10, the SD on 100 tournaments with this format is:

$$300 \text{ x } 10 \ = \ \$3,000$$

What does this number $3,000 tell us? It tells us that although you expect to break even against your competitors over the course of these 100 tournaments, minus the $900 you pay to the house in entry fees, 68% of the time you'd expect to be within $3,000 of -$900, or somewhere between -$3,900 and +$2,100 for the year. As you can see, this deviation may be positive or negative, due purely to luck. What would cause such a result? Well, instead of winning ten tournaments, you would be within one standard deviation of your expected result if you won anywhere from seven to thirteen tournaments. You might express this as: "I expect to win ten of these 100 tournaments, give or take three."

Does this mean that the worst result you might expect is to win only seven tournaments, when your break-even skill level would predict ten wins?

Unfortunately, no.

As I mentioned, you can expect to be within one standard deviation of your expected result 68% of the time. You can expect to be within two standard deviations of your expected result 95% of the time. And you can expect to be within three standard deviations of your expected result 99.7% of the time—or just about always.

This means that although your expectation is to win ten of these 100 tournaments, you can expect to be between seven and thirteen wins (one SD) 68% of the time; between four and sixteen wins (two SDs) 95% of the time; and between one and nineteen wins (3 SDs) virtually always.

You might note that you have close to a one-third chance of having a fluctuation greater than one standard deviation, so it would not be unusual for you to lose more than $3,900 over the course of this year of tournaments, and even a $6,900 loss (the result of winning only four times, instead of your expected ten) would not be all that far-fetched.

Now let's look at a more realistic tournament format. Other than super satellites, there aren't any tournaments I know of that pay all those who finish in the money the same prize. Let's again assume that you are playing in $109 tournaments, but with this more typical payout structure (shown on the following page).

Finish	Dollars
1st	$3,200
2nd	$2,000
3rd	$1,400
4th	$1,000
5th	$800
6th	$550
7th	$400
8th	$300
9th	$200
10th	$125
11th-100th	$0

Let's assume again for the moment that you are a break-even tournament player. In this case, you expect to get into the money exactly ten times, but you expect to win one 1st place, one 2nd place, one 3rd place, two 4th places, one 6th place, one 7th place, one 9th place, and two 10th places. (I'm deliberately fudging these numbers to give you exactly $10,000 in winnings for a break-even result, or an average of $1,000 each for the ten wins, just as in the satellite structure.) So again, your expectation will be to finish the year behind by $900 because of the cost of paying your entry fees.

Let's set up a chart again to calculate the standard deviation on your finishes with this payout structure:

Result	Buy-in (B)	Payout (P)	Frequency (f)	f x (P/B – 1)²
1st	$109	$3,200	0.01	8.042
2nd	$109	$2,000	0.01	3.010
3rd	$109	$1,400	0.01	1.402
4th	$109	$1,000	0.02	1.3-35
6th	$109	$550	0.01	0.164
7th	$109	$400	0.01	0.071
9th	$109	$200	0.01	0.007
10th	$109	$125	0.02	0.000
11th-100th	$109	$0	0.90	0.900
			Total:	14.931

Standard Deviation per Tournament =
Buy-in ($109) x square root of total (3.864) = $421

Note first that although you are still playing the same break-even game, the standard deviation per tournament has gone up from $300 to $421. That is a direct result of the skewed payout structure. If you intend to play 100 of these tournaments, with these payouts for your results, then one standard deviation (multiplying $421 by the square root of 100, or 10) is $4,210, instead of $3,000. And two standard deviations is $8,420. Now, despite your playing a breakeven game in these 100 tournaments, it's not inconceivable that you could end up losing more than $9,000 just due to bad fluctuations. Later you'll see that when you're playing with an edge, this gets better. But tournaments are not kind to break-even players.

Before moving on to a discussion of fluctuations with skillful play, I want to point out that there isn't really a typical break-even player that can serve as a perfect model for estimating the standard deviation on breakeven results. The finishes in the above example are just one possibility of how such a player might break even. A more aggressive break-even player might finish in the money less often, but actually capture a couple of first place finishes. A more conservative break-even player might finish in the money more often than 10% of the time, but rarely with a finish in the top two or three places. This example is meant solely to help you understand the math of fluctuations in order to get a handle on what you might expect.

Now, most serious players are not interested in what fluctuations might be for a player who has no advantage over his competition. Players who have the skill to win are much more interested in the kinds of fluctuations they might face in spite of their level of skill. So, let's take this analysis further.

Let's say you are a very skillful player, and that you enjoy a 200% advantage on the dollars you invest in tournaments—and this is not an unusual win rate for a talented tournament player. Professional tournament players often estimate their advantages as between 200% and 300%. One easy way to simulate this result would be to use the same chart as above, but assume that you finish in the money more often in the higher-payout finish positions. Here's what the chart looks like with more frequent and higher payouts at about a 200% advantage:

	200% ADVANTAGE CHART			
Result	Buy-in (B)	Payout (P)	Frequency (f)	$f \times (P/B - 1)^2$
1st	$109	$3,200	0.04	32.167
2nd	$109	$2,000	0.04	12.039
3rd	$109	$1,400	0.04	5.611
4th	$109	$1,000	0.03	2.005
6th	$109	$550	0.03	0.491
7th	$109	$400	0.02	0.143
9th	$109	$200	0.00	0.000
10th	$109	$125	0.00	0.000
11th-100th	$109	$0	0.80	0.800
			Total:	53.255

Standard Deviation per Tournament =
Buy-in ($109) x square root of total above (7.298) = $795

Note first that this skillful player's standard deviation per tournament has gone up from the break-even player's. However, since this skillful player, based on his 200% advantage, expects to finish his 100 tournaments $19,100 ahead—$20,000 in winnings minus the $900 house fees—he can afford more flux. On 100 tournaments, one standard deviation would be the square root of 100 (or 10) times $795, which is $7,950, up from $4,210 for the breakeven player. So, he has a 68% chance of being between +$11,150 and +$27,050.

And, with 95% certainty he'll be within two standard deviations of this result. Since his expected profit on these 100 tournaments is $19,100, even with miserable luck (minus two full standard deviations), a player at this skill level should still be up by $3,200 after 100 of these tournaments, and on the positive side his two standard deviation result could go up to +$35,000.

Tournament fluctuations are extreme because each tournament is a single bet, and even if you're playing a lot of tournaments, you can only make so many of these bets per year. It's not easy to get securely into your long run results unless you have a very sizeable advantage. Blackjack card counters can make a lot of money with only a 1% advantage over the house because they can play tens of thousands of hands in a reasonable period of time. For a tournament player to play with a 1% (or even a 10%) advantage would be futile.

These examples are designed to demonstrate how to compute tournament standard deviation. They are not designed as guidelines for any specific tournament. If you actually have a handle on your win rate, and how often you might place in various money positions, you can use this method to estimate your flux in the actual tournaments you enter. Remember to include the house fee in the buy-in amount.

As for the dollar payouts, most tournaments do not post these payouts until after they see exactly how many players have entered. Most do publish the payout percentages, however, so that if you know a regular tournament you play tends to get roughly eighty players, you can use that number to estimate the dollar values of the payouts, from which you can estimate the standard deviation.

If you are going to be playing tournaments regularly, you can put the formula for estimating the standard deviation into a spreadsheet, and play with the possibilities to your heart's content. Try different ways of getting a 200% advantage based on different types of finishes. What you'll find is that if you get your advantage by finishing more often up at the top, but with fewer total finishes in the money, your standard deviation will go up. If you get your advantage by many finishes in the money, but with fewer top place finishes, the standard deviation will go down. But it's not easy to get a really high percentage advantage with lower rung finishes. Also, try different win rates. Look at how much better it is to have a 200% advantage than 100%, especially insofar as your reduced bankroll requirements. A few top finishes are worth many finishes in the bottom end of the money.

But before discussing any further how to estimate your own standard deviation and required bankroll, we have to cover yet another factor in tournament standard deviation—the effect of the number of players in the field. Tournaments range from single-table satellites with ten players to major events with more than a thousand players. And, as players are added, the number of paid finishing positions and the payout percentages for each place change. As you'll see below, fluctuations increase as the number of players goes up. In these days of huge tournaments with fields in the thousands of players, field size is a huge factor in determining your bankroll requirements.

ACCOUNTING FOR THE NUMBER OF PLAYERS

Tournaments typically pay approximately 10% of the total number of players who enter. A tournament with sixty players, for example, will often pay the top six finishers. A tournament with 100 players will often pay the top ten. And a tournament with 200 players will often pay the top twenty. There is no standard payout structure that demands this, but it is the norm.

Unfortunately, as tournament fields get larger, with a greater number of players getting paid, tournaments don't adjust the prize structure to equitably handle the increased number of payouts. The best way for a tournament prize structure to minimize players' bankroll fluctuations would be to reduce each prize's payout percentage proportionately with the increase in field size. For example, if 1st place pays 32% of the prize pool with a field of 100 players, it should pay 32% total to the top 1% of players if the field gets larger. If the tournament grows to the size of the main event at the WSOP, and gets 6,000 players, then the top sixty players would have to share 32% of the total prize pool to reduce the skillful players' fluctuations.

But tournaments are interested in attracting players with humongous prizes, so they don't do this. Instead, they reduce the top prizes a far smaller percentage, and reduce the bottom prizes a far greater percentage. It's sort of like recent tax structures. The rich come out way ahead, and the poor and middle classes pay for it.

The effect of this is that variance increases as field size increases, so that it takes a larger bankroll to play in a bigger tournament even if it has the same buy-in as a smaller one and you have the same skill advantage over your opponents. And this effect is drastic with really huge fields.

As an extreme example, let's look at the main event of the 2005 WSOP, which had 5,619 players. In this tournament, the top 560 finishers, or about 10% of the field, placed in the money. But, if you finished in 501st place (or actually in any position from 501 to 560), the payout was only $12,500. These finishers essentially got back their $10,000 buy-ins, plus a profit of $2,500.

What this means is, even if you had the skill to finish in the money in 501st place seven out of ten times that you played this tournament, beating 91% of your competitors over and over after five days of play, at the end of those seven finishes in the money in ten years, you would be behind for your efforts by $12,500! Though not as distressing as always getting knocked out before you get into the money, bottom rung finishes are always painful, and for good reason.

And, no player can realistically expect to finish in the money 70% of the time in a tournament of this size, even in the bottom rungs. So, let's say you were able to finish in the money just once in ten years of playing this event. Where would you have to place in this finish in order to break even assuming the field size stayed the same? You'd have to finish between 37th and 45th place, just to get enough of a payout to cover your ten years of buy-ins. If you finished in 46th place on that one win ahead of more than 99% of the field, you'd be down by more than $26,000 overall.

I'm not trying to discourage anyone from playing this event. I'm just trying to give you a realistic picture of what you're up against in any tournament with a mammoth field of players. By contrast, if you were in the top 1% in a field of 100 players, you would take first prize and a hefty return on investment (roughly 230%) even if you only accomplish this one out of ten times. This is why you need a field size adjustment when estimating fluctuations in poker tournaments.

The mathematical effect of the number of players in a tournament is not a linear effect. That is to say, if fifty players are entered in Tournament A, and 500 players are entered in Tournament B, the player's chance of success in Tournament A is not ten times as great as in Tournament B simply because there is only one-tenth the number of competitors. You will not actually have ten times as many confrontations in Tournament B as in Tournament A. That's because, while you are facing confrontations at your table, risking your tournament life so to speak, other players are having confrontations at other tables where you have no involvement or risk whatsoever. In Tournament A, there will be four other tables besides yours when the tournament begins, and at all of these tables, players will be going through an elimination process simultaneously. In Tournament B, this elimination process will be taking place at forty-nine other tables in addition to yours.

Because of this, a tournament with ten times as many players does not take ten times as long to play out. Every time ten more players are added to a tournament, another table is added where players will go through this simultaneous elimination process. But an increased number of players in a tournament does increase the length of time a tournament takes to play out, as well as the number of confrontations each player must survive. And this increases every player's variance, independent of the payout structure effect.

It turns out that the solution to how field size affects variance, as with so many statistical problems that deal with variance, is that the fluctuations do not increase linearly according to the number of players, but according to the square root of the number of players. (This discovery was what led me to the final table ETA formula.) Doubling the number of players in a tournament has a statistically similar effect to doubling the number of coin flips before looking at the win results.

Think of it this way. Player A is playing in a tournament with 100 players, and after four hours of play, he makes the final table. Player B is playing in a similarly structured tournament—but with 200 players—and after four hours of play, he is among the top twenty players of the fifty players remaining. But Player B's tournament still has an hour or so of play before the field is reduced to just the players who are in the money.

Technically, Player B has accomplished in the same time frame exactly what Player A has accomplished. In four hours of play, both players have positioned themselves in the top 10% of the starting field. But Player A is in the money. Player B is not. He may be very well positioned to get there, but he's still flipping coins, so to speak.

SNYDER'S BANKROLL FUDGE FORMULA

My method for determining the minimum bankroll requirement for a specific tournament, assuming a tournament player has an approximate 200% advantage, is to multiply the total cost of the tournament by the square root of the number of players. Then double this number. I devised this method to mimic results obtained by calculating the standard deviation a player this skilled would encounter in various tournament structures with various numbers of players. I regard the bankroll requirement calculated by the method I'm proposing to be the minimum bankroll requirement. The recommended bankroll with this method should get a player this skilled through most of his worst negative fluctuations.

For example, if there are 200 players in a tournament, and

the buy-in is $130, then your minimum bankroll requirement for playing this tournament is the square root of 200 (14.14) x $130 x 2 = $3,676. So, if you've got a total playing bankroll in the neighborhood of $3,500 or more, and you are playing with an edge of about 150% to 200%, you should be able to withstand the bad flux you'll encounter in these $130 tournaments.

A few qualifiers—I am basing this advice on three assumptions:

1. That you intend to play *a lot* of tournaments.

2. That you are a skillful player. I'm assuming that you have a very strong advantage over your opponents, providing you with a 150% to 200% win rate.

3. That you are going to re-evaluate your bankroll position frequently. If your bankroll has substantial early negative flux, you'll have to limit yourself to cheaper tournaments or tournaments with fewer players until your bankroll recovers.

The chart at the end of Chapter 28 is based on the flux you may expect to encounter in 100 tournaments. I chose 100 tournaments for my estimates because if a player has a 150% advantage or more, he should have enough wins within 100 tournaments to replenish his bankroll from any losing streaks, and to keep him going until his wins bring him up to his long-run expectation. There is always some rare but real mathematical possibility that any player can hit a bad run worse than this, but professional gamblers work within more normal probabilities.

In addition, my chart estimates are based on withstanding fluctuations up to about two standard deviations. That's why I recommend frequent reevaluation of your bankroll and the tournaments you can afford. You would make it through the fluctuations 95% of the time without reevaluating, but frequent reassessments will protect you should you be one of the unlucky players whose negative results go beyond two standard deviations.

And don't be tempted to adjust the bankroll requirement downward based on your presumption that you possess a greater level of skill. Even if you think you have an advantage much greater than 200% because you're playing against complete poker morons, your fluctuations won't change that much. The number of players, whether they're smart players or not, is a major factor in the number of hours a tournament lasts, and this directly affects the number of confrontations you must survive. You may be a 2 to 1 favorite half a dozen times in your confrontations with lesser players, but that only means that you'd expect to win four of these battles, and lose two. Either one of those losing confrontations could cripple you, or bust you out. And the fact is—you could lose all six confrontations and it would be a meaningless blip of standard deviation to a mathematician. This stuff happens all the time. It's not like you're having thousands of these confrontations in every tournament, all at affordable chip amounts, so that your actual percentage of success will stay close to expectation. Your overall win or loss in any given tournament will result from a relative handful of very high-risk confrontations.

If you are a player of lesser skill, but still a winning tournament player, then you probably ought to have twice the bankroll this method estimates if you want to assure yourself of survival. And again, should your bankroll go into a nose-dive, be willing to start entering tournaments with either smaller buy-ins or smaller fields of players, until you rebuild your bank.

Most of the small buy-in tournaments in live poker rooms will have fields of fifty to 300 players. Small buy-in Internet tournaments, however, will often have much larger fields. Once again, look at how the size of the field affects the bankroll requirements for entry. Let's compare the bankroll requirements for entering the $130 tournament described above with 60 players, 200 players, and 1,000 players, such as you might find in a popular online poker tournament. For this comparison, note that the square root of 60 =7.75, and the square root of 1,000 = 31.62.

# of Players	Sqrt # Players		Cost			Min. Bankroll Req.
60	7.75	x	$130	x 2	=	$2,014
200	14.14	x	$130	x 2	=	$3,676
1,000	31.62	x	$130	x 2	=	$8,222

I've mentioned a number of times that in the small buy-in tournaments where I started tournament play, I made the final table in about one in five tournaments. In the graph of my initial seventy-five small buy-in tournament results in Chapter 28, the average number of players in the tournaments was 143. (I keep track of this stuff and so should you.) If you are playing in tournaments with 1,000 players, you should expect to make it into the money much less frequently, even though you may expect some substantially higher payouts when you do finish in the money. Making a final table in a tournament of 1,000 players will be a huge payday relative to such a finish in a tournament with 140 players. Likewise, a tournament with sixty players will have only about 30% of the prize pool of a tournament with 200 players, assuming the same buy-in cost, but also more frequent money finishes and lower fluctuations.

An increased number of players may raise your advantage if many of these added players are not skilled. But again, this increase in advantage due to the size of the field comes at the price of higher variance and a larger bankroll requirement.

Ideally, many other tournament-specific factors would enter into these required-bankroll calculations. Some of these factors are impossible to put numbers on—including the various skill levels of all your opponents relative to your skill. Other factors that might alter the formula would include the total number of chips in play, the exact blind structure, the number of finishers in the money, and the precise payout structure for the winners. Consider the fudge formula a general guide, and understand that you should look at the estimated bankroll requirement as the minimum amount required to get through most bad swings for a dedicated and skillful tournament player who plays lots of tournaments with no intention of stopping any time soon.

Some tournament pros have become discouraged with the huge fields now participating in the WSOP events. As recently as 2002, the $10,000 main event had only 630 participants. In 2004, this number was 2,760, and in 2005, there were 5,619 entries. Look at what these big fields do to the bankroll requirements. First, the square roots:

Square root of 630 = 25.10
Square root of 2,760 = 52.54
Square root of 5,619 = 74.96

Multiplying each of these square roots by the $10,000 buy-in cost, then multiplying by two, you get the following minimum bankroll requirements:

MINIMUM BANKROLL REQUIREMENTS	
Number of Players	Bankroll
630	$502,000
2,760	$1,050,800
5,619	$1,499,200

How can the flux be so high as to require such large bankrolls? Consider a player who will make it to tenth place at the final table in a field of 5,000 players, for a payout of about $1,000,000, just once every fifty years. That single win every half century would give this player a long-run advantage of 200% even if he never made it into the money in any of the other forty-nine years! One standard deviation on fifty of these tournaments, however, is more than $900,000. Since this player would only be investing $500,000 in fifty years time, how could he have a negative fluctuation of $900,000? Well, he couldn't, but fifty years is really too short of a time period to get a realistic handle on the possible negative fluctuation, because he has an expectation of only one occurrence of a win within this 50-year time period. With an expectation of only one such win, there's just a great chance he won't get any such win in his lifetime. This is why, incidentally, pros were stunned at the consecutive final table finishes of Dan Harrington in 2003 and 2004, and then Greg Raymer's phenomenal 25th place finish in 2005 after winning the 2004 event.

In fact, it's more realistic to assume that these top money finishes will likely occur less than once every 100 years, so that you can add a few lower money finishes which are far more likely. Either that, or you have to assume that this player actually has an advantage of 1,000 percent or more, and I just don't think *any* player has that big of a long run advantage, especially considering that when you get down to the last few hundred players, you will be competing with many of the world's top pros.

How do the tournament pros deal with this flux? Some millionaires simply cough up the $10,000 entry fee, as it's no big thing to them, and they hope for the best. Others have millionaires who stake them. Some just figure the WSOP comes around but once per year, and they can afford the $10,000 risk for a once-a-year long shot. But many tournament pros on the major tournament circuit do what many high stakes blackjack players have always done—pool their money, with each member of the team owning a piece of each other player, enabling them to share in the paydays of any team members who get into the money.

Most of the top pros in the world will not make it into the money in a field of 5,000+ players, despite thousands of players who are dead money. This is not to say that such a tournament is simply a luck-fest, where the players who get dealt the best cards win. This is not the case at all. In fact, an unskilled player who might make it on lucky cards to the final table of a fast tournament with 100 in the field, would not stand a chance of making it through a field of thousands of players in a tournament with such a slow blind structure. But neither is it inconceivable that many top players in today's 1,000+ field WSOP events could enter all forty-five events and never once make it into the money, purely as a result of suck-outs and bad beats from amateurs.

G

GLOSSARY

ace master: A hold'em player who will play any hand in any pot from any position if one of his cards is an ace.

aces up: In hold'em, to have two pair, one of which is aces.

action: General casino slang for the total amount bet by players. In poker, any betting by the players on a round is the "action."

add-on: In poker tournaments, an option to buy a specified number of chips at the end of a specified time period.

aggressive: A style of play characterized by raising and reraising frequently.

all in: In no-limit hold'em, a bet of all a player's chips.

ante: A forced bet that must be placed by *all* players at the table before any cards have been dealt.

auto-dumping: A tournament cheating technique whereby a player pockets tournament chips in order to surreptitiously introduce them into his chip stack in another tournament.

baby full: A full house that is not the best possible full house because the three-of-a-kind are made with one of the lower denomination community cards.

backdoor: To make a straight or flush by drawing to it on both the turn and river. Often an accidental improvement, as when a player with top pair backdoors a flush.

bad beat: To have a very strong hand beaten by an even stronger hand.

bad beat jackpot: A consolation prize awarded by some poker rooms to a player who suffers an extremely bad beat.

bank/bankroll: The total amount of money a player has to gamble with.

basic strategy: The mathematically correct strategy for any gambling game.

big slick: In hold'em, A-K in the hole.

blind: A forced bet that must be placed preflop by a player or players to the left of the dealer position before any cards have been dealt. Usually, only two players, on a rotating basis, are required to place blind bets.

blind level: In tournament hold'em, the current amount of the forced bets made by the player to the left of the button. As the tournament progresses, the level rises.

blinded off: In a tournament, to be eliminated by having one's chips slowly dwindled by the blinds and antes without playing a hand.

bluff: To place a bet with a weak hand in order to represent a strong hand and attempting to win a pot by causing other players to fold.

board: In hold'em, the face-up community cards on the table.

boat: A full house, also full boat.

bonus: Money added to a player's account in return for some specified deposit and action in an online poker room's games.

bot: A computer program that plays poker, either for practice, or in real games online.

bottom pair: A pair made by matching the lowest card on the board with one of your hole cards.

bounty: A cash prize awarded in some tournaments for busting out a competitor.

build (a pot): To increase the amount of money in a pot by betting and/or raising in such a way that other players are induced to call.

bust out: To lose all of your chips.

button: The disk that rotates clockwise from player to player, indicating which player has the dealer position and bets last.

buy-in: The amount you pay to obtain your initial chips for a game.

call: To match a bet without raising in order to keep your hand alive in a pot.

calling station: A derogatory term for a passive player who rarely raises, but often calls with any hand, whether weak or strong.

camouflage: Any bet or play intended to mislead an opponent, usually into thinking one's hand is weaker than it is.

card protector: A chip or other small object a player places over his face-down hole cards to indicate that his hand is alive.

card switching: A cheating move in which a player surreptitiously removes a card from play, then switches it into the game later as needed.

cash out: To withdraw your funds from a poker room by exchanging your chips for cash.

catch: To improve or make a hand by "catching" a card or cards on the flop, turn, or river.

change gears: To play more, or less, aggressively than previously.

charge: To bet in order to make other players pay to stay in a pot.

check: To stay in a pot in which no bet is required, and without betting.

check-raise: To reraise a player who has bet, after having checked to him earlier in the same round.

chip dumping: In tournaments, a cheating technique whereby one player purposely loses his chips to a cohort in order to provide the other player with a stronger chip position.

chip leader: In a tournament, the player who currently has the most chips.

chip passing: In tournaments, a cheating technique in which one player surreptitiously removes some of his chips from the table, then secretly passes them to a confederate who is playing at a different table.

chip position: In poker tournaments, the relation of a player's current chip stack to the stacks of his opponents.

chip shot: A bluff bet made with a substantial number of chips to scare an opponent out of a pot.

chopping the prize pool: In tournaments, to divide up the prize money at the final table, before the tournament ends, by mutual agreement of the remaining players.

collusion: To cheat by surreptitiously sharing information with one or more confederates at the table.

community cards: The face-up cards on the table that all players may combine with the cards in their hands to make the best possible five-card hand.

connectors: Hole cards that are consecutive in value, such as J-Q or 7-6.

counterfeit: In hold'em, for a card to come down on the turn or river that cripples a player's formerly strong hand, usually by pairing one of the cards on the board.

crunch time: In fast tournaments, the last opportunity players have to use skillful play before the rising blinds reduce the tournament to a matter of luck.

cut-off seat: The seat to the right of the button.

dead money: A weak player who has little chance of winning.

dealers' bonus chips: In tournaments, a voluntary extra chip purchase allowed to all players for a nominal fee, with the proceeds going into a pool for the dealers' compensation.

define a hand: To bet in such a way as to reveal the strength of one's hole cards.

deposit: Money placed with an online poker room cashier for the purpose of playing the games.

disguised hand: A hand whose strength is not suspected by a competitor because of misleading betting action earlier.

dominated hand: Hole cards in which one card matches another player's hole card, while the other player's kicker is stronger. K-Q is dominated by A-Q.

drawing dead: To draw to a hand with no chance of winning because another player already has a hand ranked higher than any hand that could be made.

draw out: To beat a player who had a better hand prior to the cards that appeared on the flop, turn, or river.

early position: The players who must act first—generally, the first four betting positions in a ten-handed game.

entry fee: In a gambling tournament, the amount a player pays to the house that does not go into the prize pool.

fast: In tournaments, any playing structure that requires players to play loosely and bet aggressively to stay competitive.

fifth street: The fifth community card. Also called the river.

final table: In a tournament, the last table of players remaining after all others have been eliminated.

fish: A poor player who is expected to lose.

flop: In hold'em, the first three community cards dealt onto the table after the first betting round.

flush: Any five suited cards.

flush draw: A hand in which it is possible to make a flush with one or more cards to come.

flush master: A hold'em player who will play any two suited cards, and who will stay in any pot as long as his flush draw is alive.

flux: Common gamblers' slang for fluctuations, the inevitable short-term winning and losing streaks caused by good and bad luck, as opposed to any actual advantage or disadvantage in the games.

fold: To discard a hand by refusing to call a bet.

fourth street: In hold'em, the fourth community card dealt face-up onto the table. Also called the turn.

free card: A turn or river card that any active player can see without having to put more money into the pot, because no betting occurred on the prior betting round.

free roll: Any bet or game that costs nothing but has a potential monetary return.

full house: A hand consisting of a pair and three-of-a-kind. Also called a boat or full boat.

full-ring game: In poker, a 9- or 10-handed game.

gutshot: An inside straight draw, or any straight draw that can only be made on one end. Also called a one-way straight draw, or a belly-buster.

hand history: In online poker, a feature made possible by the poker room's software that allows players to review the hands at the tables where they played after the action is over.

heads up: Betting that occurs between only two players.

hit: For the board cards to increase the value of a player's hand. If a player has a pocket pair and a trip card comes down on the flop, the flop *hit* him.

hold up: To have a hand that is not the nuts win the pot.

hole cards: In hold'em, the players' first two cards, dealt face down.

house: The poker room.

implied odds: The mathematical relationship of the current bet you must make to the total you ultimately expect to win if you take the pot, after taking into account the possible betting action after your bet.

in the dark: To play without looking at one's hole cards.

in the money: In tournaments, any finishing position that pays a portion of the prize pool.

inside straight draw: A hand in which you have four cards to a straight, but need a card that falls between two of your cards to make the straight, or can fall on only one end of your cards. Also called a gutshot, a belly-buster, or a one-way straight draw.

keep the lead: For a player who raised or led the betting on one betting round to automatically bet on the next betting round.

kicker: A hole card that will be used to determine a winner if two players otherwise have identical hands.

knock the table: To check.

last longer bet: A side-bet between players in a tournament in which the winner is the player who lasts longest among those participating in the bet.

late position: The last players to bet on a round, with the button being the latest position.

laydown: A fold of a strong hand because of perceived danger.

lead out: To enter a pot first in a betting round.

legitimate hand: Any hand that has a reasonable chance of winning a pot based on its strength.

limit: A game in which bets are limited to a specified betting structure, as opposed to no-limit.

limit the field: To raise in order to discourage marginal hands from entering a pot and possibly drawing out on you.

limp in: To enter a pot on the first betting round by calling the big blind.

limper: Any player who enters a pot preflop by just calling the big blind.

loose: A player who plays a higher percentage of hands than normal. A *loose table* is one where many players consistently enter the pot. A *loose call* is a call with a marginal hand that either could be easily beaten by many other hands given the cards on board, or a call that does not have the mathematical odds of winning necessary to justify the call as a good bet.

maniac: A very loose and aggressive player whose bets seem to have little relation to his cards or chances of winning.

marginal call: To call a bet when the odds of winning the hand are very close to the minimal odds needed to make the call a profitable bet.

middle position: Any of three seats located halfway between the first betting positions and the button. The middle positions to act on their hands.

mini-raise: A preflop raise of the minimum amount allowed.

miss: For the board cards to fail to increase the value of a player's hand.

mix up: To play the same hands in different ways at different times in order to keep competitors from figuring out their strength.

monster: Any highly ranked hand that is unlikely to be beaten, such as a full house or a straight flush.

muck: To fold. Also, the pile of already discarded cards on the table.

multiway pot: Any pot contested by more than two players.

NLH: No limit hold'em.

no-limit: A betting structure in which there is no upper limit to the amount a player can bet or raise.

nuts: A hand that, given the cards currently in play, cannot be beaten by any other hand.

odds: The chances against something occuring.

off-suit: Cards that are not suited.

on a draw: To have a potential, but not yet made, hand, that could improve if the right cards came down.

on tilt: A player who plays erratically and poorly, usually as a result of a bad beat or losing streak.

one-way straight draw: A hand with four cards to a straight that can only be completed by a card that falls between two of these cards or a card on one end, rather than either end. Also called a gutshot, a belly-buster, or inside straight draw.

open-end (straight draw): Four consecutive cards to a straight, which can be made with one more card on either end. Also called a two-way straight draw.

out: A card that will increase the value of a hand to a likely winner.

overbet: To bet an amount that seems big based on the size of the pot.

overcard: A card in the hole that is higher than the highest card on the board.

overpair: A pocket pair that is higher than the highest card on the board.

overplay: To bet too aggressively with a marginal hand.

over-the-top: To raise a bet or reraise.

passive: A non-aggressive playing style or a table with mostly checking and calling, and very little raising.

patience factor: A measure of a tournament's speed based on the number of starting chips and the blind structure.

play back: To continue to give action, particularly aggressive counter-action, to a player who is betting aggressively.

pocket: The hole cards, mostly used to describe a pair, such as "pocket pair," or "pocket jacks."

pocket rockets: In hold'em, hole-card aces.

position: The order in which a player must act on his hand.

position play: To bet in an attempt to take a pot based on having position on an opponent, not a legitimate hand.

postflop: The action that occurs after the flop.

pot: The total amount bet by all players in a current hand.

pot-committed: In a poker tournament, to have half or more of one's chips already in a pot so that abandoning the hand would leave a player with too few chips to remain competitive.

pot odds: The ratio of the total amount in the pot to the amount of the current bet.

preflop: Before the flop, usually in reference to the betting action.

price: The cost of playing a hand in relation to the potential return.

price out: To raise in order to make the price of playing mathematically incorrect for any competitor on a draw. "His all-in bet priced me out of the pot."

prize pool: In a tournament, the total amount of all prize money to be awarded to the winners.

probe bet: A bet placed, usually with a less-than-premium hand, for the purpose of seeing if a competitor will relinquish the pot without a fight.

progressive stack rebuy: A type of multiple rebuy tournament in which the rebuy chips are discounted more as the rebuy period progresses.

protecting a hand: Betting with a made hand to make it more expensive for competitors to try to draw out.

push in: For a player to bet all of his chips. Same as "all-in."

quads: Four of a kind.

rag: Any low card (usually 2-8).

rainbow: Cards of all different suits on the board after the flop.

raise: To increase the bet from the previous bet.

raising seat: In fast tournaments, the position two seats to the right of the button.

rake: The percentage of money the house takes from the pot.

read (a player): To deduce the strength of a player's hand from his actions, betting, or physical mannerisms.

read (the board): To figure out the possible hands in play based on the community cards.

rebuy: In some poker tournaments, to purchase more chips after a tournament has begun.

rebuy dumping: In multiple rebuy poker tournaments, an unethical technique whereby two or more players by mutual agreement continually push all-in on each other in order to artificially build their stacks.

reraise: To raise a prior bettor's raise.

ring game: A full-table non-tournament game, usually with 9-10 players.

river: In hold'em, the fifth and last community card to be dealt. Also known as fifth street.

rock: A very tight, conservative player.

royal flush: The highest ranking poker hand, ten through ace of the same suit.

runner-runner: To make a strong hand by catching needed cards on both the turn and river.

run over: To bully a player or players with very aggressive play.

sandbag: Same as slow play.

satellite: A poker tournament played to win a seat in a bigger tournament.

scare card: A card that appears on the board that makes premium hands possible.

semi-bluff: A bet made when you do not yet have a strong hand but might improve to a strong hand if the right card falls.

set: To make trips by holding a pocket pair and getting the third card on the board.

set a trap: To slowplay a very strong hand in order to disguise its strength and win more from your competitiors.

shark: Any highly skilled player in a field of weaker opponents.

sheriff: A player who will call down suspected bluffers, often to the detriment of his own bankroll.

shoot back: To reraise.

shot: Any bet you can make that will cause an opponent to fold and win you the pot whether or not you have the winning hand.

short bank: A playing bankroll that is dangerously small.

short-handed: A game in which there are fewer than eight players.

short stack: A small amount of chips to play with.

showdown: The revealing of active hands after all betting is completed to determine the pot winner.

sit'n'go: A popular type of tournament that has no scheduled time, but begins as soon as the required number of seats are filled with players.

slow play: To deliberately refrain from playing aggressively with a very big hand, usually to keep other players in the pot in order to draw more money out of them.

soft-play: To purposely avoid dangerous confrontations with another player out of friendship or mutual agreement, considered unethical.

split pot: A pot that is divided between two or more players holding identical hands.

standard deviation: A math term that quantifies the normal amount of fluctuation in results due to luck.

standard raise: In no-limit tournaments, a bet of three to four times the size of the big blind preflop. Also, a raise of about half the size of the current pot postflop.

starting hand: A player's hole cards.

steal: To take a pot by betting when you don't have a hand of value.

straight: A premium hand that consists of five consecutive cards with no gaps.

straight flush: One of the highest ranking poker hands. It consists of five consecutive cards, all of the same suit.

suck out: Same as draw out. To beat a player who has a better hand by making a superior hand with cards that come on the board.

suited: In hold'em, two hole cards that are the same suit. Also, any cards of the same suit.

super satellite: A multi-table satellite that will award multiple seats to a bigger tournament.

surrender: To fold.

table image: The style a player projects through his actions and demeanor, such as aggressive, timid, conservative, and crazy.

take a shot: To bet at the pot, usually hoping to win it with no callers or raises.

take a stand: To remain in a pot in the face of danger, usually by either scare cards on the board, an opponent with a superior chip position, or a bet or raise from an opponent.

take down: To win the pot.

tap out: To lose all one's funds.

tell: A player's subconscious action or mannerism that reveals something about the strength of his hand.

tight: A player who plays relatively few hands, also said of a table where there is little action because of the presence of many such players.

toke: A tip to a dealer or cocktail waitress.

top pair: To have a card in the hole that matches the top card on the board.

top set: For the highest card on the board to match a player's pocket pair.

tournament: Any gambling game that is set up with a formal structure for eliminating players until one (or some few) players remain. The winners share a prize pool composed of all players' buy-ins.

trap: Same as set a trap.

trips: Three of a kind.

turn: In hold'em, the fourth community card dealt on the board. Also known as fourth street.

two-way straight draw: To have four consecutive cards to a straight that can be made with one more card on either end. Also called an open-end straight draw.

under the gun: The first player to act on his hand preflop.

under-chipped: In a tournament, to have few chips relative to the size of the blinds and/or bets in a game.

unraised pot: A preflop pot in which all active players simply called the big blind (limped in) without raising.

variance: A math term that denotes the amount of fluctuation to be expected for a game.

WPT: World Poker Tour.

WSOP: World Series of Poker.

RECOMMENDED BOOKS

For more information on poker tournaments and information sources, see my website: www.pokertournamentformula.com.

FIVE BOOKS YOU MUST READ

1. *Super System 2: A Course in Power Poker,* Doyle Brunson (Cardoza Publishing, New York, 2005).

Brunson's chapter on no-limit hold'em is an updated version of the chapter he wrote for *Super/System 1* (1978) and it is still one of the best treatments of the no-limit game in print. All no-limit tournament players should familiarize themselves with the basics of the no-limit game in a non-tournament context. Also of interest in this book is Jennifer Harmon's treatment of limit hold'em and Mike Caro's 43 exclusive tips. I like just about everything that Caro writes because he doesn't just give advice on how to play, but how to think about playing.

2. *Caro's Book of Tells: The Body Language of Poker,* Caro, Mike (Cardoza Publishing, New York, 2003).

This is the only poker book ever written that deals exclusively with reading opponents by their body language. I've never met a player who hasn't learned a few tricks from this book. Illustrated with more than 100 photos.

3. *Championship No-Limit & Pot-Limit Hold'Em,* Cloutier, T.J. and McEvoy, Tom (Cardoza, Publishing, New York, 1997).

As one of the most successful tournament players of all time, Cloutier's thinking on the game should interest any player. Although the word "tournament" is not in the title, this is primarily a guide for tournament players, and primarily for those who play in long slow tournaments. Even if you don't play in these major events, you will profit from both authors' extensive knowledge and experience.

4. *Harrington on Hold'em, Vol. II,* Harrington, Dan and Robertie, Bill (Two Plus Two Publishing, Las Vegas, 2005).

One of the best books on tournament strategy in print by one of the world's top tournament players and creative thinkers, absolutely must reading if you intend to play major events.

5. *The Theory of Poker,* Sklansky, David (Two Plus Two Publishing, Las Vegas, 1994).

Sklansky wastes little ink on tournaments or no-limit games and really doesn't go into a lot of detail on hold'em. But this book goes into great detail on such subjects as giving free cards, raising, semi-bluffing, loose versus tight games, position, mistakes, and a dozen other topics related to the logic of all poker games.

OTHER RECOMMENDED BOOKS (BY TOPIC)

No-Limit Texas Hold'Em Tournaments

Harrington on Hold'Em, Vol. I, Harrington, Dan and Robertie, Bill (Two Plus Two Publishing, Las Vegas, 2004).

Championship Hold'Em Tournament Hands, McEvoy, Tom, and Cloutier, T.J. (formerly *Championship Tournament Practice Hands,* Cardoza Publishing, New York, 2005).

How to Win No-Limit Hold'Em Tournaments, Vines, Don, and McEvoy, Tom (Cardoza Publishing, New York, 2005).

No-Limit Texas Hold'Em

Super/System: A Course in Power Poker, Brunson, Doyle (Cardoza Publishing, New York, 2004).

No-Limit Texas Hold'Em, Daugherty, Brad and McEvoy, Tom (Cardoza Publishing, New York, 2004).

Poker Tournaments

Tournament Poker for Advanced Players, Sklansky, David (Two Plus Two Publishing, Las Vegas, 2002-3).

Poker Tournament Strategies, Suzuki, Sylvester (Two Plus Two Publishing, Las Vegas, 1998).

Poker Satellites

Win Your Way Into Big Money Hold'em Tournaments, McEvoy, Tom, and Daugherty, Brad (formerly *Championship Satellite Strategy,* Cardoza Publishing, New York, 2005).

Limit Texas Hold'Em

Middle Limit Holdem Poker, Ciaffone, Bob, and Brier, Jim (Ciaffone and Brier, 2001).

Winning Low Limit Hold'Em, Jones, Lee (ConJelCo, Pittsburgh, 2000).

Hold'Em Poker for Advanced Players, Sklansky, David, and Malmuth, Mason (Two Plus Two Publishing, Las Vegas, 1999).

Weighing the Odds in Hold'Em Poker, Yao, King (Pi Yee Press, Las Vegas, 2005).

Poker in General

Poker Wisdom of a Champion, Brunson, Doyle (formerly, *According to Doyle, 1984,* Cardoza Publishing, New York, 2003).

Caro's Fundamental Secrets of Winning Poker, Caro, Mike (Cardoza Publishing, New York, 1991, 2002).

Play Poker Like the Pros, Hellmuth, Phil, Jr. (Quill, New York, 2003).

Internet Poker

Internet Texas Hold'em, Hilger, Matthew (Dimat Enterprises, 2003).

How to Beat Internet Casinos and Poker Rooms, Snyder, Arnold (Cardoza Publishing, New York, 2006). There is little on poker strategy in this book, which focuses on how online games differ from live games and how to evaluate the deposit bonus offers at the online poker rooms.

On Cheating at Poker

Poker Protection: Cheating and the World of Poker, Forte, Steve (Forte, Las Vegas, 2006). Very comprehensive.

Poker Cheats Exposed, Piacente, Sal, 2-DVD set (Pocket Aces, LLC, Florence, KY, 2005). The finest video demonstration of poker-specific cheating techniques I've seen.

INDEX

POWERFUL POKER SIMULATIONS
A MUST FOR SERIOUS PLAYERS WITH A COMPUTER!
IBM compatible CD ROM Win 95, 98, 2000, NT, ME, XP - Full Color Graphics

---

These incredible full color poker simulation programs are the absolute best method to improve your game. Computer opponents play like real players. All games let you set the limits and rake and have fully programmable players, adjustable lineup, stat tracking, and Hand Analyzer for starting hands. MIke Caro, the world's foremost poker theoretician says, "Amazing... a steal for under $500... get it, it's great." Includes free telephone support. "Smart Advisor" gives expert advice for every play in every game!

1. TURBO TEXAS HOLD'EM FOR WINDOWS - $59.95 - Choose which players, and how many (2-10) you want to play, create loose/tight games, and control check-raising, bluffing, position, sensitivity to pot odds, and more! Also, instant replay, pop-up odds, Professional Advisor keeps track of play statistics. Free bonus: Hold'em Hand Analyzer analyzes all 169 pocket hands in detail and their win rates under any conditions you set. Caro says this "hold'em software is the most powerful ever created." Great product!

2. TURBO SEVEN-CARD STUD FOR WINDOWS - $59.95 - Create any conditions of play; choose number of players (2-8), bet amounts, fixed or spread limit, bring-in method, tight/loose conditions, position, reaction to board, number of dead cards, and stack deck to create special conditions. Features instant replay. Terrific stat reporting includes analysis of starting cards, 3-D bar charts, and graphs. Play interactively and run high speed simulation to test strategies. Hand Analyzer analyzes starting hands in detail. Wow!

3. TURBO OMAHA HIGH-LOW SPLIT FOR WINDOWS - $59.95 - Specify any playing conditions; betting limits, number of raises, blind structures, button position, aggressiveness/passiveness of opponents, number of players (2-10), types of hands dealt, blinds, position, board reaction, and specify flop, turn, and river cards! Choose opponents and use provided point count or create your own. Statistical reporting, instant replay, pop-up odds high speed simulation to test strategies, amazing Hand Analyzer, and much more!

4. TURBO OMAHA HIGH FOR WINDOWS - $59.95 - Same features as above, but tailored for Omaha High-only. Caro says program is "an electrifying research tool...it can clearly be worth thousands of dollars to any serious player. A must for Omaha High players.

5. TURBO 7 STUD 8 OR BETTER - $59.95 - Brand new with all the features you expect from the Wilson Turbo products: the latest artificial intelligence, instant advice and exact odds, play versus 2-7 opponents, enhanced data charts that can be exported or printed, the ability to fold out of turn and immediately go to the next hand, ability to peek at opponents hand, optional warning mode that warns you if a play disagrees with the advisor, and automatic testing mode that can run up to 50 tests unattended. Challenge tough computer players who vary their styles for a truly great poker game.

6. TOURNAMENT TEXAS HOLD'EM - $39.95 - Set-up for tournament practice and play, this realistic simulation pits you against celebrity look-alikes. Tons of options let you control tournament size with 10 to 300 entrants, select limits, ante, rake, blind structures, freezeouts, number of rebuys and competition level of opponents - average, tough, or toughest. Pop-up status report shows how you're doing vs. the competition. Save tournaments in progress to play again later. Additional feature allows you to quickly finish a folded hand and go on to the next.